Android™ Application Development Cookbook

93 RECIPES FOR BUILDING WINNING APPS

Wei-Meng Lee

WILEY

John Wiley & Sons, Inc.

Android™ Application Development Cookbook: 93 Recipes for Building Winning Apps

Published by
John Wiley & Sons, Inc.
10475 Crosspoint Boulevard
Indianapolis, IN 46256
www.wiley.com

Copyright © 2013 by John Wiley & Sons, Inc., Indianapolis, Indiana

Published simultaneously in Canada

ISBN: 978-1-118-17767-9
ISBN: 978-1-118-22729-9 (ebk)
ISBN: 978-1-118-24028-1 (ebk)
ISBN: 978-1-118-26491-1 (ebk)

Manufactured in the United States of America

10 9 8 7 6 5 4 3 2 1

For general information on our other products and services please contact our Customer Care Department within the United States at (877) 762-2974, outside the United States at (317) 572-3993 or fax (317) 572-4002.

Wiley publishes in a variety of print and electronic formats and by print-on-demand. Some material included with standard print versions of this book may not be included in e-books or in print-on-demand. If this book refers to media such as a CD or DVD that is not included in the version you purchased, you may download this material at http://booksupport.wiley.com. For more information about Wiley products, visit www.wiley.com.

Library of Congress Control Number: 2012948549

To my family,

Thanks for the understanding and support while I worked on getting this book ready. I love you all!

ABOUT THE AUTHOR

WEI-MENG LEE is a technologist and founder of Developer Learning Solutions (www.learn2develop .net), a technology company specializing in hands-on training on the latest mobile technologies. Wei-Meng has many years of training experience and his courses place special emphasis on the learning-by-doing approach. This hands-on approach to learning programming makes understanding the subject much easier than reading books, tutorials, and other documentation.

Wei-Meng is also the author of *Beginning iOS 5 Application Development* (Wrox, 2010) and *Beginning Android 4 Application Development* (Wrox, 2011). You can contact him at weimenglee@learn2develop.net.

ABOUT THE TECHNICAL EDITOR

CHAIM KRAUSE is a Simulation Specialist at the US Army's Command and General Staff College where he develops various software products on a multitude of platforms, from iOS and Android devices to Windows desktops and Linux servers, among other duties. Python is his preferred language, but he is multilingual and also codes in Java, JavaScript/HTML5/CSS, and others. He was fortunate to begin his professional career in the software field at Borland where he was a Senior Developer Support Engineer for Delphi. Outside of computer geek stuff, Chaim enjoys techno and dubstep music, and scootering with his two sled dogs Dasher and Minnie.

CREDITS

EXECUTIVE EDITOR
Robert Elliott

SENIOR PROJECT EDITOR
Ami Frank Sullivan

TECHNICAL EDITOR
Chaim Krause

PRODUCTION EDITOR
Christine Mugnolo

COPY EDITOR
Luann Rouff

EDITORIAL MANAGER
Mary Beth Wakefield

FREELANCER EDITORIAL MANAGER
Rosemarie Graham

ASSOCIATE DIRECTOR OF MARKETING
David Mayhew

MARKETING MANAGER
Ashley Zurcher

BUSINESS MANAGER
Amy Knies

PRODUCTION MANAGER
Tim Tate

VICE PRESIDENT AND EXECUTIVE GROUP PUBLISHER
Richard Swadley

VICE PRESIDENT AND EXECUTIVE PUBLISHER
Neil Edde

ASSOCIATE PUBLISHER
Jim Minatel

PROJECT COORDINATOR, COVER
Katie Crocker

COMPOSITOR
Craig Johnson, Happenstance Type-O-Rama

PROOFREADER
Scott Klemp, Word One New York

INDEXER
Robert Swanson

COVER DESIGNER
Ryan Sneed

COVER IMAGE
© Paul Fleet / iStockPhoto

ACKNOWLEDGMENTS

A LOT OF DEVELOPMENT in the Android world has happened since my last book, *Beginning Android 4 Application Development*, went to print. Google has released a new version of the SDK: Android 4.1 SDK. With the Android 4.1 SDK and the ADT Plugin 20.0.3, it is now much easier to write Android applications — from those that run on older devices right up to the latest and greatest.

I would like to thank some key people who have worked hard behind the scenes to make this book a reality.

First, my personal gratitude to Bob Elliott, executive editor at Wrox. Bob is always ready to lend a listening ear and offer help when it's needed. It is a great pleasure to work with Bob, as he is one of the most responsive people I have ever worked with. Thank you, Bob, for the help and guidance.

Of course, I cannot forget Ami Sullivan, my editor (and friend), who is always a pleasure to work with. Thank you for your guidance and encouragement to keep the project going, Ami.

I am also grateful to my technical editor, Chaim Krause. Chaim has been eagle-eye editing the book and testing my recipes, ensuring that my code works as written. Thanks, Chaim.

Last but not least, I want to thank my parents and my wife, Sze Wa, for all the support they have given me. They have selflessly adjusted their schedules to accommodate my busy schedule when I was working on this book. My wife, as always, has stayed up with me on numerous nights as I was furiously working to meet the deadlines, and for this I would like to say to her and my parents, "I love you all!" Finally, to our lovely dog, Ookii, thanks for staying by our side.

CONTENTS

INTRODUCTION

THE PACE OF ANDROID DEVELOPMENT has been fast and furious. Within a short time span of a few years, Android has matured into a stable platform, rivaling that of its main competitor, iOS. At the time of writing, the latest version of Android is 4.1 (aka Jelly Bean). Android 4.1 runs on both smartphones and tablets, making it the platform of choice for many developers.

This book was born out of the many frustrations I have had when developing Android applications. It is often the case that you just need a quick snapshot showing how to do a certain task, and a code snippet would be a quick fix. However, a trip to the official Android documentation often caused more confusion than help, as the code samples are not always complete. Hence, this book aims to fill the void by providing standalone examples that you can quickly "embrace and extend."

Each recipe tackles a problem that you might face in your daily life as an Android developer — whether it's as minor as using a Button view or as involved as implementing a Master-Detail application using fragments. You can read this book from the first recipe until the last recipe, or you can turn directly to the recipes that interest you most.

WHO THIS BOOK IS FOR

This book is targeted at Android programmers who already have some basic knowledge of creating Android applications. It is assumed that you know how to create an Android project using Eclipse, and that you are already familiar with the structure of an Android project.

All the code samples in this book were written and tested using the Android 4.1 SDK, together with Eclipse (Juno release) and the ADT plugin 20.0.3. All projects are able to run on Android devices beginning with Android version 2.2. In particular, all projects make use of the Android Support package that is by default included in Android 4.1 projects. Using the Android Support Package enables your applications to make use of the newer features introduced with Android version 3.0 (such as fragments) and still run on older Android devices.

> **NOTE** *While every effort has been made to ensure that all the tools used in the examples are the latest, it is always possible that by the time you read this book, newer versions may be available. If so, some of the instructions and/or screenshots may differ slightly. However, any variations should be manageable.*

WHAT THIS BOOK COVERS

This book covers all key areas of Android programming using the Android 4.1 SDK. It is divided into 11 chapters.

Chapter 1: Android Fundamentals covers basic topics such as how to link activities, pass data between activities, send and receive broadcasts, call built-in apps, and more.

Chapter 2: Using Views to Design the User Interface explains how to use the various views to build the user interface of your Android applications. Also covered are the different types of layouts supported in Android to arrange the views, including LinearLayout, RelativeLayout, FrameLayout, and others. You will also learn how to display context and option menus.

Chapter 3: Displaying Lists of Items and Images covers how to use the ListView and Spinner, and how to customize them to display a list of items. It also demonstrates how to use fragments to create Master-Detail applications.

Chapter 4: Telephony covers topics related to the phone on your Android device, such as how to block outgoing calls, auto-answering incoming calls, enabling Bluetooth, and more.

Chapter 5: Messaging covers how to send and intercept SMS messages on your Android phone. You will also learn how to monitor for SMS messages sent by your users.

Chapter 6: Network Programming covers topics related to getting your Android application connected to the outside world. You will learn about how to consume XML and JSON web services, sockets programming, and Bluetooth communications.

Chapter 7: Using Google Maps includes topics about how to display Google Maps in your Android application, how to perform reverse geocoding, and more.

Chapter 8: Location-Based Data Services covers the key techniques you need to know to build location-based services. You will also learn how to implement location data logging.

Chapter 9: Accessing the Hardware covers how to access the many hardware features from your Android application. It includes recipes demonstrating how to take pictures using the built-in camera, how to turn GPS on/off, as well as how to enable the device's flashlight.

Chapter 10: Persisting Data covers several methods for persisting your data, including internal storage, external storage, a database, and more.

Chapter 11: Deploying your Android Applications covers the different ways to deploy your Android applications, such as through an SD card, a web server, or e-mail.

HOW THIS BOOK IS STRUCTURED

Chapters in this book are divided into main topics, with each chapter containing multiple "recipes" that address specific subtopics in more detail. Instead of adopting the step-by-step approach of creating a project and then explaining how the code works, this books demonstrates the key ingredients of each recipe — the key points you need to understand in order to meet a requirement or solve a problem (or complete a common task) in Android programming. Each recipe covers the core concepts you need to understand, without any unnecessary code that can complicate an example. Using this approach, it would be easiest for you to copy-and-paste the code into your own project and then enhance it for your own purpose. This, in my opinion, is the best way to learn Android programming.

To that end, every chapter has a very defined structure. Each recipe is numbered and has a title. The recipe begins with a list of components needed to successfully complete the solution, like so:

RECIPE 0.0 THE RECIPE REQUIREMENTS

Android Versions

Each recipe uses APIs from the Android SDK. The Android Versions section states the version (level number) from which the APIs are from. For example, you might see "Level 1 and above." This indicates that the APIs used in this recipe are available from Android level 1 (i.e., version 1.0) and above.

Permissions

The Permissions section shows the permissions that you need to add into your application, specifically the `AndroidManifest.xml` file, in order to use the APIs described in the recipe. Be sure to add the permission; forgetting to do so will usually cause the application to crash during run time.

Source Code to Download from Wrox.com

The Source Code section shows the name of the ZIP file that you can download from the support web site of this book from Wrox.com. The ZIP file contains the complete project used to illustrate the concept in that recipe. If you want to quickly get the code for the recipe into your own project, downloading the source code is your fastest option.

Then, the main goal of the recipe is explained. Next the solution follows. Sometimes, the solution is short and sweet, and sometimes the solution is more complex and requires multiple steps.

A NOTE ABOUT INCLUDING PERMISSIONS IN CODE

To make the recipes succinct and easy to follow, this book assumes that you know how to add permissions in your application. For example, instead of listing the entire `AndroidManifest.xml` file and highlighting the permissions that you need to add, like this:

```xml
<manifest xmlns:android="http://schemas.android.com/apk/res/android"
    package="net.learn2develop.http"
    android:versionCode="1"
    android:versionName="1.0" >

    <uses-sdk
        android:minSdkVersion="8"
        android:targetSdkVersion="15" />

    <uses-permission android:name="android.permission.INTERNET" />
    <uses-permission
        android:name="android.permission.ACCESS_NETWORK_STATE"/>

    <application
        android:icon="@drawable/ic_launcher"
        android:label="@string/app_name"
        android:theme="@style/AppTheme" >
        <activity
            android:name=".MainActivity"
            android:label="@string/title_activity_main" >
            <intent-filter>
                <action android:name="android.intent.action.MAIN" />

                <category android:name="android.intent.category.
                LAUNCHER" />
            </intent-filter>
        </activity>
    </application>

</manifest>
```

... the recipe will simply indicate that you need to add the following permissions:

```xml
<uses-permission android:name="android.permission.INTERNET" />
<uses-permission
    android:name="android.permission.ACCESS_NETWORK_STATE"/>
```

In the event that the above step is not explicitly mentioned, you should always check the Permissions section at the beginning of each recipe and add the permission(s) to the `AndroidManifest.xml` file.

WHAT YOU NEED TO USE THIS BOOK

Most of the examples in this book run on the Android emulator, which is included as part of the Android SDK. However, to get the most out of this book, using a real Android device is recommended (though not absolutely necessary).

Additionally, each recipe begins with a list of requirements specific to that recipe (versions, permissions, and source code), as previously discussed.

CONVENTIONS

To help you get the most from the text and keep track of what's happening, a number of conventions are used throughout the book:

➤ New terms and important words are *highlighted* in italics when first introduced.

➤ Keyboard combinations are treated like this: Ctrl+R.

➤ Filenames, URLs, and code within the text are treated like so: `persistence.properties`.

➤ Code is presented in two different ways:

```
We use a monofont type with no highlighting for most code examples.
We use bolding to emphasize code that is of particular importance in the
present context.
```

> **NOTE** *Notes, tips, hints, tricks, and asides to the current discussion look like this.*

SOURCE CODE

As you work through the examples in this book, you may choose either to type in all the code manually or to use the source code files that accompany the book. All the source code used in this book is available for download at `www.wrox.com`. When at the site, simply locate the book's title (use the Search box or one of the title lists) and click the Download Code link on the book's detail page to obtain all the source code for the book.

After you download the code, just decompress it with your favorite compression tool. Alternatively, go to the main Wrox code download page at `www.wrox.com/dynamic/books/download.aspx` to see the code available for this book and all other Wrox books.

> **NOTE** *Because many books have similar titles, you may find it easiest to search by ISBN; this book's ISBN is 978-1-118-17767-9.*

ERRATA

We make every effort to ensure that there are no errors in the text or in the code. However, no one is perfect, and mistakes do occur. If you find an error in one of our books, such as a spelling mistake or a faulty piece of code, we would be very grateful for your feedback. By sending in errata, you may save another reader hours of frustration and at the same time help us provide even higher-quality information.

To find the errata page for this book, go to www.wrox.com and locate the title using the Search box or one of the title lists. Then, on the book details page, click the Book Errata link. On this page, you can view all errata that has been submitted for this book and posted by Wrox editors. A complete book list, including links to each book's errata, is also available at www.wrox.com/misc-pages/booklist.shtml.

If you don't spot "your" error on the Book Errata page, go to www.wrox.com/contact/techsupport.shtml and complete the form there to send us the error you have found. We'll check the information and, if appropriate, post a message to the book's errata page and fix the problem in subsequent editions of the book.

P2P.WROX.COM

For author and peer discussion, join the P2P forums at p2p.wrox.com. The forums are a web-based system for you to post messages relating to Wrox books and related technologies and to interact with other readers and technology users. The forums offer a subscription feature to e-mail you topics of interest of your choosing when new posts are made to the forums. Wrox authors, editors, other industry experts, and your fellow readers are present on these forums.

At p2p.wrox.com, you will find a number of different forums that will help you not only as you read this book but also as you develop your own applications. To join the forums, just follow these steps:

1. Go to p2p.wrox.com and click the Register link.
2. Read the terms of use and click Agree.
3. Complete the required information to join as well as any optional information you want to provide and click Submit.
4. You will receive an e-mail with information describing how to verify your account and complete the joining process.

NOTE *You can read messages in the forums without joining P2P, but in order to post your own messages you must join.*

After you join, you can post new messages and respond to messages that other users post. You can read messages at any time on the Web. If you want to have new messages from a particular forum e-mailed to you, click the Subscribe to This Forum icon by the forum name in the forum listing.

For more information about how to use the Wrox P2P, be sure to read the P2P FAQs for answers to questions about how the forum software works, as well as for many common questions specific to P2P and Wrox books. To read the FAQs, click the FAQ link on any P2P page.

Android Fundamentals

In this chapter, you learn about the fundamental topics in Android that most developers need to know, including how to link to other applications using the Intent object, how to communicate with other applications (or parts of the same application) using broadcast receivers, and how to pass data between activities.

RECIPE 1.1 LINKING ACTIVITIES

Android Versions
Level 1 and above

Permissions
None

Source Code to Download at Wrox.com
Linking.zip

Unless you are writing a Hello World application, chances are good that your application contains several activities that you need to connect in order to form a cohesive application. This recipe shows you the various ways to link to another activity in your Android application.

Solution

Suppose you have two activities in your application. The following `AndroidManifest.xml` file shows the two activities classes, `MainActivity` and `Activity2`:

```xml
<manifest xmlns:android="http://schemas.android.com/apk/res/android"
    package="net.learn2develop.linking"
    android:versionCode="1"
    android:versionName="1.0" >

    <uses-sdk
        android:minSdkVersion="8"
        android:targetSdkVersion="15" />

    <application
        android:icon="@drawable/ic_launcher"
        android:label="@string/app_name"
        android:theme="@style/AppTheme" >

        <activity
            android:name=".MainActivity"
            android:label="@string/title_activity_main" >
            <intent-filter>
                <action android:name="android.intent.action.MAIN" />

                <category android:name="android.intent.category.LAUNCHER" />
            </intent-filter>
        </activity>

        <activity
            android:name=".Activity2"
            android:label="@string/app_name" >
            <intent-filter>
                <action android:name="net.learn2develop.Activity2" />
                <category android:name="android.intent.category.DEFAULT" />
            </intent-filter>
        </activity>

    </application>

</manifest>
```

Assuming you are currently in the `MainActivity` activity, to link to `Activity2` you can use the following code snippet:

```java
package net.learn2develop.linking;

import android.app.Activity;
import android.content.Intent;
import android.os.Bundle;
```

```
public class MainActivity extends Activity {

    @Override
    public void onCreate(Bundle savedInstanceState) {
        super.onCreate(savedInstanceState);
        setContentView(R.layout.activity_main);

        //---link to Activity2---
        Intent i = new Intent("net.learn2develop.Activity2");
        startActivity(i);
    }

}
```

To link to another activity, you create an `Intent` object and set its constructor to the name (as set in the `<action>` element in the `AndroidManifest.xml` file) of the target activity. Then, call the `startActivity()` method to launch that activity.

Alternatively, you can create an `Intent` object and then call its `setAction()` method to set the name of the target activity:

```
//---link to Activity2---
Intent i = new Intent();
i.setAction("net.learn2develop.Activity2");
startActivity(i);
```

The previous code snippets are useful for calling an activity that is within the same application, as well as for other applications to call your activity. If you want to call an activity that is internal to your application, you can also call it using its class name, like this:

```
//---link to Activity2---
Intent i = new Intent(this, Activity2.class);
```

If you do not want other activities to call your activity from outside your application, simply remove the `<action>` element within the `<intent-filter>` element:

```
<activity
    android:name=".Activity2"
    android:label="@string/app_name" >
    <intent-filter>
        <!--
        <action android:name="net.learn2develop.Activity2" />
        -->
        <category android:name="android.intent.category.DEFAULT" />
    </intent-filter>
</activity>
```

If the activity you are trying to call does not exist on the device, your application will crash, displaying a message like the one shown in Figure 1-1.

To ensure that your application does not stop abruptly, call the `startActivity()` method together with the `Intent.createChooser()` method. The `createChooser()` method takes an `Intent` object and a string to display if an activity cannot be found (or if more than one activity has been found to satisfy your `Intent` object):

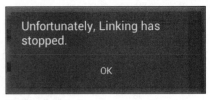

FIGURE 1-1

```
Intent i = new Intent("net.learn2develop.Activity2");
startActivity(Intent.createChooser(i, "Choose an application"));
```

Figure 1-2 shows the message that is displayed if an activity cannot be found.

FIGURE 1-2

Figure 1-3 shows the message that is displayed when more than one activity has been found.

Note that when using the `createChooser()` method, you need to specify the name of the activity (such as `net.learn2develop.Activity2` as seen in the previous example) that you are launching, not its class name. The following code snippet will not work:

```
//---the following will never link to Activity2---
Intent i = new Intent(this, Activity2.class);
startActivity(Intent.createChooser(i, "Choose an application"));
```

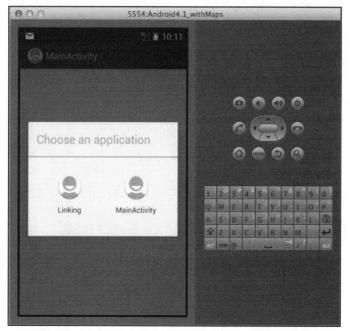

FIGURE 1-3

RECIPE 1.2 PASSING DATA BETWEEN ACTIVITIES

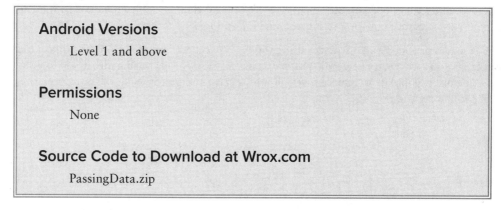

Android Versions

Level 1 and above

Permissions

None

Source Code to Download at Wrox.com

PassingData.zip

The preceding recipe demonstrated how to launch another activity using the `startActivity()` method. One common task you need to perform when launching another activity is passing some data to it. For example, you might want to launch another activity to collect some user-related data, so you pass the name of the user to another activity. When the user has finished collecting all the data, the data also needs to be passed back to the calling activity. Hence, you need to be able to pass data back and forth between activities. This recipe shows you how.

Solution

You can make use of the `Intent` class to pass data to another activity. To pass primitive data types to another activity, you can use the `putExtra()` method, as the following code snippet shows:

```
package net.learn2develop.passingdata;

import android.app.Activity;
import android.content.Intent;
import android.os.Bundle;
import android.view.View;

public class MainActivity extends Activity {

    @Override
    public void onCreate(Bundle savedInstanceState) {
        super.onCreate(savedInstanceState);
        setContentView(R.layout.activity_main);
    }

    public void onClick(View view) {
        Intent i = new
                Intent("net.learn2develop.SecondActivity");

        //---use putExtra() to add new key/value pairs---
        i.putExtra("str1", "This is a string");
        i.putExtra("age1", 25);
    }
}
```

The preceding statements create an `Intent` object and then attach two values to it using the `putExtra()` method: one for a string and one for an integer.

You can also pass in a `Bundle` object using the `Intent` object. A `Bundle` object is like a dictionary object, as you can specify key/value pairs. To pass a `Bundle` object using an `Intent` object, create a `Bundle` object, populate it, and then attach it to the `Intent` object using the `putExtras()` method, as the following code shows:

```
    public void onClick(View view) {
        Intent i = new
                Intent("net.learn2develop.SecondActivity");

        //---use putExtra() to add new key/value pairs---
        i.putExtra("str1", "This is a string");
        i.putExtra("age1", 25);

        //---use a Bundle object to add new key/values
        // pairs---
        Bundle extras = new Bundle();
        extras.putString("str2", "This is another string");
        extras.putInt("age2", 35);

        //---attach the Bundle object to the Intent object---
        i.putExtras(extras);
    }
```

When you start another activity using the `Intent` object, the data attached to the `Intent` object is passed to the destination activity. To call another activity with the intention of getting some data back from it, use the `startActivityForResult()` method:

```
public void onClick(View view) {
    Intent i = new
            Intent("net.learn2develop.SecondActivity");

    //---use putExtra() to add new key/value pairs---
    i.putExtra("str1", "This is a string");
    i.putExtra("age1", 25);

    //---use a Bundle object to add new key/values
    // pairs---
    Bundle extras = new Bundle();
    extras.putString("str2", "This is another string");
    extras.putInt("age2", 35);

    //---attach the Bundle object to the Intent object---
    i.putExtras(extras);

    //---start the activity to get a result back---
    startActivityForResult(i, 1);
}
```

The `startActivityForResult()` method takes an `Intent` object as well as a request code. The request code is an integer value that is greater than or equal to zero. This request code is used to identify returning activities, as you may call more than one activity simultaneously. If you set the request code to -1, then the call of `startActivityForResult()` is equivalent to `startActivity()`. That is, you will not be able to obtain data passed back from the destination activity.

On the target activity, to retrieve the data that was passed to it, you use the `getIntent()` method to obtain the instance of the `Intent` object that was passed to it. To get the simple data type passed in through the `putExtra()` method, use the `get<type>Extra()` method, where the type may be `String`, `int`, `float`, and so on. The following code shows how the two primitive data types are retrieved:

```
package net.learn2develop.passingdata;

import android.app.Activity;
import android.os.Bundle;
import android.widget.Toast;

public class SecondActivity extends Activity {

    @Override
    public void onCreate(Bundle savedInstanceState) {
        super.onCreate(savedInstanceState);
        setContentView(R.layout.activity_second);

        //---get the data passed in using getStringExtra()---
        Toast.makeText(this,getIntent().getStringExtra("str1"),
            Toast.LENGTH_SHORT).show();
```

```
            //---get the data passed in using getIntExtra()---
            Toast.makeText(this,Integer.toString(
                getIntent().getIntExtra("age1", 0)),
                Toast.LENGTH_SHORT).show();
    }

}
```

To retrieve the data passed in through the `Bundle` object, use the `getExtras()` method of the `Intent` object. The `getExtras()` method returns a `Bundle` object, which you can use to retrieve the various key/values using the `get<type>()` method, where type may be `String`, `int`, and so on:

```
@Override
public void onCreate(Bundle savedInstanceState) {
    super.onCreate(savedInstanceState);
    setContentView(R.layout.activity_second);

    //---get the data passed in using getStringExtra()---
    Toast.makeText(this,getIntent().getStringExtra("str1"),
        Toast.LENGTH_SHORT).show();

    //---get the data passed in using getIntExtra()---
    Toast.makeText(this,Integer.toString(
        getIntent().getIntExtra("age1", 0)),
        Toast.LENGTH_SHORT).show();

    //---get the Bundle object passed in---
    Bundle bundle = getIntent().getExtras();

    //---get the data using the getString()---
    Toast.makeText(this, bundle.getString("str2"),
        Toast.LENGTH_SHORT).show();

    //---get the data using the getInt() method---
    Toast.makeText(this,Integer.toString(bundle.getInt("age2")),
        Toast.LENGTH_SHORT).show();
    }
```

The destination may also pass data back to the calling activity. To pass data back, you can create another `Intent` object and set the values as described earlier. You can also use the `setData()` method to pass a `Uri` object through the `Intent` object. To pass the result back to the calling activity, use the `setResult()` method, as shown in the following code:

```
package net.learn2develop.passingdata;

import android.app.Activity;
import android.content.Intent;
import android.net.Uri;
import android.os.Bundle;
import android.view.View;
import android.widget.Toast;

public class SecondActivity extends Activity {
```

```
    @Override
    public void onCreate(Bundle savedInstanceState) {
        super.onCreate(savedInstanceState);
        setContentView(R.layout.activity_second);

        //---get the data passed in using getStringExtra()---
        Toast.makeText(this,getIntent().getStringExtra("str1"),
            Toast.LENGTH_SHORT).show();

        //---get the data passed in using getIntExtra()---
        Toast.makeText(this,Integer.toString(
            getIntent().getIntExtra("age1", 0)),
            Toast.LENGTH_SHORT).show();

        //---get the Bundle object passed in---
        Bundle bundle = getIntent().getExtras();

        //---get the data using the getString()---
        Toast.makeText(this, bundle.getString("str2"),
            Toast.LENGTH_SHORT).show();

        //---get the data using the getInt() method---
        Toast.makeText(this,Integer.toString(bundle.getInt("age2")),
            Toast.LENGTH_SHORT).show();
    }

    public void onClick(View view) {
        //---use an Intent object to return data---
        Intent i = new Intent();

        //---use the putExtra() method to return some
        // value---
        i.putExtra("age3", 45);

        //---use the setData() method to return some value---
        i.setData(Uri.parse(
            "http://www.learn2develop.net"));

        //---set the result with OK and the Intent object---
        setResult(RESULT_OK, i);

        finish();
    }

}
```

The RESULT_OK constant enables you to indicate to the calling activity whether the data returned should be ignored. If you want the calling activity to ignore the result, you can use the RESULT_ CANCELLED constant. How the calling activity interprets the result is really up to it, but the use of these two constants serves as an indication.

Back in the main calling activity, implement the onActivityResult() method. You need to check for the request code to ensure that you are getting the result from the correct activity. The request code is the number that you earlier passed to the `startActivityForResult()` method, which is 1 in this example:

```
//---start the activity to get a result back---
startActivityForResult(i, 1);
```

You can also check the result code to see if it is RESULT_OK:

```
package net.learn2develop.passingdata;

import android.app.Activity;
import android.content.Intent;
import android.net.Uri;
import android.os.Bundle;
import android.view.View;
import android.widget.Toast;

public class MainActivity extends Activity {

    @Override
    public void onCreate(Bundle savedInstanceState) {
        super.onCreate(savedInstanceState);
        setContentView(R.layout.activity_main);
    }

    public void onClick(View view) {
        Intent i = new
                Intent("net.learn2develop.SecondActivity");

        //---use putExtra() to add new key/value pairs---
        i.putExtra("str1", "This is a string");
        i.putExtra("age1", 25);

        //---use a Bundle object to add new key/values
        // pairs---
        Bundle extras = new Bundle();
        extras.putString("str2", "This is another string");
        extras.putInt("age2", 35);

        //---attach the Bundle object to the Intent object---
        i.putExtras(extras);

        //---start the activity to get a result back---
        startActivityForResult(i, 1);
    }

    public void onActivityResult(int requestCode,
            int resultCode, Intent data)
    {
        //---check if the request code is 1---
        if (requestCode == 1) {

            //---if the result is OK---
            if (resultCode == RESULT_OK) {
```

```
            //---get the result using getIntExtra()---
            Toast.makeText(this, Integer.toString(
                    data.getIntExtra("age3", 0)),
                    Toast.LENGTH_SHORT).show();

            //---get the result using getData()---
            Uri url = data.getData();
            Toast.makeText(this, url.toString(),
                    Toast.LENGTH_SHORT).show();
        }
    }
  }
}
```

To retrieve the data sent using the setData() method, use the getData() method of the Intent object (passed in as the second argument of the onActivityResult() method).

RECIPE 1.3 PASSING OBJECTS BETWEEN ACTIVITIES

Android Versions

Level 1 and above

Permissions

None

Source Code to Download at Wrox.com

PassingData.zip

In the previous recipe, you saw how to pass simple data (such as strings and integers) between activities. This recipe demonstrates how to pass objects between activites. For example, you might have encapsulated the information of a customer (such as the customer ID, name, company, and so on) within an object and you need to pass it over to another activity for processing. Instead of passing the various pieces of the information of the customer individually, it would be easier to simply pass that object.

Solution

Besides passing simple data types using the putExtra() and putExtras() methods, you can also pass objects using an Intent object. If you have your own custom class, you need to ensure that your class implements the Serializable base class. The following MyCustomClass class is an example:

```
package net.learn2develop.passingdata;

import java.io.Serializable;
```

```
public class MyCustomClass implements Serializable {
    private static final long serialVersionUID = 1L;
    String _name;
    String _email;

    public void setName(String name) {
        _name = name;
    }

    public String Name() {
        return _name;
    }

    public void setEmail(String email) {
        _email = email;
    }

    public String Email() {
        return _email;
    }
}
```

To pass an object to another activity, use the `putExtra()` method:

```
public void onClick(View view) {
    Intent i = new
            Intent("net.learn2develop.SecondActivity");

    //---use putExtra() to add new key/value pairs---
    i.putExtra("str1", "This is a string");
    i.putExtra("age1", 25);

    //---use a Bundle object to add new key/values
    // pairs---
    Bundle extras = new Bundle();
    extras.putString("str2", "This is another string");
    extras.putInt("age2", 35);

    //---attach the Bundle object to the Intent object---
    i.putExtras(extras);

    //---create my own custom object---
    MyCustomClass myObject = new MyCustomClass();
    myObject.setName("Wei-Meng Lee");
    myObject.setEmail("weimenglee@learn2develop.net");
    i.putExtra("MyObject", myObject);

    //---start the activity to get a result back---
    startActivityForResult(i, 1);
}
```

To retrieve the object passed to another activity, use the `getSerializableExtra()` method of the `Intent` object, passing it the key that you set earlier in the `putExtra()` method. Then, typecast the result returned by this method to the `MyCustomClass` class and assign it to a variable of this type:

```
@Override
public void onCreate(Bundle savedInstanceState) {
    super.onCreate(savedInstanceState);
    setContentView(R.layout.activity_second);

    //---get the data passed in using getStringExtra()---
    Toast.makeText(this,getIntent().getStringExtra("str1"),
        Toast.LENGTH_SHORT).show();

    //---get the data passed in using getIntExtra()---
    Toast.makeText(this,Integer.toString(
        getIntent().getIntExtra("age1", 0)),
        Toast.LENGTH_SHORT).show();

    //---get the Bundle object passed in---
    Bundle bundle = getIntent().getExtras();

    //---get the data using the getString()---
    Toast.makeText(this, bundle.getString("str2"),
        Toast.LENGTH_SHORT).show();

    //---get the data using the getInt() method---
    Toast.makeText(this,Integer.toString(bundle.getInt("age2")),
        Toast.LENGTH_SHORT).show();

    //---get the custom object passed in---
    MyCustomClass obj = (MyCustomClass)
        getIntent().getSerializableExtra("MyObject");
    Toast.makeText(this, obj.Name(), Toast.LENGTH_SHORT).show();
    Toast.makeText(this, obj.Email(), Toast.LENGTH_SHORT).show();
}
```

RECIPE 1.4 SENDING AND RECEIVING BROADCASTS

Android Versions

Level 1 and above

Permissions

None

Source Code to Download at Wrox.com

UsingBroadcastReceiver.zip

In Android, a broadcast enables you to send a message to another part of your application (or another application) so that you can inform it of something happening. In this recipe, you learn how to create a broadcast receiver to listen for broadcasts, as well as send broadcasts to other applications.

Solution

There are two ways to create a broadcast receiver: programmatically through code and declaratively via the AndroidManifest.xml file. The following sections address each possible solution.

Programmatically Registering a Broadcast Receiver

Consider the following activity:

```
package net.learn2develop.usingbroadcastreceiver;

import android.app.Activity;
import android.content.BroadcastReceiver;
import android.content.Context;
import android.content.Intent;
import android.content.IntentFilter;
import android.os.Bundle;
import android.view.View;
import android.widget.Toast;

public class MainActivity extends Activity {
    MyBroadcastReceiver myReceiver;
    IntentFilter intentFilter;

    @Override
    public void onCreate(Bundle savedInstanceState) {
        super.onCreate(savedInstanceState);
        setContentView(R.layout.activity_main);

        myReceiver = new MyBroadcastReceiver();
        intentFilter = new IntentFilter("MY_SPECIFIC_ACTION");
    }

    @Override
    public void onResume() {
        super.onResume();
        //---register the receiver---
        registerReceiver(myReceiver, intentFilter);
    }

    @Override
    public void onPause() {
        super.onPause();
        //---unregister the receiver---
        unregisterReceiver(myReceiver);
    }
```

```
public void onClick(View view) {
    Intent i = new Intent("MY_SPECIFIC_ACTION");
    i.putExtra("key", "some value from intent");
    sendBroadcast(i);
}

public class MyBroadcastReceiver extends BroadcastReceiver {
    @Override
    public void onReceive(Context context, Intent i) {
        Toast.makeText(context,
                "Received broadcast in MyBroadcastReceiver, " +
                " value received: " + i.getStringExtra("key"),
                Toast.LENGTH_LONG).show();
    }
}

}
```

The preceding code snippet shows the inner class MyBroadcastReceiver extending from the BroadcastReceiver base class. In this class, you need to override the onReceive() method so that when the broadcast is received, you can perform the action that you want to perform. To get the data that is passed to the receiver, you can make use of the Intent object in the second argument of the onReceive() method.

To use this class, you need to create an instance of it, as well as create an IntentFilter object:

```
myReceiver = new MyBroadcastReceiver();
intentFilter = new IntentFilter("MY_SPECIFIC_ACTION");
```

You specify a user-defined action in the IntentFilter's constructor, and use your own string to define this action.

To register the BroadcastReceiver object, use the registerReceiver() method, passing it the BroadcastReceiver object as well as the IntentFilter object:

```
registerReceiver(myReceiver, intentFilter);
```

Now that you have registered a BroadcastReceiver object, you can send a broadcast to test whether it works. To send a broadcast, you use the sendBroadcast() method, passing it an Intent object:

```
public void onClick(View view) {
    Intent i = new Intent("MY_SPECIFIC_ACTION");
    i.putExtra("key", "some value from intent");
    sendBroadcast(i);
}
```

If you want to pass data to the receiver, you can use the putExra() method. To unregister the broadcast receiver, use the unregisterReceiver() method:

```
unregisterReceiver(myReceiver);
```

Figure 1-4 shows the receiver receiving the broadcast.

FIGURE 1-4

The broadcast receiver will work even if the broadcast was sent by another application.

Registering the BroadcastReceiver in the AndroidManifest.xml File

In the previous example, if the application is in the background, the broadcast receiver will no longer work because you have unregistered the broadcast receiver when the application goes to the background:

```
@Override
public void onPause() {
    super.onPause();
    //---unregister the receiver---
    unregisterReceiver(myReceiver);
}
```

If you want a more persistent way to receive broadcasts, you need to register the BroadcastReceiver class in the AndroidManifest.xml file.

To do so, you create the BroadcastReceiver class in another Java class. The following code snippet shows the content of the MySecondBroadcastReceiver.java file:

```
package net.learn2develop.usingbroadcastreceiver;

import android.content.BroadcastReceiver;
import android.content.Context;
```

```
import android.content.Intent;
import android.widget.Toast;

public class MySecondBroadcastReceiver extends BroadcastReceiver {
    @Override
    public void onReceive(Context context, Intent i) {
        Toast.makeText(context,
                "Received broadcast in MySecondBroadcastReceiver; " +
                " value received: " + i.getStringExtra("key"),
                Toast.LENGTH_LONG).show();
    }
}
```

To register this receiver in the `AndroidManifest.xml` file, add the `<receiver>` element:

```
<manifest xmlns:android="http://schemas.android.com/apk/res/android"
    package="net.learn2develop.usingbroadcastreceiver"
    android:versionCode="1"
    android:versionName="1.0" >

    <uses-sdk
        android:minSdkVersion="8"
        android:targetSdkVersion="15" />

    <application
        android:icon="@drawable/ic_launcher"
        android:label="@string/app_name"
        android:theme="@style/AppTheme" >
        <activity
            android:name=".MainActivity"
            android:label="@string/title_activity_main" >
            <intent-filter>
                <action android:name="android.intent.action.MAIN" />

                <category android:name="android.intent.category.LAUNCHER" />
            </intent-filter>
        </activity>

        <receiver android:name=".MySecondBroadcastReceiver" >
            <intent-filter>
                <action android:name="MY_SPECIFIC_ACTION" />
            </intent-filter>
        </receiver>

    </application>

</manifest>
```

Your application now has two `BroadcastReceiver` objects: one you registered programmatically in the `onResume()` method and one in the `AndroidManifest.xml` file. If you send a broadcast now, both receivers will be called. Figure 1-5 shows the second broadcast receiver being called.

FIGURE 1-5

RECIPE 1.5 ASSIGNING PRIORITIES TO BROADCAST RECEIVERS

Android Versions

Level 1 and above

Permissions

None

Source Code to Download at Wrox.com

UsingBroadcastReceiver.zip

When you send a broadcast using the sendBroadcast() method, all the broadcast receivers that match the specified action are called in random fashion. What if you want to assign a particular order to the broadcast receivers so that some broadcast receivers will be called before others? To do that, you need to assign a priority to the broadcast receivers.

Solution

To programmatically assign a priority to a broadcast receiver, use the `setPriority()` method:

```
public class MainActivity extends Activity {
    MyBroadcastReceiver myReceiver;
    IntentFilter intentFilter;

    @Override
    public void onCreate(Bundle savedInstanceState) {
        super.onCreate(savedInstanceState);
        setContentView(R.layout.activity_main);

        myReceiver = new MyBroadcastReceiver();
        intentFilter = new IntentFilter("MY_SPECIFIC_ACTION");
    }

    @Override
    public void onResume() {
        super.onResume();
        intentFilter.setPriority(10);
        registerReceiver(myReceiver, intentFilter);
    }
}
```

The `setPriority()` method takes a priority value between 0 (default) and 1,000. The larger the number, the higher priority it has, and hence broadcast receivers with a higher priority are called before those with lower priority. If more than one broadcast receiver has the same priority, they are called randomly. The preceding code snippet sets the priority to 10.

To set the priority of broadcast receivers in the `AndroidManifest.xml` file, use the `android:priority` attribute:

```
<receiver android:name=".MySecondBroadcastReceiver" >
    <intent-filter android:priority="50">
        <action android:name="MY_SPECIFIC_ACTION" />
    </intent-filter>
</receiver>
```

The preceding example sets the priority to 50.

To send a broadcast that is delivered to broadcast receivers with higher priority first, you cannot use the `sendBroadcast()` method. Instead, you need to use the `sendOrderedBroadcast()` method, passing it an `Intent` object, plus any additional permission that the receiver must have in order to receive your broadcast:

```
public void onClick(View view) {
    Intent i = new Intent("MY_SPECIFIC_ACTION");
    i.putExtra("key", "some value from intent");
    //sendBroadcast(i);

    //---allows broadcast to be aborted---
    //---allows broadcast receivers to set priority---
    sendOrderedBroadcast(i, null);
}
```

If you try to send the broadcast now, you will notice that the broadcast receiver declared in the AndroidManifest.xml file is called first, before the one declared programmatically through code.

If you want to send a broadcast to only broadcast receivers with the permission to access the Internet, you will specify the permission in the second argument of the sendOrderedBroadcast() method, like this:

```
sendOrderedBroadcast(i, "android.permission.INTERNET");
```

Aborting a Broadcast

When broadcasts are sent using the sendOrderedBroadcast() method, broadcast receivers are called in the order of the priorities defined. When a broadcast receiver of higher priority receives the broadcast, it will handle that and the broadcast will be passed to the next broadcast receiver in line. In some scenarios, you might want to handle the broadcast and stop the broadcast from being propagated to the next receiver. To do that, you can use the abortBroadcast() method:

```
package net.learn2develop.UsingBroadcastReceiver;

import android.content.BroadcastReceiver;
import android.content.Context;
import android.content.Intent;
import android.widget.Toast;

public class MySecondBroadcastReceiver extends BroadcastReceiver {
    @Override
    public void onReceive(Context context, Intent i) {
        Toast.makeText(context,
                "Received broadcast in MySecondBroadcastReceiver; " +
                "value received: " + i.getStringExtra("key"),
                Toast.LENGTH_LONG).show();
        //---abort the broadcast----
        abortBroadcast();
    }
}
```

In the preceding code snippet, the MySecondBroadcastReceiver class aborts the broadcast after receiving it. Once it aborts the broadcast, other receivers who are waiting in line will not be able to receive it.

> **NOTE** In order to call the abortBroadcast() method to abort a broadcast, you need to send the broadcast using the sendOrderedBroadcast() method. Using the sendBroadcast() method has no effect on the priority and will not cause a broadcast to be aborted.

RECIPE 1.6 AUTO-LAUNCHING YOUR APPLICATION AT BOOT TIME

Android Versions

Level 1 and above

Permissions

android.permission.RECEIVE_BOOT_COMPLETED

Source Code to Download at Wrox.com

AutoStartApp.zip

If you need to automatically start your application whenever the device starts up, you need to register a `BroadcastReceiver`. This recipe shows you how.

Solution

To auto-launch your app during device boot-up, add a new class to your package and ensure that it extends the `BroadcastReceiver` base class. The following `BootupReceiver` class is an example:

```
package net.learn2develop.autostartapp;

import android.content.BroadcastReceiver;
import android.content.Context;
import android.content.Intent;
import android.widget.Toast;

public class BootupReceiver extends BroadcastReceiver {
    @Override
    public void onReceive(Context context, Intent intent) {
        Toast.makeText(context, "App started", Toast.LENGTH_LONG).show();

        //---start the main activity of our app---
        Intent i = new Intent(context,MainActivity.class);
        i.addFlags(Intent.FLAG_ACTIVITY_NEW_TASK);
        context.startActivity(i);
    }
}
```

When the device boots up, it will fire this broadcast receiver and call the `onReceiver()` method. To display your activity when the device boots up, you will use an `Intent` object. Remember to add the `FLAG_ACTIVITY_NEW_TASK` flag to the `Intent` object.

To register the broadcast receiver, you need to add the `<receiver>` element to the `AndroidManifest.xml` file. You also need the `RECEIVE_BOOT_COMPLETED` permission:

```
<manifest xmlns:android="http://schemas.android.com/apk/res/android"
    package="net.learn2develop.autostartapp"
```

```
        android:versionCode="1"
        android:versionName="1.0" >

        <uses-sdk
            android:minSdkVersion="8"
            android:targetSdkVersion="15" />

        <uses-permission android:name="android.permission.RECEIVE_BOOT_COMPLETED"/>

        <application
            android:icon="@drawable/ic_launcher"
            android:label="@string/app_name"
            android:theme="@style/AppTheme" >
            <activity
                android:name=".MainActivity"
                android:label="@string/title_activity_main" >
                <intent-filter>
                    <action android:name="android.intent.action.MAIN" />

                    <category android:name="android.intent.category.LAUNCHER" />
                </intent-filter>
            </activity>

            <receiver android:name=".BootupReceiver">
                <intent-filter>
                    <action android:name="android.intent.action.BOOT_COMPLETED" />
                    <category android:name="android.intent.category.DEFAULT" />
                </intent-filter>
            </receiver>

        </application>

    </manifest>
```

Your application will now be automatically launched when the device has booted up.

RECIPE 1.7 CALLING BUILT-IN APPS

Android Versions
Level 1 and above

Permissions
None

Source Code to Download at Wrox.com
CallingApps.zip

One of the key features of Android is the functionality it provides for applications to call other applications seamlessly. This enable you to integrate various applications on the device to form a coherent experience for your users. This recipe shows you the various ways to call the applications on your device.

Solution

There are many ways to call built-in apps, and how depends on which application you are calling. For this recipe's solution, you will learn how to call some of the commonly installed applications on your Android device, such as:

➤   How to display maps

➤   How to direct the user to a particular application on Google Play

➤   How to send e-mails

➤   How to send text and graphic content to applications that can handle them

Displaying Maps

To display maps in your application, you can launch an activity using the geo: scheme, as shown in here:

```
package net.learn2develop.callingapps;

import android.app.Activity;
import android.content.Intent;
import android.net.Uri;
import android.os.Bundle;

public class MainActivity extends Activity {

    @Override
    public void onCreate(Bundle savedInstanceState) {
        super.onCreate(savedInstanceState);
        setContentView(R.layout.activity_main);

        Intent i = new Intent(android.content.Intent.ACTION_VIEW);
        i.setData(Uri.parse("geo:37.827500,-122.481670"));
        startActivity(i);
    }

}
```

Figure 1-6 shows the application displaying a list of applications able to handle the geo: scheme when the preceding code is run on an Android device (you may see more on your device).

To launch an application from the list, select the application (say, Google Earth) and select either Always or Just once. If you select Always, the application you have just selected (in this case, Google Earth) will always be launched automatically. If you select Just once, you will see this prompt (asking if you want to launch it Always or Just once) each time you run this application.

When you select the Earth application, the Google Earth application will launch (see Figure 1-7).

Similarly, selecting the Maps application launches the Google Maps application (see Figure 1-8).

FIGURE 1-6

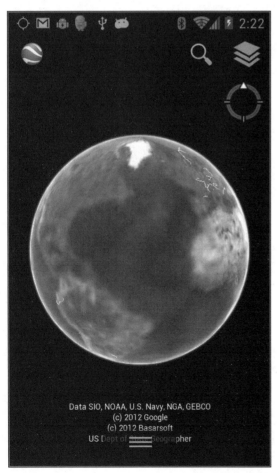

FIGURE 1-7

FIGURE 1-8

Launching Google Play

If you want to redirect the user to another application that is available on Google Play (formerly known as Google Market), use the `market:` scheme:

```
Intent i = new Intent(android.content.Intent.ACTION_VIEW);
i.setData(Uri.parse(
    "market://details?id=com.zinio.mobile.android.reader"));
startActivity(i);
```

The preceding code snippet will display the Zinio application available on Google Play (see Figure 1-9).

FIGURE 1-9

Sending E-mail

To send an e-mail message from within your application, use the following code snippet:

```
Intent i = new Intent(Intent.ACTION_SEND);
i.setData(Uri.parse("mailto:"));
String[] to = { "someone1@example.com" , "someone2@example.com" };
String[] cc = { "someone3@example.com" , "someone4@example.com" };
i.putExtra(Intent.EXTRA_EMAIL, to);
i.putExtra(Intent.EXTRA_CC, cc);
i.putExtra(Intent.EXTRA_SUBJECT, "Subject here...");
i.putExtra(Intent.EXTRA_TEXT, "Message here...");
i.setType("message/rfc822");
startActivity(Intent.createChooser(i, "Email"));
```

Figure 1-10 shows the E-mail application displaying the content of the e-mail.

FIGURE 1-10

Sending Content to Other Apps

Occasionally, you may want to launch another activity and send some content to it. For example, you might want to send some content to Facebook as well as the E-mail application. In this case, instead of targeting a particular application to invoke, you can use the generic ACTION_SEND constant to invoke a list of applications from which to choose. Consider the following code snippet:

```
Intent i = new Intent(android.content.Intent.ACTION_SEND);
i.setType("text/plain");
i.putExtra(Intent.EXTRA_SUBJECT, "Subject...");
i.putExtra(Intent.EXTRA_TEXT, "Text...");
startActivity(Intent.createChooser(i, "Apps that can respond to this"));
```

When run on a real device, the preceding code might invoke the list of applications shown in Figure 1-11.

If you selected the Messaging app, the data you set in the Intent object will then be sent as an SMS message (see Figure 1-12).

FIGURE 1-11

FIGURE 1-12

If you selected Gmail, the data you set in the `Intent` object will then be sent as an e-mail (see Figure 1-13).

If you selected Twitter (assuming you have Twitter installed on your device), the data you set in the `Intent` object will then be sent as a tweet (see Figure 1-14).

FIGURE 1-13   **FIGURE 1-14**

Sending Binary Content

If you have some images in your `drawable` folders, you can also send them to other applications using the following code snippet:

```
//---sending binary content---
Uri uriToImage =
    Uri.parse(
    "android.resource://net.learn2develop.CallingApps/drawable/" +
    Integer.toString(R.drawable.android));
```

```
Intent i = new Intent(android.content.Intent.ACTION_SEND);
i.setType("image/jpeg");
i.putExtra(Intent.EXTRA_STREAM, uriToImage);
i.putExtra(Intent.EXTRA_TEXT, "Text...");
startActivity(Intent.createChooser(i, "Apps that can respond to this"));
```

The preceding code assumes that you have a file named android.jpg located in one of the drawable folders in your project (see Figure 1-15). You set the image type to image/jpeg and then use the putExtra() method to put the image into the Intent object.

If you send the data to Twitter, the image will be used by Twitter as part of your tweet (see Figure 1-16).

FIGURE 1-15   **FIGURE 1-16**

To send multiple images, you can use the following code snippet:

```
import java.util.ArrayList;
...
...
        Uri uriToImage1 =
            Uri.parse(
            "android.resource://net.learn2develop.CallingApps/drawable/" +
            Integer.toString(R.drawable.android));
        Uri uriToImage2 =
            Uri.parse(
            "android.resource://net.learn2develop.CallingApps/drawable/" +
            Integer.toString(R.drawable.google));

        ArrayList<Uri> urisToImages = new ArrayList<Uri>();
        urisToImages.add(uriToImage1);
        urisToImages.add(uriToImage2);
```

```
Intent i = new Intent(android.content.Intent.ACTION_SEND_MULTIPLE);
i.setType("image/*");
i.putExtra(Intent.EXTRA_STREAM, urisToImages);
i.putExtra(Intent.EXTRA_SUBJECT, "Subject...");
i.putExtra(Intent.EXTRA_TEXT, "Text...");
startActivity(Intent.createChooser(i, "Apps that can respond to this"));
```

Figure 1-17 shows the two images sent to the Gmail application.

FIGURE 1-17

If you simply want to launch an application that enables you to view images, use the following code snippet:

```
Intent i = new Intent(android.content.Intent.ACTION_VIEW);
//---indicates the type that the target activity will handle---
i.setType("image/jpeg");
startActivity(i);
```

The preceding code snippet will list all the applications that allow you to view images (see Figure 1-18).

If you want to send an image (say located on the SD card) to an image viewer application, you can use the following code snippet:

```
Intent i = new Intent(android.content.Intent.ACTION_VIEW);
i.setDataAndType(
    Uri.parse("file:///storage/sdcard0/MyPhoto.jpg"), "image/*");
startActivity(i);
```

Figure 1-19 shows the Galley Viewer displaying the image located on the SD card.

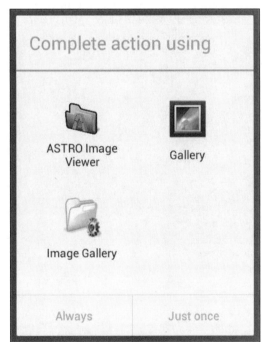

FIGURE 1-18

FIGURE 1-19

RECIPE 1.8 MAKING YOUR APPLICATION CALLABLE BY OTHERS

Android Versions

Level 1 and above

Permissions

android.permission.INTERNET

Source Code to Download at Wrox.com

IntentFilters.zip

In all the previous recipes you have launched other apps by using the Intent object. What about your own apps? How do you allow other apps to call yours using the Intent object? This recipe shows you how.

Solution

Assume you have the following class in your application:

```
package net.learn2develop.intentfilters;

import android.app.Activity;
import android.net.Uri;
import android.os.Bundle;
import android.webkit.WebView;
import android.webkit.WebViewClient;

public class MyBrowserActivity extends Activity {
    @Override
    public void onCreate(Bundle savedInstanceState)
    {
        super.onCreate(savedInstanceState);
        setContentView(R.layout.browser);

        Uri url = getIntent().getData();
        WebView webView = (WebView) findViewById(R.id.webView);
        webView.setWebViewClient(new Callback());

        if (url!=null) {
            webView.loadUrl(url.toString());
        } else {
            webView.loadUrl("http://www.google.com");
        }
    }
```

```
    private class Callback extends WebViewClient {
        @Override
        public boolean shouldOverrideUrlLoading(
                WebView view, String url) {
            return(false);
        }
    }
}
```

Basically, the preceding class loads an XML file named `browser.xml` (shown next) that contains a `WebView`. It displays a web page based on the data passed in through the `Intent` object:

```
<?xml version="1.0" encoding="utf-8"?>
<LinearLayout
    xmlns:android="http://schemas.android.com/apk/res/android"
    android:layout_width="fill_parent"
    android:layout_height="fill_parent"
    android:orientation="vertical" >

    <WebView
        android:id="@+id/webView"
        android:layout_width="wrap_content"
        android:layout_height="wrap_content" />

</LinearLayout>
```

The class is also declared in your `AndroidManifest.xml` file as follows:

```
<manifest xmlns:android="http://schemas.android.com/apk/res/android"
    package="net.learn2develop.intentfilters"
    android:versionCode="1"
    android:versionName="1.0" >

    <uses-sdk
        android:minSdkVersion="8"
        android:targetSdkVersion="15" />

    <uses-permission android:name="android.permission.INTERNET"/>

    <application
        android:icon="@drawable/ic_launcher"
        android:label="@string/app_name"
        android:theme="@style/AppTheme" >
        <activity
            android:name=".MainActivity"
            android:label="@string/title_activity_main" >
            <intent-filter>
                <action android:name="android.intent.action.MAIN" />

                <category android:name="android.intent.category.LAUNCHER" />
            </intent-filter>
        </activity>
```

```
<activity
    android:name=".MyBrowserActivity"
    android:label="@string/app_name" >
    <intent-filter>
        <action android:name="android.intent.action.VIEW" />
        <action android:name="net.learn2develop.MyBrowser" />
        <category android:name="android.intent.category.DEFAULT" />
        <data android:scheme="http" />
    </intent-filter>
</activity>

</application>

</manifest>
```

Note the elements contained within the <intent-filter> element for the MyBrowserActivity class. It has two actions: android.intent.action.VIEW and net.learn2develop.MyBrowser. This means that it can be called using the android.intent.action.VIEW action constant, or directly using the net.learn2develop.MyBrowser name. It also specifies the data scheme of http:. This means that this activity requires data passed to it to have the http: prefix, such as http:// www.amazon.com, http://www.google.com, and http://www.wrox.com.

To invoke the MyBrowserActivity class, you can use the following statements in your main activity:

```
package net.learn2develop.intentfilters;

import android.app.Activity;
import android.content.Intent;
import android.net.Uri;
import android.os.Bundle;

public class MainActivity extends Activity {

    @Override
    public void onCreate(Bundle savedInstanceState) {
        super.onCreate(savedInstanceState);
        setContentView(R.layout.activity_main);

        Intent i = new Intent("net.learn2develop.MyBrowser");
        i.setData(Uri.parse("http://www.amazon.com"));
        startActivity(i);
    }

}
```

Figure 1-20 shows the MyBrowserActivity class displaying the Amazon.com site. In this case, you are directly calling the MyBrowserActivity class using its "net.learn2develop.MyBrowser" action.

FIGURE 1-20

Alternatively, you can use the `android.content.Intent.ACTION_VIEW` constant (which evaluates to the same value as "`android.intent.action.VIEW`") to call it. However, this time you will see a dialog asking you to choose an application to complete the action (see Figure 1-21):

```
Intent i = new Intent(android.content.Intent.ACTION_VIEW);
i.setData(Uri.parse("http://www.amazon.com"));
startActivity(i);
```

This is because now more than one application can handle this action.

FIGURE 1-21

Now go to the `AndroidManifest.xml` file and modify the `<data>` element:

```xml
<activity
    android:name=".MyBrowserActivity"
    android:label="@string/app_name" >
    <intent-filter>
        <action android:name="android.intent.action.VIEW" />
        <action android:name="net.learn2develop.MyBrowser" />
        <category android:name="android.intent.category.DEFAULT" />
        <!--
            <data android:scheme="http" />
        -->
        <data android:mimeType="text/html" />
    </intent-filter>
</activity>
```

The `<data>` element in this case specifies the MIME media type that the activity is capable of handling.

To call the activity with this MIME type, you have to use the `setType()` method:

```java
Intent i = new Intent(android.content.Intent.ACTION_VIEW);

//---if you are using setType(), no need to use setData()---
//i.setData(Uri.parse("http://www.amazon.com"));

//---indicates the type that the target activity will handle---
i.setType("text/html");
i.putExtra("URL", "http://www.amazon.com");
startActivity(i);
```

Note that the `setType()` method automatically clears any data you set using the `setData()` method; hence, you do not need to use the `setData()` method. To pass data to the activity in this case, you can use the `putExtra()` method.

The preceding code snippet will show a list of applications that are capable of handling the MIME type you specified (see Figure 1-22).

To retrieve the data passed in using the `putExtra()` method, you can use the `getStringExtra()` method:

```java
@Override
public void onCreate(Bundle savedInstanceState)
{
    super.onCreate(savedInstanceState);
    setContentView(R.layout.browser);

    //Uri url = getIntent().getData();
    Uri url = Uri.parse(getIntent().getStringExtra("URL"));

    WebView webView = (WebView) findViewById(R.id.webView);
    webView.setWebViewClient(new Callback());
```

```
        if (url!=null) {
            webView.loadUrl(url.toString());
        } else {
            webView.loadUrl("http://www.google.com");
        }
    }
```

FIGURE 1-22

2

Using Views to Design the User Interface

In the previous chapter, you learned about some of the fundamental concepts in Android programming. This chapter takes a look at the various views that you can use to design the user interface for your applications. In particular, you will learn about the following views:

➤   `Button`, `ToggleButton`, `ImageButton`, and `RadioButton`

➤   `CheckBox`

➤   `WebView`

➤   `DatePicker` and `TimePicker`

You will also learn about the various ways to lay out your views using ViewGroups. In particular, you will learn about the following ViewGroups:

➤   `LinearLayout`

➤   `RelativeLayout`

➤   `FrameLayout`

➤   `TableLayout`

➤   `ScrollView`

Finally, this chapter demonstrates how to display context and options menus, as well as how to display dialogs and implement page swiping.

RECIPE 2.1 USING BUTTONS

Android Versions

Level 1 and above

Permissions

None

Source Code to Download from Wrox.com

Buttons.zip

The Button view is one of the most commonly used views on an activity. This recipe shows you the basic types of Button views and the various ways to handle their events.

Solution

Assume you have the following code snippet in the `activity_main.xml` file:

```xml
<LinearLayout xmlns:android="http://schemas.android.com/apk/res/android"
    android:layout_width="match_parent"
    android:layout_height="match_parent"
    android:orientation="vertical" >

    <Button
        android:layout_width="match_parent"
        android:layout_height="wrap_content"
        android:text="Button 1"
        android:onClick="onClick" />

    <Button
        android:layout_width="match_parent"
        android:layout_height="wrap_content"
        android:text="Button 2"
        android:onClick="onClick" />

    <Button
        android:id="@+id/button3"
        android:layout_width="match_parent"
        android:layout_height="wrap_content"
        android:text="Button 3" />

    <Button
        android:id="@+id/button4"
        android:layout_width="match_parent"
        android:layout_height="wrap_content"
        android:text="Button 4" />
```

```
    <Button
        android:id="@+id/button5"
        android:layout_width="match_parent"
        android:layout_height="wrap_content"
        android:text="Button 5" />

    <ToggleButton
        android:id="@+id/toggleButton"
        android:layout_width="wrap_content"
        android:layout_height="wrap_content"
        android:text="ToggleButton"
        android:onClick="onToggle" />

</LinearLayout>
```

The most common way to handle a Button event is to implement its onClick event. There are a few ways to do this:

```
package net.learn2develop.buttons;

import android.app.Activity;
import android.os.Bundle;
import android.view.View;
import android.view.View.OnClickListener;
import android.widget.Button;
import android.widget.Toast;
import android.widget.ToggleButton;

public class MainActivity extends Activity {

    @Override
    public void onCreate(Bundle savedInstanceState) {
        super.onCreate(savedInstanceState);
        setContentView(R.layout.activity_main);

        //---Button view---
        Button btn = (Button) findViewById(R.id.button3);
        btn.setOnClickListener(new View.OnClickListener() {
            public void onClick(View view) {
                Toast.makeText(getBaseContext(), "Button 3 was clicked!",
                        Toast.LENGTH_SHORT).show();
            }
        });

        //---the two buttons are wired to the same event handler---
        Button btn4 = (Button) findViewById(R.id.button4);
        btn4.setOnClickListener(btnListener);

        Button btn5 = (Button) findViewById(R.id.button5);
        btn5.setOnClickListener(btnListener);
    }

    //---create an anonymous class to act as a button click listener---
    private OnClickListener btnListener = new OnClickListener() {
```

```
        public void onClick(View view)
        {
            Toast.makeText(getBaseContext(),
                    ((Button) view).getText() + " was clicked!",
                    Toast.LENGTH_LONG).show();
        }
    };

    public void onClick(View view) {
        Button btn = (Button) view;
        Toast.makeText(this, btn.getText() + " was clicked!",
                Toast.LENGTH_SHORT).show();
    }

    public void onToggle(View view) {
        ToggleButton btn = (ToggleButton) view;
        Toast.makeText(this, "Toggle mode: " + btn.isChecked(),
                Toast.LENGTH_SHORT).show();
    }

}
```

The first two buttons (Button 1 and Button 2) have no `android:id` attributes in their declaration. Instead, they have the `android:onClick` attribute, which is set to `onClick`. The `onClick` refers to the name of the method in the activity:

```
public void onClick(View view) {
    Button btn = (Button) view;
    Toast.makeText(this, btn.getText() + " was clicked!",
            Toast.LENGTH_SHORT).show();
}
```

When these two buttons are clicked, they both fire the same `onClick()` method as shown above. You can programmatically differentiate them by typecasting the `view` argument that is passed in through the method and examining their text value.

The next button (Button 3) has the `android:id` attribute set, but not the `android:onClick` attribute. To programmatically handle the click event for the button, you need to get a reference to the button, call its `setOnClickListener()` method, and then set it an instance of the `OnClickListener` class. In the `OnClickListener` class, implement the `onClick()` method:

```
//---Button view---
Button btn = (Button) findViewById(R.id.button3);
btn.setOnClickListener(new View.OnClickListener() {
    public void onClick(View view) {
        Toast.makeText(getBaseContext(), "Button 3 was clicked!",
                Toast.LENGTH_SHORT).show();
    }
});
```

The next two buttons are similar to Button 3, but instead of creating an inner class to handle the event, you created an anonymous class:

```
//---create an anonymous class to act as a button click listener---
private OnClickListener btnListener = new OnClickListener() {
```

```
        public void onClick(View view)
        {
            Toast.makeText(getBaseContext(),
                    ((Button) view).getText() + " was clicked!",
                    Toast.LENGTH_LONG).show();
        }
    };
```

You then set the two buttons' click event handler to this class:

```
        //---the two buttons are wired to the same event handler---
        Button btn4 = (Button) findViewById(R.id.button4);
        btn4.setOnClickListener(btnListener);

        Button btn5 = (Button) findViewById(R.id.button5);
        btn5.setOnClickListener(btnListener);
```

The `ToggleButton` behaves just like the `Button` except that it displays a blue line indicating whether it is toggled:

```
        public void onToggle(View view) {
            ToggleButton btn = (ToggleButton) view;
            Toast.makeText(this, "Toggle mode: " + btn.isChecked(),
                    Toast.LENGTH_SHORT).show();
        }
```

You can check whether a `ToggleButton` is toggled by checking its `isChecked()` method.

Figure 2-1 shows the buttons in action.

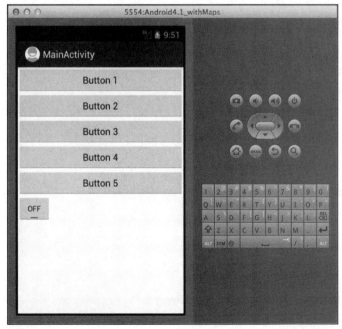

FIGURE 2-1

RECIPE 2.2 USING IMAGE BUTTONS

Android Versions

Level 1 and above

Permissions

None

Source Code to Download from Wrox.com

ImageButtons.zip

The previous recipe showed the `Button` and `ToggleButton` in action and the various ways to handle their events. This recipe describes how to display images on buttons. As the saying goes, a picture is worth a thousand words. Hence, sometimes it would be more intuitive and descriptive to display a picture on top of a button rather than words.

Solution

Consider the following code snippet in the `activity_main.xml` file:

```xml
<LinearLayout xmlns:android="http://schemas.android.com/apk/res/android"
    android:layout_width="match_parent"
    android:layout_height="match_parent"
    android:orientation="vertical" >

    <ImageButton
        android:id="@+id/imageButton"
        android:layout_width="wrap_content"
        android:layout_height="wrap_content"
        android:src="@drawable/ic_launcher"
        android:onClick="onToggle" />

    <Button
        android:id="@+id/imageTextButton1"
        android:layout_width="wrap_content"
        android:layout_height="wrap_content"
        android:drawableTop="@drawable/ic_launcher"
        android:text="Android"/>

    <Button
        android:id="@+id/imageTextButton2"
        android:layout_width="wrap_content"
        android:layout_height="wrap_content"
        android:drawableLeft="@drawable/ic_launcher"
        android:text="Android"/>

    <Button
        android:id="@+id/imageTextButton3"
        android:layout_width="wrap_content"
```

```
        android:layout_height="wrap_content"
        android:drawableRight="@drawable/ic_launcher"
        android:text="Android"/>

    <Button
        android:id="@+id/imageTextButton4"
        android:layout_width="wrap_content"
        android:layout_height="wrap_content"
        android:drawableBottom="@drawable/ic_launcher"
        android:text="Android"/>

</LinearLayout>
```

The preceding code snippet results in the appearance shown in Figure 2-2.

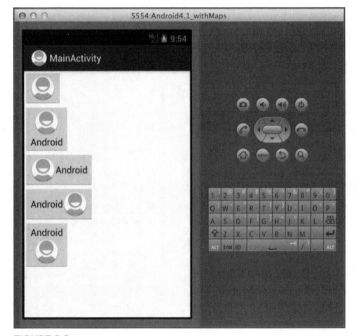

FIGURE 2-2

Note that the first button is an ImageButton, which enables you to display an image on top of a button. However, you cannot display text inside an ImageButton.

To display text along with text on a button, you have to use the android:drawableLeft, android:drawableRight, android:drawableTop, or android:drawableBottom attribute within a Button view. This enables you to display an image at the left, right, top, or bottom of the button. You can also combine all these attributes, like this:

```
    <Button
        android:id="@+id/imageTextButton5"
        android:layout_width="wrap_content"
        android:layout_height="wrap_content"
        android:drawableTop="@drawable/ic_launcher"
```

```
        android:drawableBottom="@drawable/ic_launcher"
        android:drawableLeft="@drawable/ic_launcher"
        android:drawableRight="@drawable/ic_launcher"
        android:text="Android"/>
```

The preceding code snippet produces the button shown in Figure 2-3.

You can also programmatically set a button with images. Assume you have the
following Button in your UI:

```
<Button
        android:id="@+id/imageTextButton6"
        android:layout_width="wrap_content"
        android:layout_height="wrap_content"
        android:text=""/>
```

FIGURE 2-3

The following code snippet sets the button with the text "Android" and the
image at the top of the button (see Figure 2-4):

```
//---Button view---
Button btn = (Button) findViewById(R.id.imageTextButton6);
btn.setText("Android");
btn.setCompoundDrawablesWithIntrinsicBounds(
        0,                             // left
        R.drawable.ic_launcher,   // top
        0,                             // right
        0);                            // bottom
```

FIGURE 2-4

RECIPE 2.3 USING RADIO BUTTONS

Android Versions

Level 1 and above

Permissions

None

Source Code to Download from Wrox.com

RadioButtons.zip

Radio buttons enable users to select one item from a list of available options. This recipe shows how
to use radio buttons in your Android application.

Solution

Assume you have the following code snippet in your activity_main.xml file:

```
<LinearLayout xmlns:android="http://schemas.android.com/apk/res/android"
        android:layout_width="match_parent"
```

```
        android:layout_height="match_parent"
        android:orientation="vertical" >

    <RadioGroup
        android:id="@+id/rdbGp1"
        android:layout_width="match_parent"
        android:layout_height="wrap_content"
        android:orientation="vertical" >

        <RadioButton
            android:id="@+id/rdb1"
            android:layout_width="match_parent"
            android:layout_height="wrap_content"
            android:drawableLeft="@drawable/ic_launcher"
            android:text="Option 1" />

        <RadioButton
            android:id="@+id/rdb2"
            android:layout_width="match_parent"
            android:layout_height="wrap_content"
            android:drawableLeft="@drawable/ic_launcher"
            android:text="Option 2"
            android:checked="true"/>
    </RadioGroup>

</LinearLayout>
```

The `RadioButton` element represents a two-state button that can be either checked or unchecked. Once a radio button is checked, it cannot be unchecked by tapping on it. Instead, radio buttons are contained within a `RadioGroup` element, which contains a set of radio buttons. Checking one radio button in a radio group unchecks the rest of the radio buttons in the same group.

Figure 2-5 shows the result of the preceding code snippet in the Android emulator.

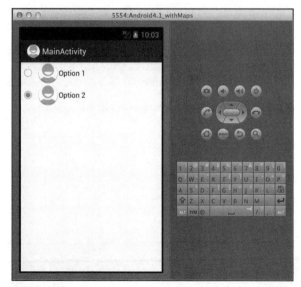

FIGURE 2-5

The following code snippet shows how to determine whether a radio button is checked:

```
package net.learn2develop.radiobuttons;

import android.app.Activity;
import android.os.Bundle;
import android.widget.RadioButton;
import android.widget.RadioGroup;
import android.widget.RadioGroup.OnCheckedChangeListener;
import android.widget.Toast;

public class MainActivity extends Activity {

    @Override
    public void onCreate(Bundle savedInstanceState) {
        super.onCreate(savedInstanceState);
        setContentView(R.layout.activity_main);

        //---RadioButton---
        RadioGroup radioGroup = (RadioGroup) findViewById(R.id.rdbGp1);
        radioGroup.setOnCheckedChangeListener(new OnCheckedChangeListener()
        {
            public void onCheckedChanged(RadioGroup group, int checkedId) {
                RadioButton rb1 = (RadioButton) findViewById(R.id.rdb1);
                if (rb1.isChecked()) {
                    Toast.makeText(getBaseContext(),
                            "Option 1 checked!",
                            Toast.LENGTH_LONG).show();
                } else {
                    Toast.makeText(getBaseContext(),
                            "Option 2 checked!",
                            Toast.LENGTH_LONG).show();
                }
            }
        });
    }
}
```

You can determine whether a radio button is checked by listening to the onCheckedChanged event on of the RadioGroup element. This event is fired whenever a radio button contained within it is checked or unchecked. To determine the state of a radio button, examine its isChecked() method.

Figure 2-6 shows the Toast class displaying a message when a radio button is clicked on the emulator.

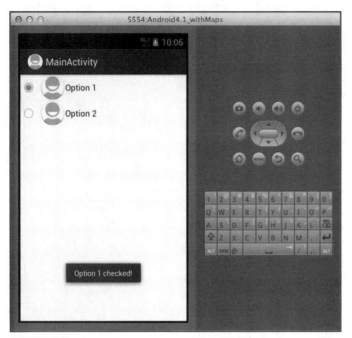

FIGURE 2-6

RECIPE 2.4 USING CHECKBOXES

Android Versions

Level 1 and above

Permissions

None

Source Code to Download from Wrox.com

CheckBoxes.zip

Like radio buttons, checkboxes enable users to select one or more options from a list. A `CheckBox` has two states: checked or unchecked. Unlike radio buttons, checkboxes can be checked and unchecked by the user without regard to the state of other checkboxes. This recipe shows how to use checkboxes in your Android application.

Solution

Assume you have the following code snippet in the `activity_main.xml` file:

```xml
<LinearLayout xmlns:android="http://schemas.android.com/apk/res/android"
    android:layout_width="match_parent"
    android:layout_height="match_parent"
    android:orientation="vertical" >

    <CheckBox
        android:id="@+id/chkAutosave"
        android:layout_width="match_parent"
        android:layout_height="wrap_content"
        android:text="Autosave" />

    <CheckBox
        android:id="@+id/star"
        style="?android:attr/starStyle"
        android:layout_width="wrap_content"
        android:layout_height="wrap_content" />

</LinearLayout>
```

The `CheckBox` element defines an item for users to check or uncheck. Android supports a special type of checkbox known as the *star checkbox*. You display a star checkbox by setting the `style` attribute and setting its value to `?android:attr/starStyle`.

Figure 2-7 shows the default checkbox and the star checkbox. The top part shows the unchecked state of the two checkboxes, and the lower portion shows the checked state.

The following code snippet shows how to determine whether a checkbox is checked:

```java
package net.learn2develop.checkboxes;

import android.app.Activity;
import android.os.Bundle;
import android.view.View;
import android.widget.CheckBox;
import android.widget.Toast;

public class MainActivity extends Activity {

    @Override
    public void onCreate(Bundle savedInstanceState) {
        super.onCreate(savedInstanceState);
        setContentView(R.layout.activity_main);
```

FIGURE 2-7

```
//---CheckBox---
CheckBox checkBox = (CheckBox) findViewById(R.id.chkAutosave);
checkBox.setOnClickListener(new View.OnClickListener()
{
    public void onClick(View v) {
        if (((CheckBox)v).isChecked())
            Toast.makeText(getBaseContext(),
                    "CheckBox is checked",
                    Toast.LENGTH_LONG).show();
        else
            Toast.makeText(getBaseContext(),
                    "CheckBox is unchecked",
                    Toast.LENGTH_LONG).show();
    }
});
        }
    }
```

To determine the state of a checkbox, you need to listen to its onClick event. The isChecked() method of the checkbox returns true if the checkbox is checked, or false if it is not. Figure 2-8 shows the Toast class displaying the state of the Autosave checkbox.

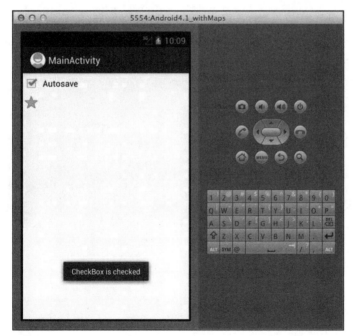

FIGURE 2-8

RECIPE 2.5 IMPLEMENTING A STAR RATING SYSTEM

Android Versions

Level 1 and above

Permissions

None

Source Code to Download from Wrox.com

CheckBoxesRating.zip

The previous recipe introduced you to the checkbox, in particular the star checkbox. One popular use of the star checkbox is to implement a star rating system, whereby users tap on the stars to provide a rating for a particular item (such as user reviews for books, music, or venues). This recipe demonstrates how to implement this rating system.

Solution

Assume you have the following code snippet in the `activity_main.xml` file:

```xml
<LinearLayout xmlns:android="http://schemas.android.com/apk/res/android"
    android:layout_width="match_parent"
    android:layout_height="match_parent"
    android:orientation="horizontal"
    android:id="@+id/ratings" >

    <CheckBox
        android:id="@+id/star1"
        style="?android:attr/starStyle"
        android:layout_width="wrap_content"
        android:layout_height="wrap_content"
        android:tag="1" />

    <CheckBox
        android:id="@+id/star2"
        style="?android:attr/starStyle"
        android:layout_width="wrap_content"
        android:layout_height="wrap_content"
        android:tag="2" />

    <CheckBox
        android:id="@+id/star3"
        style="?android:attr/starStyle"
        android:layout_width="wrap_content"
        android:layout_height="wrap_content"
        android:tag="3" />
```

```
<CheckBox
    android:id="@+id/star4"
    style="?android:attr/starStyle"
    android:layout_width="wrap_content"
    android:layout_height="wrap_content"
    android:tag="4" />

<CheckBox
    android:id="@+id/star5"
    style="?android:attr/starStyle"
    android:layout_width="wrap_content"
    android:layout_height="wrap_content"
    android:tag="5" />

</LinearLayout>
```

Note that the checkboxes are arranged horizontally and displayed using the star style. Also note that each checkbox is tagged using the `android:tag` attribute. This will be useful later when you need to programmatically locate the individual checkbox.

The following code snippet shows how to implement the star rating system:

```
package net.learn2develop.checkboxesratings;

import android.app.Activity;
import android.os.Bundle;
import android.view.View;
import android.view.View.OnClickListener;
import android.widget.CheckBox;
import android.widget.LinearLayout;

public class MainActivity extends Activity {
    LinearLayout rating;
    CheckBox star;

    @Override
    public void onCreate(Bundle savedInstanceState) {
        super.onCreate(savedInstanceState);
        setContentView(R.layout.activity_main);

        //---get the layout containing the stars---
        rating = (LinearLayout) findViewById(R.id.ratings);

        for (int i = 1; i <= 5; i++) {
            star = (CheckBox) rating.findViewWithTag(String.valueOf(i));
            star.setOnClickListener(starsListener);
        }
    }

    private OnClickListener starsListener = new OnClickListener() {
        public void onClick(View view) {

            //---get the tag of the star selected---
            int tag = Integer.valueOf((String) view.getTag());

            //---check all the stars up to the one touched---
```

```
                    for (int i = 1; i <= tag; i++) {
                        star = (CheckBox) rating.findViewWithTag(String.valueOf(i));
                        star.setChecked(true);
                    }

                    //---uncheck all remaining stars---
                    for (int i = tag + 1; i <= 5; i++) {
                        star = (CheckBox) rating.findViewWithTag(String.valueOf(i));
                        star.setChecked(false);
                    }
                }
            };

        }
```

Here, you first locate all five checkboxes and listen to each checkbox's `onClick()` event. You locate the individual checkboxes using the `findViewWithTag()` method of the `LinearLayout` instance (because the checkboxes are all embedded within a `LinearLayout`).

When a checkbox is tapped, you check all the checkboxes up to the checkbox that was tapped and uncheck all the checkboxes thereafter.

Figure 2-9 shows the star rating system in action.

FIGURE 2-9

RECIPE 2.6 USING AUTOCOMPLETETEXTVIEW

Android Versions

Level 1 and above

Permissions

None

Source Code to Download from Wrox.com

AutoComplete.zip

While you can use an `EditText` view for entering text, it is sometimes useful to provide users with suggestions to automatically complete what they are typing. For example, if a user is typing a search string into an `EditText`, you can offer possible suggestions to complete the search string while the user is typing. In this case, you can use the `AutoCompleteTextView` to do so. This recipe shows you how.

Solution

The `AutoCompleteTextView` is an editable text view that shows completion suggestions while the user is typing. The suggestions are displayed as a drop-down menu that contains content that is supplied by you.

Assume you have the following code snippet in the `activity_main.xml` file:

```
<LinearLayout xmlns:android="http://schemas.android.com/apk/res/android"
    android:layout_width="match_parent"
    android:layout_height="match_parent"
    android:orientation="vertical" >

    <TextView
        android:layout_width="match_parent"
        android:layout_height="wrap_content"
        android:text="Name of President" />

    <AutoCompleteTextView
        android:id="@+id/txtCountries"
        android:layout_width="match_parent"
        android:layout_height="wrap_content" />

</LinearLayout>
```

The following code snippet shows how to use the `AutoCompleteTextView`:

```
package net.learn2develop.autocomplete;

import android.app.Activity;
import android.os.Bundle;
import android.widget.ArrayAdapter;
import android.widget.AutoCompleteTextView;

public class MainActivity extends Activity {
    String[] presidents = {
            "Dwight D. Eisenhower",
            "John F. Kennedy",
            "Lyndon B. Johnson",
            "Richard Nixon",
            "Gerald Ford",
            "Jimmy Carter",
            "Ronald Reagan",
            "George H. W. Bush",
            "Bill Clinton",
            "George W. Bush",
            "Barack Obama"
    };

    @Override
    public void onCreate(Bundle savedInstanceState) {
        super.onCreate(savedInstanceState);
        setContentView(R.layout.activity_main);

        ArrayAdapter<String> adapter = new ArrayAdapter<String>(this,
            android.R.layout.simple_dropdown_item_1line, presidents);

        AutoCompleteTextView textView = (AutoCompleteTextView)
            findViewById(R.id.txtCountries);

        textView.setThreshold(3);
        textView.setAdapter(adapter);
    }
}
```

You first created an array containing a list of presidents' names. You then created an `ArrayAdapter` object, specifying how you want to display the list of names, as well as the array containing the names.

You set the `AutoCompleteTextView`'s threshold to 3 so that the suggestions will appear only after the user has typed at least three characters. You then need to set the `AutoCompleteTextView` to use the array adapter you have just created.

Figure 2-10 shows the suggestions displayed in a list as the user types the characters "joh" into the `AutoCompleteTextView`.

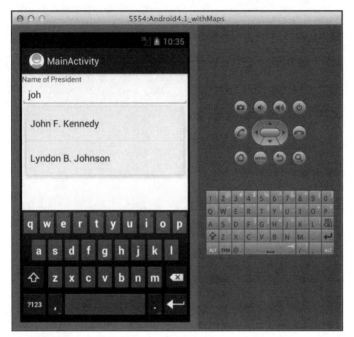

FIGURE 2-10

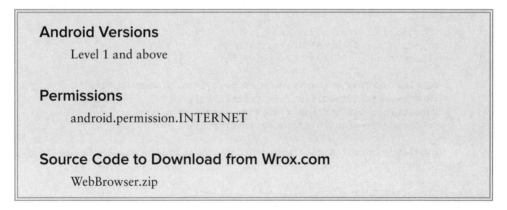

RECIPE 2.7   DISPLAYING WEB PAGES

Android Versions

Level 1 and above

Permissions

android.permission.INTERNET

Source Code to Download from Wrox.com

WebBrowser.zip

Oftentimes your Android application needs to load content from the web, such as images or web pages. This recipe shows you how to embed a web browser in your application and use it to load content from the web, as well as content stored locally in your application.

Solution

Assume you have the following code snippet in your `activity_main.xml` file:

```xml
<LinearLayout xmlns:android="http://schemas.android.com/apk/res/android"
    android:layout_width="match_parent"
    android:layout_height="match_parent"
    android:orientation="vertical" >

    <WebView
        android:id="@+id/WebView01"
        android:layout_width="wrap_content"
        android:layout_height="wrap_content" />

</LinearLayout>
```

The `WebView` element defines a web browser in your Android activity. You can use it to load content from the web or resources stored locally in your application.

The following code snippet shows how to load the `WebView` with an image from the web:

```java
package net.learn2develop.webbrowser;

import android.app.Activity;
import android.os.Bundle;
import android.webkit.WebSettings;
import android.webkit.WebView;
import android.webkit.WebViewClient;

public class MainActivity extends Activity {

    @Override
    public void onCreate(Bundle savedInstanceState) {
        super.onCreate(savedInstanceState);
        setContentView(R.layout.activity_main);

        WebView webView = (WebView) findViewById(R.id.WebView01);
        webView.setWebViewClient(new Callback());
        WebSettings webSettings = webView.getSettings();
        webSettings.setBuiltInZoomControls(true);

        webView.loadUrl("http://www.android.com/images/whatsnew/jb-new-logo.png");
    }

    private class Callback extends WebViewClient {
        @Override
        public boolean shouldOverrideUrlLoading(WebView view,
        String url) {
            return (false);
        }
    }
}
```

To display the built-in zoom controls, you need to first get the `WebSettings` property from the `WebView` and then call its `setBuiltInZoomControls()` method.

> **NOTE** *Although most Android devices support multi-touch screens, the built-in zoom controls are useful for zooming your web content when testing your application on the Android emulator.*

Sometimes when you load a page that redirects you (such as loading `www.wrox.com` redirects you to `www.wrox.com/wileyCDA`), the `WebView` will cause your application to launch the device's browser application to load the desired page. For example, if you ask the `WebView` to load `www.wrox.com`, Wrox .com will automatically redirect you to `www.wrox.com/WileyCDA/`. In this case, your application will automatically launch the device's browser application to load your page. To prevent this from happening, you need to implement the `WebViewClient` class and override the `shouldOverrideUrlLoading()` method, as shown in the preceding example.

Finally, to use the `WebView` in your application, you need to remember to add the `INTERNET` permission to your `AndroidManifest.xml` file:

```
<uses-permission android:name="android.permission.INTERNET" />
```

> **NOTE** *This book makes the assumption that you are familiar with how permissions work in context, so it will list only the permission line itself; see the section titled "A Note About Permissions" in the Introduction.*

Figure 2-11 shows the `WebView` displaying an image loaded from the web.

FIGURE 2-11

Loading from a String

Besides loading the content of the WebView from the web, you can also load it from a string, like this:

```
@Override
public void onCreate(Bundle savedInstanceState) {
    super.onCreate(savedInstanceState);
    setContentView(R.layout.activity_main);

    WebView webView = (WebView) findViewById(R.id.WebView01);
    webView.setWebViewClient(new Callback());
    WebSettings webSettings = webView.getSettings();
    webSettings.setBuiltInZoomControls(true);

    //---Part 1---
    //webView.loadUrl(
        "http://www.android.com/images/whatsnew/jb-new-logo.png");

    final String mimeType = "text/html";
    final String encoding = "UTF-8";
    String html =
    "<H1>A simple HTML page</H1><body>" +
    "<p>The quick brown fox jumps over the lazy dog</p></body>";

    webView.loadDataWithBaseURL("", html, mimeType, encoding, "");
}
```

The preceding code snippet loads the WebView with a string containing HTML content using the loadDataWithBaseURL() method. Figure 2-12 shows the WebView displaying the content loaded.

FIGURE 2-12

Loading from an Assets Folder

If you want to load content from a file, perhaps located in the assets folder of your project (see Figure 2-13), you can also load the WebView with the content stored in the file.

Assume that the index.html file shown in Figure 2-13 contains the following:

```
<H1>A simple HTML page</H1>
<body>
<p>The quick brown fox jumps over the lazy dog</p>
<img src="http://developer.android.com/images/home/
market_icon.png" />
</body>
```

The following code snippet loads the WebView using the content of index.html:

FIGURE 2-13

```
@Override
public void onCreate(Bundle savedInstanceState) {
    super.onCreate(savedInstanceState);
    setContentView(R.layout.activity_main);

    WebView webView = (WebView) findViewById(R.id.WebView01);
    webView.setWebViewClient(new Callback());
    WebSettings webSettings = webView.getSettings();
    webSettings.setBuiltInZoomControls(true);

    //---Part 1---
    //webView.loadUrl(
        "http://www.android.com/images/whatsnew/jb-new-logo.png");

    //---Part 2---
    final String mimeType = "text/html";
    final String encoding = "UTF-8";
    String html =
    "<H1>A simple HTML page</H1><body>" +
    "<p>The quick brown fox jumps over the lazy dog</p></body>";
    //webView.loadDataWithBaseURL("", html, mimeType, encoding, "");

    //---Part 3---
    webView.loadUrl("file:///android_asset/index.html");
}
```

Figure 2-14 shows the WebView displaying the content of the file.

FIGURE 2-14

RECIPE 2.8 USING THE TIMEPICKER

Android Versions

Level 1 and above

Permissions

None

Source Code to Download from Wrox.com

UsingTimePicker.zip

The `TimePicker` view enables users to select a time of the day, in either 24-hour mode or AM/PM mode. This recipe shows you how to use it.

Solution

Assume you have the following code snippet in the `activity_main.xml` file, which contains a TimePicker and a Button view:

```
<RelativeLayout xmlns:android="http://schemas.android.com/apk/res/android"
    xmlns:tools="http://schemas.android.com/tools"
```

```
    android:layout_width="match_parent"
    android:layout_height="match_parent" >

    <TimePicker
        android:id="@+id/timePicker"
        android:layout_width="wrap_content"
        android:layout_height="wrap_content"
        android:layout_alignParentTop="true"
        android:layout_centerHorizontal="true" />

    <Button
        android:id="@+id/btnSet"
        android:layout_width="wrap_content"
        android:layout_height="wrap_content"
        android:layout_alignParentLeft="true"
        android:layout_alignParentRight="true"
        android:layout_below="@+id/timePicker"
        android:layout_marginTop="29dp"
        android:text="I am all set!"
        android:onClick="btnClick"/>

</RelativeLayout>
```

The `TimePicker` displays a standard UI to enable users to set a time. By default, it displays the time in the AM/PM format.

The following code snippet shows how you can get the time set by the user using the `TimePicker` view:

```java
package com.example.usingtimepicker;

import java.text.DecimalFormat;
import java.text.NumberFormat;

import android.app.Activity;
import android.os.Bundle;
import android.view.View;
import android.widget.TimePicker;
import android.widget.Toast;

public class MainActivity extends Activity {
    TimePicker timePicker;
    @Override
    public void onCreate(Bundle savedInstanceState) {
        super.onCreate(savedInstanceState);
        setContentView(R.layout.activity_main);

        timePicker = (TimePicker) findViewById(R.id.timePicker);
        timePicker.setIs24HourView(true);
    }

    public void btnClick(View view) {
        NumberFormat formatter = new DecimalFormat("00");
        Toast.makeText(getBaseContext(),
                "Time selected:" +
```

```
            timePicker.getCurrentHour() +
        ":" + formatter.format(timePicker.getCurrentMinute()),
        Toast.LENGTH_SHORT).show();
    }

}
```

If you want to display the time in the 24-hour format, you use the setIs24HourView() method. To programmatically get the time set by the user, use the getCurrentHour() and getCurrentMinute() methods. Figure 2-15 shows the TimePicker in action.

FIGURE 2-15

RECIPE 2.9 USING THE DATEPICKER

Android Versions
Level 1 and above

Permissions
None

Source Code to Download from Wrox.com
UsingDatePicker.zip

Another view that is similar to the `TimePicker` is the `DatePicker`. Using the `DatePicker`, you can enable users to select a particular date on the activity. This recipe shows you how to use the `DatePicker`.

Solution

Assume you have the following code snippet in your `activity_main.xml` file, which contains a Button and a DatePicker view:

```xml
<RelativeLayout xmlns:android="http://schemas.android.com/apk/res/android"
    xmlns:tools="http://schemas.android.com/tools"
    android:layout_width="match_parent"
    android:layout_height="match_parent" >

    <Button
        android:id="@+id/btnSet"
        android:layout_width="wrap_content"
        android:layout_height="wrap_content"
        android:layout_alignParentLeft="true"
        android:onClick="btnClick"
        android:text="I am all set!" />

    <DatePicker
        android:id="@+id/datePicker"
        android:layout_width="wrap_content"
        android:layout_height="wrap_content"
        android:layout_alignParentLeft="true"
        android:layout_below="@+id/btnSet" />

</RelativeLayout>
```

The following code snippet shows the date selected by the user:

```java
package net.learn2develop.usingdatepicker;

import android.app.Activity;
import android.os.Bundle;
import android.view.View;
import android.widget.DatePicker;
import android.widget.Toast;

public class MainActivity extends Activity {
    DatePicker datePicker;

    @Override
    public void onCreate(Bundle savedInstanceState) {
        super.onCreate(savedInstanceState);
        setContentView(R.layout.activity_main);

        datePicker = (DatePicker) findViewById(R.id.datePicker);
    }

    public void btnClick(View view) {
        Toast.makeText(getBaseContext(),
```

```
            "Date selected:" + (datePicker.getMonth() + 1) +
            "/" + datePicker.getDayOfMonth() +
            "/" + datePicker.getYear(),
            Toast.LENGTH_SHORT).show();
        }
    }
```

Like the `TimePicker`, you call the `getMonth()`, `getDayOfMonth()`, and `getYear()` methods
of the `DatePicker` to get the selected month, day, and year, respectively. Figure 2-16 shows the
`DatePicker` in action.

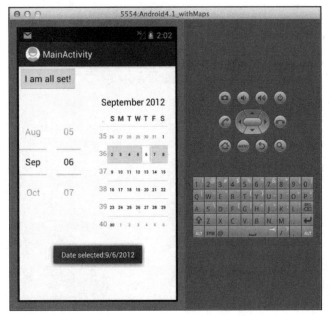

FIGURE 2-16

RECIPE 2.10 USING LINEARLAYOUT FOR VIEW POSITIONING

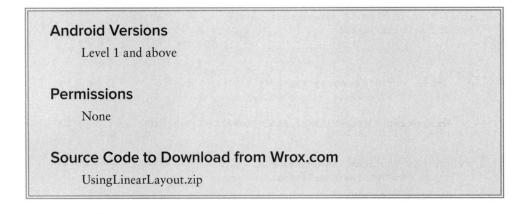

Android Versions
Level 1 and above

Permissions
None

Source Code to Download from Wrox.com
UsingLinearLayout.zip

An activity contains Views and ViewGroups. A view is a widget that has an appearance on screen. Examples of views are Buttons, TextViews, and EditTexts. A view derives from the base class `android.view.View`.

One or more Views can be grouped together into a ViewGroup. A ViewGroup (which is itself a special type of view) provides the layout in which you can order the appearance and sequence of views. Examples of ViewGroups include `LinearLayout` and `FrameLayout`. A ViewGroup derives from the base class `android.view.ViewGroup`.

Android supports the following ViewGroups:

➤ `LinearLayout`

➤ `TableLayout`

➤ `RelativeLayout`

➤ `FrameLayout`

➤ `ScrollView`

The following recipes describe each of these ViewGroups in more detail. Note that in practice it is common to combine different types of layouts to create the UI you want. This recipe discusses the `LinearLayout` ViewGroup.

Solution

You have several options when arranging views using the `LinearLayout`:

➤ They can be arranged in a single column or a single row.

➤ Child views can be arranged either vertically or horizontally.

➤ Views can be aligned to certain sides of a screen, using weight specifications.

The following sections discuss these in more details.

Orientations

You can set the orientation to display horizontally or vertically, so items appear in a single column or a single row.

Assume you have the following code snippet in the `activity_main.xml` file:

```
<LinearLayout xmlns:android="http://schemas.android.com/apk/res/android"
    android:layout_width="match_parent"
    android:layout_height="match_parent"
    android:orientation="horizontal" >

    <Button
        android:layout_width="100dp"
        android:layout_height="wrap_content"
        android:text="Button 1" />
```

```
    <Button
        android:layout_width="100dp"
        android:layout_height="wrap_content"
        android:text="Button 2" />

    <Button
        android:layout_width="100dp"
        android:layout_height="wrap_content"
        android:text="Button 3" />

</LinearLayout>
```

The preceding code produces the layout shown in Figure 2-17. Note that the buttons are displayed next to each other, from left to right. This is because the orientation of the LinearLayout is set to horizontal.

FIGURE 2-17

If you set the orientation of the LinearLayout to vertical, as shown in the following example, the buttons are stacked on top of one another (see Figure 2-18):

```
    <LinearLayout xmlns:android="http://schemas.android.com/apk/res/android"
        android:layout_width="match_parent"
        android:layout_height="match_parent"
        android:orientation="vertical" >

        <Button
            android:layout_width="100dp"
            android:layout_height="wrap_content"
            android:text="Button 1" />
```

```
    <Button
        android:layout_width="100dp"
        android:layout_height="wrap_content"
        android:text="Button 2" />

    <Button
        android:layout_width="100dp"
        android:layout_height="wrap_content"
        android:text="Button 3" />

</LinearLayout>
```

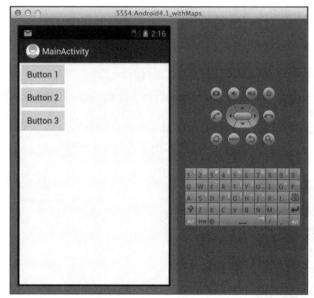

FIGURE 2-18

Gravity and Weight

Besides aligning views either horizontally or vertically, you can also specify a view's gravity and weight. A view's gravity indicates how the view should be placed in its container (so, alignment to the left, right or center). A view's weight specifies its positioning with respect to the other views in the same container (it can be positioned above or below other items).

Assume you have added the attributes highlighted in the following code snippet:

```
<LinearLayout xmlns:android="http://schemas.android.com/apk/res/android"
    android:layout_width="match_parent"
    android:layout_height="match_parent"
    android:orientation="vertical" >

    <Button
        android:layout_width="100dp"
        android:layout_height="wrap_content"
        android:layout_gravity="left"
```

```
            android:layout_weight="1"
            android:text="Button 1" />

        <Button
            android:layout_width="100dp"
            android:layout_height="wrap_content"
            android:layout_gravity="center"
            android:layout_weight="2"
            android:text="Button 2" />

        <Button
            android:layout_width="100dp"
            android:layout_height="wrap_content"
            android:layout_gravity="right"
            android:layout_weight="3"
            android:text="Button 3" />

    </LinearLayout>
```

Figure 2-19 shows the positioning of the views as well as their height. The layout_gravity attribute indicates the position of the content, while the layout_weight attribute specifies the distribution of available space. In the preceding example, the three buttons occupy about **16.6%** (1/(1+2+3) * 100), **33.3%** (2/(1+2+3) * 100), and **50%** (3/(1+2+3) * 100) of the available height, respectively.

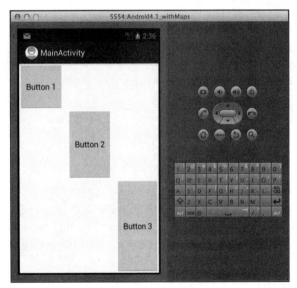

FIGURE 2-19

If you added one more button to the activity_main.xml file, the new layout of the buttons would look like what is shown in Figure 2-20:

```
    <LinearLayout xmlns:android="http://schemas.android.com/apk/res/android"
        android:layout_width="match_parent"
```

```
    android:layout_height="match_parent"
    android:orientation="vertical" >

<Button
    android:layout_width="100dp"
    android:layout_height="wrap_content"
    android:layout_gravity="left"
    android:layout_weight="1"
    android:text="Button 1" />

<Button
    android:layout_width="100dp"
    android:layout_height="wrap_content"
    android:layout_gravity="center"
    android:layout_weight="2"
    android:text="Button 2" />

<Button
    android:layout_width="100dp"
    android:layout_height="wrap_content"
    android:layout_gravity="right"
    android:layout_weight="3"
    android:text="Button 3" />

<Button
    android:layout_width="100dp"
    android:layout_height="wrap_content"
    android:layout_gravity="right"
    android:layout_weight="2"
    android:text="Button 4" />

</LinearLayout>
```

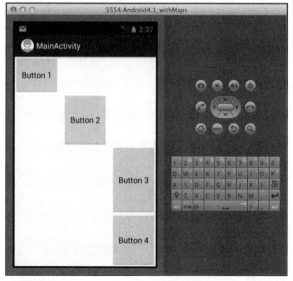

FIGURE 2-20

RECIPE 2.11 USING RELATIVELAYOUT FOR VIEW POSITIONING

Android Versions

Level 1 and above

Permissions

None

Source Code to Download from Wrox.com

UsingRelativeLayout.zip

The `RelativeLayout` ViewGroup enables you to specify how child views are positioned relative to each other. This recipe demonstrates how to use the `RelativeLayout`.

Solution

Assume you have the following code snippet in the `activity_main.xml` file:

```xml
<RelativeLayout xmlns:android="http://schemas.android.com/apk/res/android"
    xmlns:tools="http://schemas.android.com/tools"
    android:layout_width="match_parent"
    android:layout_height="match_parent" >

    <TextView
        android:id="@+id/lblComments"
        android:layout_width="wrap_content"
        android:layout_height="wrap_content"
        android:text="Comments"
        android:layout_alignParentTop="true"
        android:layout_alignParentLeft="true" />

    <EditText
        android:id="@+id/txtComments"
        android:layout_width="match_parent"
        android:layout_height="170dp"
        android:textSize="18sp"
        android:layout_alignLeft="@+id/lblComments"
        android:layout_below="@+id/lblComments"
        android:layout_centerHorizontal="true" />

    <Button
        android:id="@+id/btnSave"
        android:layout_width="125dp"
        android:layout_height="wrap_content"
        android:text="Save"
        android:layout_below="@+id/txtComments"
        android:layout_alignRight="@+id/txtComments" />
```

```
<Button
    android:id="@+id/btnCancel"
    android:layout_width="124dp"
    android:layout_height="wrap_content"
    android:text="Cancel"
    android:layout_below="@+id/txtComments"
    android:layout_alignLeft="@+id/txtComments" />

</RelativeLayout>
```

Figure 2-21 shows the layout of the various views.

FIGURE 2-21

Notice that each view embedded within the RelativeLayout has attributes that enable it to align with another view. These attributes are as follows:

- ➤ layout_alignParentTop
- ➤ layout_alignParentLeft
- ➤ layout_alignLeft
- ➤ layout_alignRight
- ➤ layout_below
- ➤ layout_centerHorizontal

The value for each of these attributes is the ID for the view that you are referencing.

RECIPE 2.12 USING FRAMELAYOUT FOR VIEW POSITIONING

Android Versions

Level 1 and above

Permissions

None

Source Code to Download from Wrox.com

UsingFrameLayout.zip

The `FrameLayout` is a placeholder on screen that you can use to display a single view. Views that you add to a `FrameLayout` are always anchored to the top left of the layout. This recipe shows how to use the `FrameLayout` to create a simple image viewer.

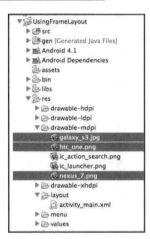

Solution

For this recipe, assume you have three images located in the `res/drawable-mdpi` folder (see Figure 2-22).

You also need to add the following code snippet in the `activity_main .xml` file:

FIGURE 2-22

```
<RelativeLayout
    android:id="@+id/RLayout"
    android:layout_width="match_parent"
    android:layout_height="match_parent"
    xmlns:android="http://schemas.android.com/apk/res/android">

    <TextView
        android:id="@+id/lblComments"
        android:layout_width="wrap_content"
        android:layout_height="wrap_content"
        android:text="Hello, Android!"
        android:layout_alignParentTop="true"
        android:layout_alignParentLeft="true" />

    <FrameLayout
        android:id="@+id/framelayout"
        android:layout_width="wrap_content"
        android:layout_height="wrap_content"
        android:layout_alignLeft="@+id/lblComments"
        android:layout_below="@+id/lblComments"
        android:layout_centerHorizontal="true" >
```

```
<ImageView
    android:src = "@drawable/galaxy_s3"
    android:layout_width="wrap_content"
    android:layout_height="wrap_content"
    android:tag="1" />

<ImageView
    android:src = "@drawable/htc_one"
    android:layout_width="wrap_content"
    android:layout_height="wrap_content"
    android:tag="2"
    android:visibility="invisible" />

<ImageView
    android:src = "@drawable/nexus_7"
    android:layout_width="wrap_content"
    android:layout_height="wrap_content"
    android:tag="3"
    android:visibility="invisible"/>

</FrameLayout>

<Button
    android:layout_width="wrap_content"
    android:layout_height="wrap_content"
    android:layout_alignParentRight="true"
    android:layout_alignParentTop="true"
    android:text="Next"
    android:onClick="btnClick" />

</RelativeLayout>
```

The preceding code snippet will display the activity as shown in Figure 2-23.

FIGURE 2-23

Note that multiple image views are added to the `FrameLayout`, but each is stacked on top of the previous one. In this example, the second and third images are set to invisible. To make the second and third images visible one by one, use the following code snippet:

```
package net.learn2develop.usingframelayout;

import android.app.Activity;
import android.os.Bundle;
import android.view.View;
import android.widget.FrameLayout;
import android.widget.ImageView;

public class MainActivity extends Activity {
    int count = 1;
    FrameLayout frame;
    ImageView imageview;

    @Override
    public void onCreate(Bundle savedInstanceState) {
        super.onCreate(savedInstanceState);
        setContentView(R.layout.activity_main);
        frame = (FrameLayout) findViewById(R.id.framelayout);
    }

    public void btnClick(View view) {
        //---hide the current one---
        imageview = (ImageView) frame.findViewWithTag(String.valueOf(count));
        imageview.setVisibility(android.view.View.INVISIBLE);

        //---go to the next image---
        count++;
        if (count>3) count = 1;

        //---show the next image---
        imageview = (ImageView) frame.findViewWithTag(String.valueOf(count));
        imageview.setVisibility(android.view.View.VISIBLE);
    }
}
```

The preceding snippet programmatically locates the image views contained within the `FrameLayout` and hides and shows the respective views. Figure 2-24 shows that the second image view is displayed when the user clicks the Next button.

FIGURE 2-24

RECIPE 2.13 USING TABLELAYOUT FOR VIEW POSITIONING

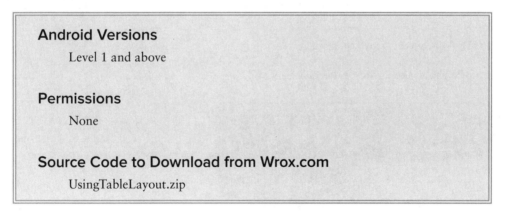

Android Versions

Level 1 and above

Permissions

None

Source Code to Download from Wrox.com

UsingTableLayout.zip

The `TableLayout` groups views into rows and columns. You use the `<TableRow>` element to desig-
nate a row in the table. Each row can contain one or more views. Each view you place within a row
forms a cell. The width of each column is determined by the largest width of each cell in that column.
This recipe shows how to use the `TableLayout`.

Solution

Assume you have the following code snippet in the `activity_main.xml` file, which contains the
`TableLayout` ViewGroup:

```
<TableLayout
    xmlns:android="http://schemas.android.com/apk/res/android"
```

```
        android:layout_height="match_parent"
        android:layout_width="match_parent">
    <TableRow>
        <TextView
            android:text="User Name:"
            android:width ="120dp" />
        <EditText
            android:id="@+id/txtUserName"
            android:width="200dp" />
    </TableRow>
    <TableRow>
        <TextView
            android:text="Password:"/>
        <EditText
            android:id="@+id/txtPassword"
            android:password="true" />
    </TableRow>
    <TableRow>
        <TextView />
        <CheckBox android:id="@+id/chkRememberPassword"
            android:layout_width="match_parent"
            android:layout_height="wrap_content"
            android:text="Remember Password" />
    </TableRow>
    <TableRow>
        <Button
            android:id="@+id/buttonSignIn"
            android:text="Log In" />
    </TableRow>
</TableLayout>
```

Figure 2-25 shows the layout of the various views.

FIGURE 2-25

Note that in this example, there are two columns and four rows in the `TableLayout`. The cell directly under the Password `TextView` is populated with an empty `<TextView/>` element.

RECIPE 2.14 | USING THE SCROLLVIEW

Android Versions
Level 1 and above

Permissions
None

Source Code to Download from Wrox.com
UsingScrollView.zip

A `ScrollView` is a special type of `FrameLayout` in that it enables users to scroll through a list of views that occupy more space than the physical display provides. The `ScrollView` can contain only one child view or ViewGroup, which normally is a `LinearLayout`. This recipe shows how to use the `ScrollView`.

Solution

Assume you have the following code snippet in the `activity_main.xml` file:

```xml
<ScrollView
    android:layout_width="match_parent"
    android:layout_height="match_parent"
    xmlns:android="http://schemas.android.com/apk/res/android" >

    <LinearLayout
        android:layout_width="match_parent"
        android:layout_height="wrap_content"
        android:orientation="vertical" >

        <Button
            android:id="@+id/button1"
            android:layout_width="match_parent"
            android:layout_height="wrap_content"
            android:text="Button 1" />

        <Button
            android:id="@+id/button2"
            android:layout_width="match_parent"
            android:layout_height="wrap_content"
            android:text="Button 2" />
```

```
<Button
    android:id="@+id/button3"
    android:layout_width="match_parent"
    android:layout_height="wrap_content"
    android:text="Button 3" />

<EditText
    android:id="@+id/txt"
    android:layout_width="match_parent"
    android:layout_height="600px" />

<Button
    android:id="@+id/button4"
    android:layout_width="match_parent"
    android:layout_height="wrap_content"
    android:text="Button 4" />

<Button
    android:id="@+id/button5"
    android:layout_width="match_parent"
    android:layout_height="wrap_content"
    android:text="Button 5" />

<Button
    android:id="@+id/button6"
    android:layout_width="match_parent"
    android:layout_height="wrap_content"
    android:text="Button 6" />

<Button
    android:id="@+id/button7"
    android:layout_width="match_parent"
    android:layout_height="wrap_content"
    android:text="Button 7" />

<Button
    android:id="@+id/button8"
    android:layout_width="match_parent"
    android:layout_height="wrap_content"
    android:text="Button 8" />

    </LinearLayout>

</ScrollView>
```

If you try to load the preceding code on the Android emulator, you will see something like what is shown in Figure 2-26.

FIGURE 2-26

Because the EditText automatically gets the focus, it fills up the entire activity (as you have set the height to 600dp). To prevent it from getting the focus, add the following two attributes to the <LinearLayout> element:

```
<ScrollView
    android:layout_width="match_parent"
    android:layout_height="match_parent"
    xmlns:android="http://schemas.android.com/apk/res/android" >

    <LinearLayout
        android:layout_width="match_parent"
        android:layout_height="wrap_content"
        android:orientation="vertical"
        android:focusable="true"
        android:focusableInTouchMode="true" >
    ...
```

You will now be able to scroll through the list of views (see Figures 2-27 and 2-28).

FIGURE 2-27

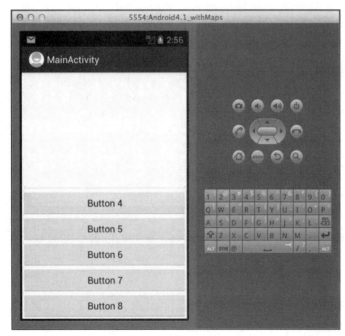

FIGURE 2-28

RECIPE 2.15 DISPLAYING CONTEXT AND OPTIONS MENUS

Android Versions

Level 1 and above

Permissions

None

Source Code to Download from Wrox.com

ContextAndOptionsMenu.zip

Menus are useful for displaying additional options that are not directly visible on the main UI of an application. You can add two main types of menus in Android:

➤ **Options menu** — Displays information related to the current activity. In Android, you activate the options menu by pressing the MENU key. The menu items displayed vary according to the current activity that is running.

➤ **Context menu** — Displays information related to a particular view on an activity. In Android, to activate a context menu you tap and hold it.

This recipe shows how to create the options and context menus for your Android application.

Solution

To create either an options menu or a context menu, populate the `activity_main.xml` file in the `res/menu` folder as follows:

```xml
<menu xmlns:android="http://schemas.android.com/apk/res/android" >

    <item
        android:id="@+id/menu1"
        android:icon="@drawable/ic_action_search"
        android:orderInCategory="100"
        android:showAsAction="always"
        android:title="Item 1"/>
    <item
        android:id="@+id/menu2"
        android:orderInCategory="100"
        android:showAsAction="ifRoom"
        android:title="Item 2">
        <menu>
            <item
                android:id="@+id/menu21"
                android:title="Item 2.1"/>
            <item
                android:id="@+id/menu22"
                android:title="Item 2.2"/>
```

```
            <item
                android:id="@+id/menu23"
                android:title="Item 2.3"/>
        </menu>
    </item>
    <item
        android:id="@+id/menu3"
        android:orderInCategory="100"
        android:showAsAction="never"
        android:title="Item 3"/>
    <item
        android:id="@+id/menu4"
        android:orderInCategory="100"
        android:showAsAction="ifRoom"
        android:title="Item 4">
        <menu>
            <group
                android:id="@+id/group"
                android:checkableBehavior="single" >
                <item
                    android:id="@+id/group_item1"
                    android:onClick="onGroupItemClick"
                    android:title="Red"/>
                <item
                    android:id="@+id/group_item2"
                    android:onClick="onGroupItemClick"
                    android:title="Green"/>
                <item
                    android:id="@+id/group_item3"
                    android:onClick="onGroupItemClick"
                    android:title="Blue"/>
            </group>
        </menu>
    </item>

</menu>
```

The preceding code snippet creates the following:

➤ Four main menu items, as indicated by the `<item>` element.

➤ The second menu item contains a submenu (as indicated by the `<menu>` element) with three items.

➤ The fourth menu item contains a submenu with three radio buttons (as indicated by the `<group>` element).

Assume you have the following code snippet in the `activity_main.xml` file located in the `res/layout` folder:

```
<RelativeLayout xmlns:android="http://schemas.android.com/apk/res/android"
    xmlns:tools="http://schemas.android.com/tools"
    android:layout_width="match_parent"
    android:layout_height="match_parent" >
```

```
<TextView
    android:id="@+id/textView1"
    android:layout_width="wrap_content"
    android:layout_height="wrap_content"
    android:layout_centerHorizontal="true"
    android:layout_centerVertical="true"
    android:text="@string/hello_world"
    tools:context=".MainActivity" />

<Button
    android:id="@+id/button1"
    android:layout_width="wrap_content"
    android:layout_height="wrap_content"
    android:layout_below="@+id/textView1"
    android:layout_centerHorizontal="true"
    android:text="Click and hold on this button" />

</RelativeLayout>
```

The following code snippet enables the options and context menus to be shown for the activity:

```java
package net.learn2develop.contextandoptionsmenu;

import android.app.Activity;
import android.os.Bundle;
import android.view.ContextMenu;
import android.view.ContextMenu.ContextMenuInfo;
import android.view.Menu;
import android.view.MenuItem;
import android.view.View;
import android.widget.Button;
import android.widget.Toast;

public class MainActivity extends Activity {

    @Override
    public void onCreate(Bundle savedInstanceState) {
        super.onCreate(savedInstanceState);
        setContentView(R.layout.activity_main);

        Button btn = (Button) findViewById(R.id.button1);
        btn.setOnCreateContextMenuListener(this);
    }

    //---Options Menu---
    @Override
    public boolean onCreateOptionsMenu(Menu menu) {
        getMenuInflater().inflate(R.menu.activity_main, menu);
        return true;
    }

    public void onGroupItemClick (MenuItem item) {
        if (item.isChecked()) {
            item.setChecked(false);
```

```
        } else {
            item.setChecked(true);
        }
    }

    @Override
    public boolean onOptionsItemSelected(MenuItem item)
    {
        Toast.makeText(this, item.getTitle(), Toast.LENGTH_LONG).show();
        return true;
    }

    //---Context Menu---
    @Override
    public void onCreateContextMenu(ContextMenu menu, View view,
    ContextMenuInfo menuInfo)
    {
        getMenuInflater().inflate(R.menu.activity_main, menu);
    }

    @Override
    public boolean onContextItemSelected(MenuItem item)
    {
        Toast.makeText(this, item.getTitle(), Toast.LENGTH_LONG).show();
        return true;
    }
}
```

When the activity is first loaded, the onCreateOptionsMenu() method is called. Here, you display the menu contained in the activitiy_main.xml file located in the res/menu folder. Figure 2-29 shows that the activity's action bar contains two menu items:

➤ **A Search menu item** — The icon is set by the android:icon attribute in the <item> element. It will always be shown in the action bar if specified by the attribute android:showAsAction with its value set to "always".

➤ **ITEM 2** — This menu item will be shown whenever there is room on the action bar if its android:showAsAction attribute's value is set to "ifRoom".

The third menu is not shown in the action bar, as its android:showAsAction attribute's value is set to "never". The fourth menu is not shown in the action bar because no more room is available in the action bar for another menu item.

Clicking ITEM 2 will also reveal the submenu containing three menu items (see Figure 2-29).

Clicking the MENU button will reveal the third and fourth menu items, as shown in Figure 2-30.

FIGURE 2-29

FIGURE 2-30

If you click Item 4, you will see the list of menu items with radio buttons (see Figure 2-31).

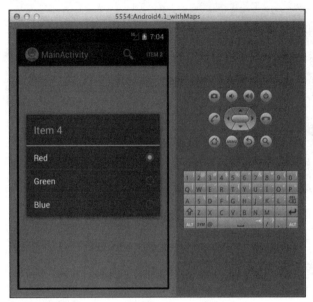

FIGURE 2-31

When you click another of the menu items in a group (as specified by the `<group>` element), the `onGroupItemClick()` method will fire:

```
public void onGroupItemClick (MenuItem item) {
    if (item.isChecked()) {
        item.setChecked(false);
    } else {
        item.setChecked(true);
    }
}
```

You need to manually check/uncheck the item that was selected. In this example, because the group's `android:checkableBehavior` attribute value was set to `"single"`, only one item can be checked at any time.

When a menu item is selected, it will fire the `onOptionsItemSelected()` method:

```
@Override
public boolean onOptionsItemSelected(MenuItem item)
{
    Toast.makeText(this, item.getTitle(), Toast.LENGTH_LONG).show();
    return true;
}
```

If you long-click the button on the activity, it will fire the `onCreateContextMenu()` method to display the menu as a context menu (see Figure 2-32):

```
//---Context Menu---
@Override
```

```
public void onCreateContextMenu(ContextMenu menu, View view,
ContextMenuInfo menuInfo)
{
    getMenuInflater().inflate(R.menu.activity_main, menu);
}
```

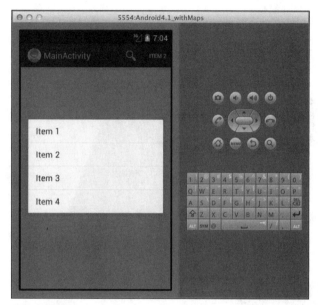

FIGURE 2-32

If you select Item 2, the submenu shown in Figure 2-33 will be displayed.

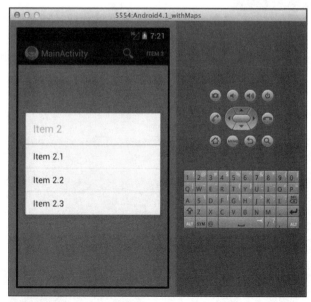

FIGURE 2-33

When a menu item in the context menu is selected, it fires the `onContextItemSelected()` method:

```
@Override
public boolean onContextItemSelected(MenuItem item)
{
    Toast.makeText(this, item.getTitle(), Toast.LENGTH_LONG).show();
    return true;
}
```

Finally, if you change the orientation of the emulator to landscape, ITEM 4 will be displayed in the action bar (see Figure 2-34).

FIGURE 2-34

RECIPE 2.16 DISPLAYING DIALOGS

Android Versions
Level 1 and above

Permissions
None

Source Code to Download from Wrox.com
Dialogs.zip

A dialog is usually a small floating window that appears in front of the current activity. When a dialog appears, the current activity loses focus and all user interaction becomes focused on the dialog. A dialog is usually used to get a response from the user.

In Android, a dialog is implemented as a dialog fragment, which floats on top of an activity and is displayed modally. Dialog fragments are useful when you need to obtain the user's response before continuing with the execution. To create a dialog fragment, you need to extend the `DialogFragment` base class. This recipe shows you how to create two types of dialogs: an input dialog and a Yes/No dialog.

Solution

For this recipe, add two Android XML layout files to the `res/layout` folder and name them as shown in Figure 2-35.

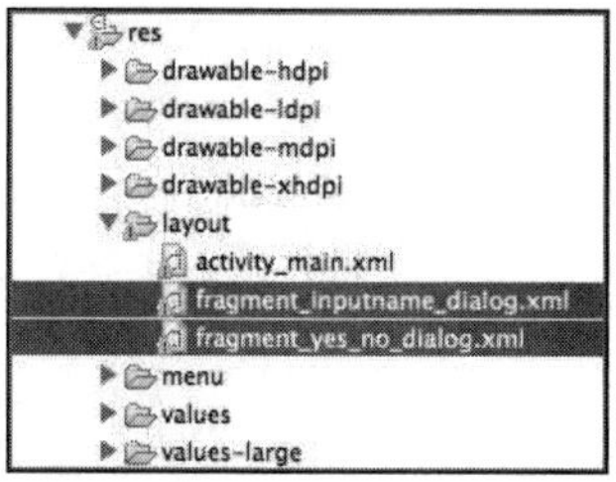

FIGURE 2-35

Populate the `fragment_inputname_dialog.xml` file with the following:

```
<LinearLayout
    xmlns:android="http://schemas.android.com/apk/res/android"
    android:layout_width="wrap_content"
    android:layout_height="wrap_content"
    android:layout_gravity="center"
    android:orientation="vertical"  >

    <TextView
        android:text="Please enter your name"
        android:layout_width="wrap_content"
        android:layout_height="wrap_content"
        android:paddingLeft="10dp"
        android:paddingRight="10dp" />

    <EditText
        android:id="@+id/txtName"
        android:layout_width="match_parent"
        android:layout_height="wrap_content"
        android:inputType="text"
        android:imeOptions="actionDone" />

    <Button
        android:id="@+id/btnDone"
        android:layout_width="match_parent"
        android:layout_height="wrap_content"
        android:text="Done" />

</LinearLayout>
```

This basically contains a page with a label, a text box, and a button.

Populate the `fragment_yes_no_dialog.xml` file as follows:

```
<LinearLayout xmlns:android="http://schemas.android.com/apk/res/android"
    android:id="@+id/edit_name"
    android:layout_width="wrap_content"
```

```
        android:layout_height="wrap_content"
        android:layout_gravity="center"
        android:orientation="vertical" >

    <TextView
        android:layout_width="wrap_content"
        android:layout_height="wrap_content"
        android:paddingLeft="10dp"
        android:paddingRight="10dp"
        android:text="Are you sure?" />

    <LinearLayout
        android:layout_width="wrap_content"
        android:layout_height="wrap_content"
        android:layout_gravity="center"
        android:orientation="horizontal" >

        <Button
            android:id="@+id/btnYes"
            android:layout_width="match_parent"
            android:layout_height="wrap_content"
            android:text="Yes" />

        <Button
            android:id="@+id/btnNo"
            android:layout_width="match_parent"
            android:layout_height="wrap_content"
            android:text="No" />
    </LinearLayout>

</LinearLayout>
```

This contains a label and two buttons.

Add two Java classes to the project as shown in Figure 2-36.

Populate the `InputNameDialogFragment.java` file as follows:

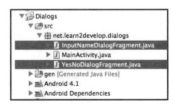

FIGURE 2-36

```java
package net.learn2develop.dialogs;

import android.os.Bundle;
import android.support.v4.app.DialogFragment;
import android.view.LayoutInflater;
import android.view.View;
import android.view.ViewGroup;
import android.view.WindowManager.LayoutParams;
import android.widget.Button;
import android.widget.EditText;

public class InputNameDialogFragment extends DialogFragment {
    EditText txtName;
    Button btn;
    static String dialogTitle;
```

```
//---Interface containing methods to be implemented
// by calling activity---
public interface InputNameDialogListener {
    void onFinishInputDialog(String inputText);
}

public InputNameDialogFragment() {
    //---empty constructor required---
}

//---set the title of the dialog window---
public void setDialogTitle(String title) {
    dialogTitle = title;
}

@Override
public View onCreateView(LayoutInflater inflater, ViewGroup container,
Bundle savedInstanceState) {
    View view = inflater.inflate(
        R.layout.fragment_inputname_dialog, container);

    //---get the EditText and Button views---
    txtName = (EditText) view.findViewById(R.id.txtName);
    btn = (Button) view.findViewById(R.id.btnDone);

    //---event handler for the button---
    btn.setOnClickListener(new View.OnClickListener()
    {
        public void onClick(View view) {
            //---gets the calling activity---
            InputNameDialogListener activity =
                (InputNameDialogListener) getActivity();

            activity.onFinishInputDialog(txtName.getText().toString());
            //---dismiss the alert---
            dismiss();
        }
    });

    //---show the keyboard automatically---
    txtName.requestFocus();
    getDialog().getWindow().setSoftInputMode(
        LayoutParams.SOFT_INPUT_STATE_VISIBLE);

    //---set the title for the dialog---
    getDialog().setTitle(dialogTitle);

    return view;
}
}
```

This class extends the `DialogFragment` base class and loads the UI defined in the `fragment_inputname_dialog.xml` file. In this class, you created an interface called `InputNameDialogListener` with an abstract method named `onFinishInputDialog()`. This method will be implemented by the activity that calls this class. In essence, it is fired when the user clicks the button to close the dialog. The text entered into the text box is then sent back to the calling activity through this method.

Populate the `YesNoDialogFragment.java` file with the following:

```java
package net.learn2develop.dialogs;

import android.os.Bundle;
import android.support.v4.app.DialogFragment;
import android.view.LayoutInflater;
import android.view.View;
import android.view.View.OnClickListener;
import android.view.ViewGroup;
import android.widget.Button;

public class YesNoDialogFragment extends DialogFragment{
    Button btnYes, btnNo;
    static String dialogTitle;

    //---Interface containing methods to be implemented
    // by calling activity---
    public interface YesNoDialogListener {
        void onFinishYesNoDialog(boolean state);
    }

    public YesNoDialogFragment() {
        //---empty constructor required---
    }

    //---set the title of the dialog window---
    public void setDialogTitle(String title) {
        dialogTitle = title;
    }

    @Override
    public View onCreateView(LayoutInflater inflater, ViewGroup container,
    Bundle savedInstanceState) {
        View view = inflater.inflate(R.layout.fragment_yes_no_dialog, container);

        //---get the Button views---
        btnYes = (Button) view.findViewById(R.id.btnYes);
        btnNo = (Button) view.findViewById(R.id.btnNo);

        btnYes.setOnClickListener(btnListener);
        btnNo.setOnClickListener(btnListener);

        //---set the title for the dialog---
        getDialog().setTitle(dialogTitle);

        return view;
    }
```

```
//---create an anonymous class to act as a button click
// listener---
private OnClickListener btnListener = new OnClickListener()
{
    public void onClick(View v)
    {
        //---gets the calling activity---
        YesNoDialogListener activity = (YesNoDialogListener) getActivity();
        boolean state =
            ((Button) v).getText().toString().equals("Yes") ? true : false;
        activity.onFinishYesNoDialog(state);

        //---dismiss the alert---
        dismiss();
    }
};

}
```

Like the `InputNameDialogFragment` class, this class extends the `DialogFragment` class and implements an interface.

Populate the `activity_main.xml` file as follows:

```
<LinearLayout xmlns:android="http://schemas.android.com/apk/res/android"
    xmlns:tools="http://schemas.android.com/tools"
    android:layout_width="match_parent"
    android:layout_height="match_parent"
    android:orientation="vertical" >

    <Button
        android:layout_width="match_parent"
        android:layout_height="wrap_content"
        android:text="Show Dialog"
        android:onClick="btnShowDialog" />

    <Button
        android:layout_width="match_parent"
        android:layout_height="wrap_content"
        android:text="Show Yes/No Dialog"
        android:onClick="btnShowYesNoDialog" />

</LinearLayout>
```

Add the following statements in bold to the `MainActivity.java` file:

```
package net.learn2develop.dialogs;

import net.learn2develop.dialogs.InputNameDialogFragment.InputNameDialogListener;
import net.learn2develop.dialogs.YesNoDialogFragment.YesNoDialogListener;
import android.os.Bundle;
import android.support.v4.app.FragmentActivity;
import android.support.v4.app.FragmentManager;
import android.view.View;
import android.widget.Toast;
```

```java
public class MainActivity extends FragmentActivity
    implements InputNameDialogListener, YesNoDialogListener {

    @Override
    public void onCreate(Bundle savedInstanceState) {
        super.onCreate(savedInstanceState);
        setContentView(R.layout.activity_main);
    }

    //===Input Name Dialog===
    public void btnShowDialog(View view) {
        showInputNameDialog();
    }

    private void showInputNameDialog() {
        FragmentManager fragmentManager = getSupportFragmentManager();
        InputNameDialogFragment inputNameDialog = new InputNameDialogFragment();
        inputNameDialog.setCancelable(false);
        inputNameDialog.setDialogTitle("Enter Name");
        inputNameDialog.show(fragmentManager, "input dialog");
    }

    @Override
    public void onFinishInputDialog(String inputText) {
        Toast.makeText(this, "Returned from dialog: " + inputText,
                Toast.LENGTH_SHORT).show();
    }

    //===YES/No Dialog===
    public void btnShowYesNoDialog(View view) {
        showYesNoDialog();
    }

    private void showYesNoDialog() {
        FragmentManager fragmentManager = getSupportFragmentManager();
        YesNoDialogFragment yesnoDialog = new YesNoDialogFragment();
        yesnoDialog.setCancelable(false);
        yesnoDialog.setDialogTitle("Status change");
        yesnoDialog.show(fragmentManager, "yes/no dialog");
    }

    @Override
    public void onFinishYesNoDialog(boolean state) {
        Toast.makeText(this, "Returned from dialog: " + state,
                Toast.LENGTH_SHORT).show();
    }

}
```

Run the project and deploy it onto an Android emulator. Click the Show Dialog button and you should see the dialog displayed in Figure 2-37.

FIGURE 2-37

Enter a name and click the Done button. The Toast class will display the value (the name you entered). Next, click the Show Yes/No Dialog button. You should see the dialog shown in Figure 2-38.

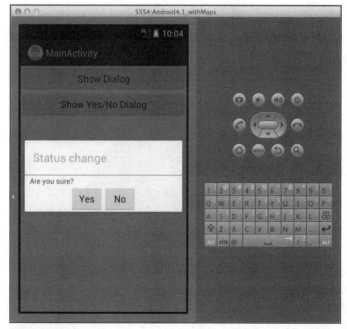

FIGURE 2-38

Click either the Yes or the No button. The Toast class will display true if you clicked Yes and false if you clicked No.

RECIPE 2.17 IMPLEMENTING PAGING

Android Versions

Level 1 and above

Permissions

None

Source Code to Download from Wrox.com

Swiping.zip

In Chapter 1, you learned how to link multiple activities using the `Intent` object. When you link to another activity, the target activity simply appears on the screen. Sometimes, you would like the user to swipe across the screen so that you can reveal the next page. This recipe describes how to perform swiping on the screen to reveal additional pages.

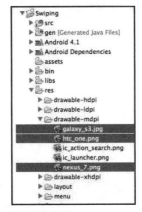

FIGURE 2-39

Solution

For this recipe, suppose you have the three images shown in Figure 2-39 in the `/res/drawable-mdpi` folder.

Also, add three XML files to the `res/layout` folder and name them `page1.xml`, `page2.xml`, and `page3.xml` (see Figure 2-40).

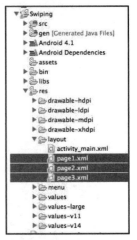

FIGURE 2-40

Populate the `page1.xml` file as follows:

```xml
<LinearLayout xmlns:android="http://schemas.android.com/apk/res/android"
    android:layout_width="match_parent"
    android:layout_height="match_parent"
    android:orientation="vertical" >

    <TextView
        android:id="@+id/textView1"
        android:layout_width="wrap_content"
        android:layout_height="wrap_content"
```

```
            android:text="Page 1" />

        <ImageView
            android:layout_width="wrap_content"
            android:layout_height="300dp"
            android:src="@drawable/htc_one" />

        <Button
            android:layout_width="wrap_content"
            android:layout_height="wrap_content"
            android:onClick="onClick"
            android:tag="1"
            android:text="Button 1" />

    </LinearLayout>
```

Populate the `page2.xml` file as follows:

```
    <LinearLayout xmlns:android="http://schemas.android.com/apk/res/android"
        android:layout_width="match_parent"
        android:layout_height="match_parent"
        android:orientation="vertical" >

        <TextView
            android:id="@+id/textView1"
            android:layout_width="wrap_content"
            android:layout_height="wrap_content"
            android:text="Page 2" />

        <ImageView
            android:layout_width="wrap_content"
            android:layout_height="300dp"
            android:src="@drawable/galaxy_s3" />

        <Button
            android:layout_width="wrap_content"
            android:layout_height="wrap_content"
            android:onClick="onClick"
            android:tag="2"
            android:text="Button 2" />

    </LinearLayout>
```

Populate the `page3.xml` file as follows:

```
    <LinearLayout xmlns:android="http://schemas.android.com/apk/res/android"
        android:layout_width="match_parent"
        android:layout_height="match_parent"
        android:orientation="vertical" >

        <TextView
            android:id="@+id/textView1"
            android:layout_width="wrap_content"
            android:layout_height="wrap_content"
            android:text="Page 3" />
```

```
<ImageView
    android:layout_width="wrap_content"
    android:layout_height="300dp"
    android:src="@drawable/nexus_7" />

<Button
    android:layout_width="wrap_content"
    android:layout_height="wrap_content"
    android:onClick="onClick"
    android:tag="3"
    android:text="Button 3" />

</LinearLayout>
```

What you have done so far is create three pages, each showing a `TextView`, `ImageButton`, and `Button`.

Now add a new Java class to the `src` folder and name it `MyPageAdapter.java` (see Figure 2-41).

Populate the `MyPageAdapter.java` file as follows:

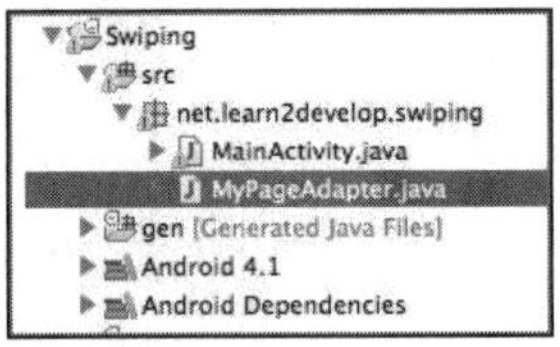

```
package net.learn2develop.swiping;

import android.content.Context;
import android.os.Parcelable;
import android.support.v4.view.PagerAdapter;
import android.support.v4.view.ViewPager;
import android.view.LayoutInflater;
import android.view.View;

public class MyPageAdapter extends PagerAdapter {
    //---return the total number of pages---
    public int getCount() {
        return 3;
    }

    public Object instantiateItem(View collection, int position) {
        LayoutInflater inflater = (LayoutInflater) collection.getContext()
                .getSystemService(Context.LAYOUT_INFLATER_SERVICE);
        int resId = 0;
        switch (position) {
        case 0:
            resId = R.layout.page1;
            break;
        case 1:
            resId = R.layout.page2;
            break;
        case 2:
            resId = R.layout.page3;
            break;
        }

        View view = inflater.inflate(resId, null);
        ((ViewPager) collection).addView(view, 0);
```

FIGURE 2-41

```
            return view;
        }

        @Override
        public void destroyItem(View arg0, int arg1, Object arg2) {
            ((ViewPager) arg0).removeView((View) arg2);
        }

        @Override
        public boolean isViewFromObject(View arg0, Object arg1) {
            return arg0 == ((View) arg1);
        }

        @Override
        public Parcelable saveState() {
            return null;
        }
    }
}
```

The `MyPageAdapter` class extends the `PagerAdapter` class, which enables multiple pages to be displayed when the user swipes across the screen. The `getCount()` method returns the total number of pages you want to display. The `instantiateItem()` method retrieves the page to display depending on the current position of the page.

Populate the `activity_main.xml` file as follows:

```xml
<LinearLayout xmlns:android="http://schemas.android.com/apk/res/android"
    android:layout_width="match_parent"
    android:layout_height="match_parent"
    android:orientation="vertical" >

    <android.support.v4.view.ViewPager
        android:id="@+id/viewPager"
        android:layout_width="match_parent"
        android:layout_height="match_parent" />

</LinearLayout>
```

To use the `MyPageAdapter` class that you have just defined, add the following statements in bold to your activity:

```java
package net.learn2develop.swiping;

import android.app.Activity;
import android.os.Bundle;
import android.support.v4.view.ViewPager;
import android.view.View;
import android.widget.Toast;

public class MainActivity extends Activity {
    @Override
    public void onCreate(Bundle savedInstanceState) {
        super.onCreate(savedInstanceState);
```

```
        setContentView(R.layout.activity_main);

        MyPageAdapter adapter = new MyPageAdapter();
        ViewPager viewPager = (ViewPager) findViewById(R.id.viewPager);
        viewPager.setAdapter(adapter);

        //---starts with the second page---
        viewPager.setCurrentItem(1);
    }

    public void onClick(View view) {
        int buttonTag = Integer.valueOf(view.getTag().toString());
        Toast.makeText(this, "Button " + Integer.toString(buttonTag)+
                " clicked", Toast.LENGTH_LONG).show();
    }
}
```

In the onCreate() method, you create an instance of the MyPageAdapter class and then retrieve the ViewPager view from the UI and set it to the instance of the MyPageAdapter class. By default, the ViewPager always displays the first page, but you can customize it by calling the setCurrentItem() method to display a particular page. The onClick() method demonstrates that even though you have three buttons spread across three pages, their events are all handled in the same activity.

Figure 2-42 shows how the application looks when run.

FIGURE 2-42

You can swipe it left or right to reveal additional pages (see Figure 2-43).

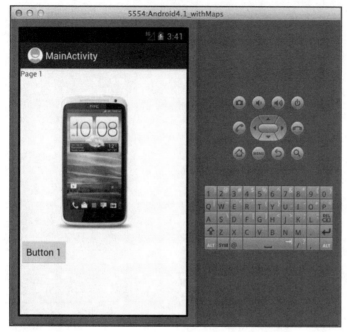

FIGURE 2-43

3

Displaying Lists of Items and Images

One of the common tasks you need to perform in Android application development is displaying long lists of items or images. For example, you might have a list of names and images that you want to display in your activity so that when the user selects a name, you can do some further processing, such as using another activity to display details about the selected name. In Android, you have a number of ways to do that. This chapter covers how to use the following views:

➤ ListView

➤ Spinner

➤ GridView

➤ Gallery

➤ ImageSwitcher

RECIPE 3.1 DISPLAYING A LIST OF ITEMS USING THE LISTVIEW

Android Versions
Level 1 and above

Permissions
None

Source Code to Download from Wrox.com
ListView.zip

If you have a long list of items that you want to display to the user, the `ListView` view is the answer. This recipe demonstrates how to use the `ListView` to display a list of items contained within an array.

Solution

To use the `ListView`, use the `<ListView>` element and put it into your UI file, such as the `activity_main.xml` file:

```
<RelativeLayout xmlns:android="http://schemas.android.com/apk/res/android"
    xmlns:tools="http://schemas.android.com/tools"
    android:layout_width="match_parent"
    android:layout_height="match_parent" >

    <ListView
        android:id="@+id/android:list"
        android:layout_width="fill_parent"
        android:layout_height="fill_parent" />

</RelativeLayout>
```

> **NOTE** *Note the value of the attribute – its value must be* `"@+id/android:list"`.
> *You need to use this value if your activity that is displaying the* `ListView`
> *extends the* `ListActivity` *base class. If your activity that uses the* `ListView`
> *does not extend the base class, then you can set it to a normal value, such as*
> `"@+id/listView1"`. *You will see this in the next recipe.*

In the activity, extend the `ListActivity` base class and use the `setListAdapter()` method to bind the `ListView` to an `ArrayAdapter` object (which in turn loads the string array). You specify the type of `ListView` you want by specifying the `android.R.layout.simple_list_item_1` constant, which will simply display a list of items within the `ListView`:

```
package net.learn2develop.listview;

import android.app.ListActivity;
import android.os.Bundle;
import android.view.View;
import android.widget.ArrayAdapter;
import android.widget.ListView;
import android.widget.Toast;

public class MainActivity extends ListActivity {

    String[] presidents = {
            "Dwight D. Eisenhower",
            "John F. Kennedy",
            "Lyndon B. Johnson",
            "Richard Nixon",
            "Gerald Ford",
            "Jimmy Carter",
            "Ronald Reagan",
            "George H. W. Bush",
            "Bill Clinton",
            "George W. Bush",
            "Barack Obama"
    };

    @Override
    public void onCreate(Bundle savedInstanceState) {
        super.onCreate(savedInstanceState);
        setContentView(R.layout.activity_main);

        //---List View---
        setListAdapter(new ArrayAdapter<String>(this,
            android.R.layout.simple_list_item_1, presidents));
    }

    public void onListItemClick(ListView parent, View v,
    int position, long id) {
        Toast.makeText(this, "You have selected " + presidents[position],
            Toast.LENGTH_SHORT).show();
    }

}
```

The `onListItemClick()` method is the callback method used when the user has selected an item inside the `ListView`. The second argument indicates the index of the items inside the `ListView` that was selected. Using this information, you can reference it against your array and obtain the name of the item selected. Figure 3-1 shows what the `ListView` looks like.

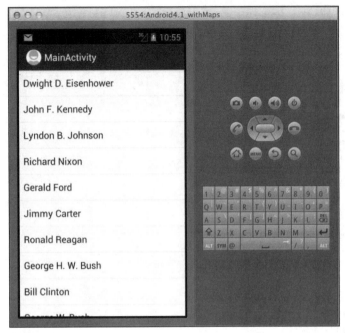

FIGURE 3-1

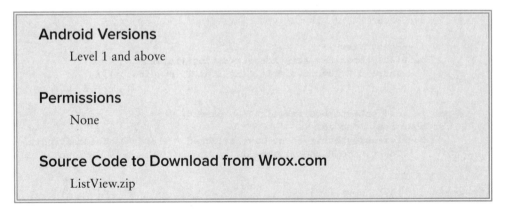

RECIPE 3.2 CUSTOMIZING THE LISTVIEW

Android Versions

Level 1 and above

Permissions

None

Source Code to Download from Wrox.com

ListView.zip

By default, the `ListView` allows one item to be selected. To enable multiple items to be selected, you can configure the `ListView` to display a checkbox next to each item.

Solution

To configure the `ListView`, you first need to get a reference to the `ListView`. If your activity is extending the `ListActivity` base class, you can use the `getListView()` method to return an instance of the ListView in your activity. Once you obtain an instance of the ListView, you can call the setChoiceMode() method to set the display mode of the ListView:

```
@Override
public void onCreate(Bundle savedInstanceState) {
    super.onCreate(savedInstanceState);
    setContentView(R.layout.activity_main);

    ListView lstView = getListView();
    //lstView.setChoiceMode(ListView.CHOICE_MODE_NONE);
    //lstView.setChoiceMode(ListView.CHOICE_MODE_SINGLE);
    lstView.setChoiceMode(ListView.CHOICE_MODE_MULTIPLE);

    setListAdapter(new ArrayAdapter<String>(this,
        android.R.layout.simple_list_item_checked, presidents));
}
```

The ListView.CHOICE_MODE_MULTIPLE constant displays a checkbox next to each item in the ListView (see Figure 3-2). As the user selects each item, the onListItemClick() method is called.

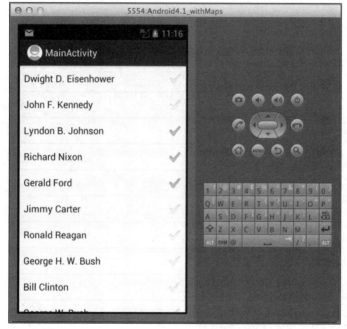

FIGURE 3-2

To determine whether an item in the ListView is checked or unchecked, you can use the second argument of the onListItemClick() method:

```
import android.widget.CheckedTextView;
...
```

. . .

```
    public void onListItemClick(ListView parent, View v,
    int position, long id) {
        CheckedTextView item = (CheckedTextView) v;
        Toast.makeText(this, presidents[position] + " checked : " +
            !item.isChecked(), Toast.LENGTH_SHORT).show();
    }
```

The second argument returns the view of the item that was selected in the ListView. In this case, it returns a CheckedTextView object. Using this object, you can check whether it has been checked or not using its isChecked() method. Note that in this example, you have to negate the isChecked() method because when an item is selected, the onListItemClick() method will fire first before checking (or unchecking) the checkbox for the item.

Another nice feature of the ListView is its support for text filtering. If your device has a hardware keyboard, typing in the names of the items in your ListView will automatically cause the ListView to display only those items that match the text you enter. To enable filtering on the ListView, call the setTextFilterEnabled() method:

```
    ListView lstView = getListView();
    //lstView.setChoiceMode(ListView.CHOICE_MODE_NONE);
    //lstView.setChoiceMode(ListView.CHOICE_MODE_SINGLE);
    lstView.setChoiceMode(ListView.CHOICE_MODE_MULTIPLE);
    lstView.setTextFilterEnabled(true);
```

Figure 3-3 shows what the ListView will look like when you type the characters "joh".

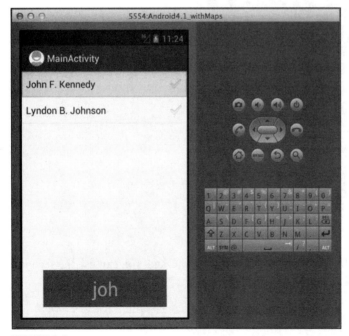

FIGURE 3-3

NOTE *By default, the Android emulator does not support keyboard inputs (even though a keyboard appears next to the screen of the emulator). To enable keyboard support for your Android emulator (AVD), you need to perform the following steps:*

1. *In Eclipse, select Window | AVD Manager*

2. *Select the particular AVD and click on Edit...*

3. *Under the Hardware section, click on New...*

4. *Select the Keyboard Support property*

5. *By default, it is added with a value of 'no'. Click on the value column and change it to 'yes'*

6. *Click on Edit AVD to save the changes*

RECIPE 3.3   DISPLAYING MULTIPLE LISTVIEWS

Android Versions

Level 1 and above

Permissions

None

Source Code to Download from Wrox.com

ListView2.zip

So far, the first two recipes in this chapter showed a single `ListView` in your activity; but it is common to have more than one `ListView` in an activity. This recipe demonstrates how to include multiple `ListViews` in your activity.

Solution

To display multiple `ListViews` in your activity, simply add multiple `<ListView>` elements to your UI, such as the `activity_main.xml` file:

```
<LinearLayout xmlns:android="http://schemas.android.com/apk/res/android"
    android:layout_width="fill_parent"
    android:layout_height="fill_parent"
    android:orientation="vertical" >
```

```xml
    <TextView
        android:layout_width="fill_parent"
        android:layout_height="wrap_content"
        android:text="List 1" />

    <ListView
        android:id="@+id/ListView1"
        android:layout_width="fill_parent"
        android:layout_height="200dp" />

    <TextView
        android:layout_width="fill_parent"
        android:layout_height="wrap_content"
        android:text="List 2" />

    <ListView
        android:id="@+id/ListView2"
        android:layout_width="fill_parent"
        android:layout_height="200dp" />

</LinearLayout>
```

The preceding example contains two `ListViews`, each of which has a unique id: `"@+id/ListView1"` and `"@+id/ListView2"`.

To fill each `ListView` with items, you need to get a reference to the `ListView` using the `find-ViewById()` method (see the following code). Once that is done, you can then bind it to an `ArrayAdapter` object:

```java
package net.learn2develop.listview2;

import android.app.Activity;
import android.os.Bundle;
import android.view.View;
import android.widget.AdapterView;
import android.widget.AdapterView.OnItemClickListener;
import android.widget.ArrayAdapter;
import android.widget.ListView;
import android.widget.Toast;

public class MainActivity extends Activity {
    ListView l1, l2;
    String[] presidents = {
            "Dwight D. Eisenhower",
            "John F. Kennedy",
            "Lyndon B. Johnson",
            "Richard Nixon",
            "Gerald Ford",
            "Jimmy Carter",
            "Ronald Reagan",
            "George H. W. Bush",
```

```
                        "Bill Clinton",
                        "George W. Bush",
                        "Barack Obama"
        };

        @Override
        public void onCreate(Bundle savedInstanceState) {
            super.onCreate(savedInstanceState);
            setContentView(R.layout.activity_main);

            ArrayAdapter<String> adapter = new ArrayAdapter<String>(
                    this, android.R.layout.simple_list_item_1, presidents);

            //---List View---
            l1 = (ListView) findViewById(R.id.ListView1);
            l1.setAdapter(adapter);
            l1.setOnItemClickListener(new OnItemClickListener() {
                @Override
                public void onItemClick(AdapterView<?> arg0, View arg1, int arg2,
                        long arg3) {
                    int index = arg2;
                    Toast.makeText(getBaseContext(),
                        "You have selected item : " + presidents[index],
                        Toast.LENGTH_SHORT).show();
                }
            });

            //---List View---
            l2 = (ListView) findViewById(R.id.ListView2);
            l2.setAdapter(adapter);
            l2.setOnItemClickListener(new OnItemClickListener() {
                @Override
                public void onItemClick(AdapterView<?> arg0, View arg1, int arg2,
                        long arg3) {
                    int index = arg2;
                    Toast.makeText(getBaseContext(),
                        "You have selected item : " + presidents[index],
                        Toast.LENGTH_SHORT).show();
                }
            });
        }

    }
```

To handle the selection of the item inside the `ListView`, you need to call the
`setOnItemClickListener()` method to assign it an instance of the `OnItemClickListener`
class and override the `onItemClick()` method.

Figure 3-4 shows the activity displaying two `ListViews`.

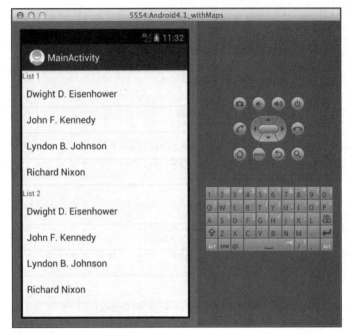

FIGURE 3-4

RECIPE 3.4 CREATING CUSTOM LISTVIEWS

Android Versions

    Level 1 and above

Permissions

    None

Source Code to Download from Wrox.com

    CustomListView.zip

The standard `ListView` simply displays a list of items. While it may suffice when you just want to display a list of text, it is not enough for more sophisticated applications. In this recipe, you will see how you can customize the `ListView` so that you can display images, multiple lines of text, and more.

Solution

To display a `ListView` in your activity, you need to add the `<ListView>` element to your UI, such as the `activity_main.xml` file:

```
<RelativeLayout xmlns:android="http://schemas.android.com/apk/res/android"
    xmlns:tools="http://schemas.android.com/tools"
    android:layout_width="match_parent"
    android:layout_height="match_parent" >

    <ListView
        android:id="@+id/android:list"
        android:layout_width="fill_parent"
        android:layout_height="fill_parent" />

</RelativeLayout>
```

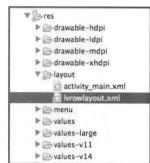

The first thing you will learn in this recipe is how to display an image next to each item in the `ListView`. To do that, add an XML file in your `res/layout` folder and name it, for example, `lvrowlayout.xml` (see Figure 3-5).

FIGURE 3-5

Populate the `lvrowlayout.xml` file as follows:

```
<LinearLayout xmlns:android="http://schemas.android.com/apk/res/android"
    android:layout_width="fill_parent"
    android:layout_height="fill_parent"
    android:orientation="horizontal" >

    <ImageView
        android:id="@+id/icon"
        android:layout_width="50dp"
        android:layout_height="50dp"
        android:layout_marginBottom="5dp"
        android:layout_marginLeft="5dp"
        android:layout_marginRight="5dp"
        android:layout_marginTop="5dp"
        android:src="@drawable/ic_launcher" />

    <TextView
        android:id="@+id/txtPresidentName"
        android:layout_width="wrap_content"
        android:layout_height="wrap_content"
        android:textSize="20sp" />

</LinearLayout>
```

The preceding code will serve as the layout for each row in the `ListView`. As you can see, each row will contain an `ImageView` and a `TextView`.

Modify the `MainActivity.java` file as follows:

> **NOTE** *This example uses the* `ListActivity` *class as the base class for the activity.*

```
package net.learn2develop.customlistview;

import android.app.ListActivity;
import android.os.Bundle;
import android.widget.ArrayAdapter;

public class MainActivity extends ListActivity  {
    String[] presidents = {
            "Dwight D. Eisenhower",
            "John F. Kennedy",
            "Lyndon B. Johnson",
            "Richard Nixon",
            "Gerald Ford",
            "Jimmy Carter",
            "Ronald Reagan",
            "George H. W. Bush",
            "Bill Clinton",
            "George W. Bush",
            "Barack Obama"
    };

    @Override
    public void onCreate(Bundle savedInstanceState) {
        super.onCreate(savedInstanceState);
        setContentView(R.layout.activity_main);

        this.setListAdapter(new ArrayAdapter<String>(
                this,
                R.layout.lvrowlayout,
                R.id.txtPresidentName,
                presidents));
    }

}
```

Note that instead of using one of the predefined layout types, in this case you are using your own self-defined layout:

```
this.setListAdapter(new ArrayAdapter<String>(
        this,
        R.layout.lvrowlayout,
        R.id.txtPresidentName,
        presidents));
```

Figure 3-6 shows how the ListView looks now.

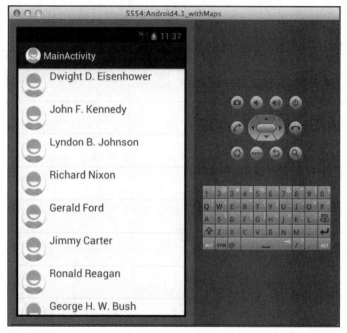

FIGURE 3-6

Observe that each row now has an icon. However, the icon for each row is the same. If you want different icons for each row, you need to create your own custom adapter. The next recipe shows you how to achieve this.

RECIPE 3.5 FURTHER CUSTOMIZING EACH ROW WITH ADDITIONAL TEXTVIEWS

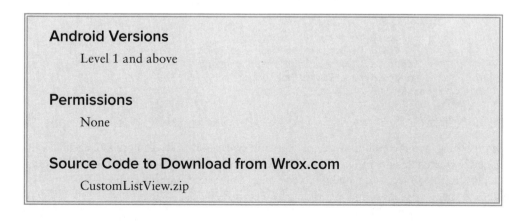

Android Versions

Level 1 and above

Permissions

None

Source Code to Download from Wrox.com

CustomListView.zip

The previous recipe showed how to customize each row within a
ListView with various views. This recipe shows you how to further
customize each row with more views.

Solution Part One: Adding Additional TextViews

Let's further customize the content of each row by adding additional
TextViews to it. You may want to add another layout XML document
to the res/layout folder (see Figure 3-7).

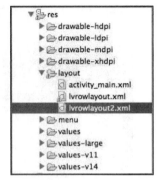

Populate the content of the lvrowlayout2.xml file as follows:

FIGURE 3-7

```xml
<LinearLayout xmlns:android="http://schemas.android.com/apk/res/android"
    android:layout_width="fill_parent"
    android:layout_height="fill_parent"
    android:orientation="horizontal" >

    <ImageView
        android:id="@+id/icon"
        android:layout_width="60dp"
        android:layout_height="60dp"
        android:layout_marginBottom="5dp"
        android:layout_marginLeft="5dp"
        android:layout_marginRight="5dp"
        android:layout_marginTop="5dp"
        android:src="@drawable/ic_launcher" />

    <LinearLayout
        android:layout_width="fill_parent"
        android:layout_height="90dp"
        android:orientation="vertical" >

        <TextView
            android:id="@+id/txtPresidentName"
            android:layout_width="wrap_content"
            android:layout_height="wrap_content"
            android:textSize="25sp" />

        <TextView
            android:id="@+id/txtDescription"
            android:layout_width="wrap_content"
            android:layout_height="wrap_content"
            android:textSize="15sp" />
    </LinearLayout>

</LinearLayout>
```

The preceding layout contains an ImageView and two TextViews. To populate each row using
this newly created layout, you need to create a new custom array adapter. To do that, add a new
Java class to the project and name it CustomArrayAdapter.java (see Figure 3-8). You also add 11
images to the res/drawable-mdpi folder (see Figure 3-9).

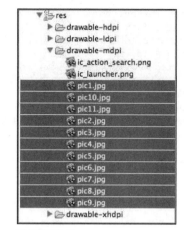

FIGURE 3-8   FIGURE 3-9

Populate the `CustomArrayAdapter.java` file as follows:

```java
package net.learn2develop.customlistview;

import android.app.Activity;
import android.util.Log;
import android.view.LayoutInflater;
import android.view.View;
import android.view.ViewGroup;
import android.widget.ArrayAdapter;
import android.widget.ImageView;
import android.widget.TextView;

public class CustomArrayAdapter extends ArrayAdapter<String>{
    private final Activity context;
    private final String[] presidents;
    private final Integer[] imageIds;

    public CustomArrayAdapter(Activity context,
    String[] presidents, Integer[] imageIds) {
        super(context, R.layout.lvrowlayout2, presidents);
        this.context = context;
        this.presidents = presidents;
        this.imageIds = imageIds;
    }

    @Override
    public View getView(int position, View view, ViewGroup parent) {
        //---print the index of the row to examine---
        Log.d("CustomArrayAdapter",String.valueOf(position));

        LayoutInflater inflater = context.getLayoutInflater();
        View rowView= inflater.inflate(R.layout.lvrowlayout2, null, true);
```

```
        //---get a reference to all the views on the xml layout---
        TextView txtTitle = (TextView) rowView.findViewById(R.id.txtPresidentName);
        TextView txtDescription = (TextView)
rowView.findViewById(R.id.txtDescription);
        ImageView imageView = (ImageView) rowView.findViewById(R.id.icon);

        //---customize the content of each row based on position---
        txtTitle.setText(presidents[position]);
        txtDescription.setText(presidents[position] + "...Some
descriptions here...");
        imageView.setImageResource(imageIds[position]);
        return rowView;
    }
}
```

The `CustomArrayAdapter` class extends the `ArrayAdapter` base class. You want it to bind the array to the new layout that you have just created. Observe that the constructor of the `CustomArrayAdapter` class takes three arguments (see bold code): the context of the application, an array containing the presidents' names, and an integer array containing the IDs of the picture of each president.

To display the `ListView` using the new layout, add the following code to the `MainActivity` `.java` file:

```
package net.learn2develop.customlistview;

import android.app.ListActivity;
import android.os.Bundle;
import android.widget.ArrayAdapter;

public class MainActivity extends ListActivity {
    String[] presidents = {
            "Dwight D. Eisenhower",
            "John F. Kennedy",
            "Lyndon B. Johnson",
            "Richard Nixon",
            "Gerald Ford",
            "Jimmy Carter",
            "Ronald Reagan",
            "George H. W. Bush",
            "Bill Clinton",
            "George W. Bush",
            "Barack Obama"
    };

    Integer[] imageIDs = {
            R.drawable.pic1,
            R.drawable.pic2,
            R.drawable.pic3,
            R.drawable.pic4,
            R.drawable.pic5,
            R.drawable.pic6,
            R.drawable.pic7,
            R.drawable.pic8,
```

```
                    R.drawable.pic9,
                    R.drawable.pic10,
                    R.drawable.pic11
    };

    @Override
    public void onCreate(Bundle savedInstanceState) {
        super.onCreate(savedInstanceState);
        setContentView(R.layout.activity_main);

        /*
        this.setListAdapter(new ArrayAdapter<String>(
                this,
                R.layout.lvrowlayout,
                R.id.txtPresidentName,
                presidents));
        */

        //---using custom array adapter---
        CustomArrayAdapter adapter = new
            CustomArrayAdapter(this, presidents, imageIDs);
        setListAdapter(adapter);
    }

}
```

Figure 3-10 shows the new ListView with the different images for each row.

FIGURE 3-10

Solution Part Two: Recycling Each Row

The previous section demonstrates how to create a `ListView` with rows showing different images and text. However, it is not optimized, as each row requires a certain amount of memory to store the images and text; therefore, a long list of items will definitely impact your application's performance, causing it to consume large amounts of memory. It would be better to reuse some of the memory consumed by the rows that are no longer visible to the user. This section shows you how to improve the memory usage of your `ListView`.

Add another Java class to your project and name it `AdvancedCustomArrayAdapter.java` (see Figure 3-11).

Populate the `AdvancedCustomArrayAdapter.java` file as follows:

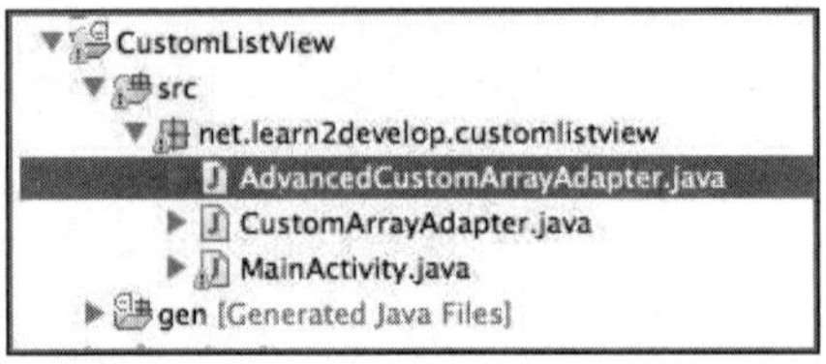

FIGURE 3-11

```java
package net.learn2develop.customlistview;

import android.app.Activity;
import android.util.Log;
import android.view.LayoutInflater;
import android.view.View;
import android.view.ViewGroup;
import android.widget.ArrayAdapter;
import android.widget.ImageView;
import android.widget.TextView;

public class AdvancedCustomArrayAdapter extends ArrayAdapter<String>{
    private final Activity context;
    private final String[] presidents;
    private final Integer[] imageIds;

    public AdvancedCustomArrayAdapter(
    Activity context, String[] presidents, Integer[] imageIds) {
        super(context, R.layout.lvrowlayout2, presidents);
        this.context = context;
        this.presidents = presidents;
        this.imageIds = imageIds;
    }

    static class ViewContainer {
        public ImageView imageView;
        public TextView txtTitle;
        public TextView txtDescription;
    }

    @Override
    public View getView(int position, View view, ViewGroup parent) {
        ViewContainer viewContainer;
        View rowView = view;

        //---print the index of the row to examine---
        Log.d("CustomArrayAdapter",String.valueOf(position));
```

```
//---if the row is displayed for the first time---
if (rowView == null) {

    Log.d("CustomArrayAdapter", "New");
    LayoutInflater inflater = context.getLayoutInflater();
    rowView = inflater.inflate(R.layout.lvrowlayout2, null, true);

    //---create a view container object---
    viewContainer = new ViewContainer();

    //---get the references to all the views in the row---
    viewContainer.txtTitle = (TextView)
        rowView.findViewById(R.id.txtPresidentName);
    viewContainer.txtDescription = (TextView)
        rowView.findViewById(R.id.txtDescription);
    viewContainer.imageView = (ImageView)
        rowView.findViewById(R.id.icon);

    //---assign the view container to the rowView---
    rowView.setTag(viewContainer);
} else {

    //---view was previously created; can recycle---
    Log.d("CustomArrayAdapter", "Recycling");
    //---retrieve the previously assigned tag to get
    // a reference to all the views; bypass the findViewByID() process,
    // which is computationally expensive---
    viewContainer = (ViewContainer) rowView.getTag();
}

//---customize the content of each row based on position---
viewContainer.txtTitle.setText(presidents[position]);
viewContainer.txtDescription.setText(presidents[position] +
    " ...Some descriptions here...");
viewContainer.imageView.setImageResource(imageIds[position]);
return rowView;
    }
}
```

Notice that it is very similar to the one in the previous section, except that now you make use of a ViewContainer object (which you have defined to contain the ImageView and two TextViews) to store the individual rows in the ListView. As each row is displayed, you check if it was previously created. If it was not, you create a new ViewContainer object to store the row. If it was previously created, you retrieve the saved ViewContainer object and then reuse it.

To use this new custom adapter, add the following statements to the MainActivity.java file:

```
@Override
public void onCreate(Bundle savedInstanceState) {
    super.onCreate(savedInstanceState);
    setContentView(R.layout.main);
```

```
        /*
        //---using custom layout---
        this.setListAdapter(new ArrayAdapter<String>(
                this,
                R.layout.lvrowlayout,
                R.id.txtPresidentName,
                presidents));
        */

        /*
        //---using custom array adapter---
        CustomArrayAdapter adapter = new CustomArrayAdapter(this, presidents);
        setListAdapter(adapter);
        */

        //---using custom array adapter (with recycling)---
        AdvancedCustomArrayAdapter adapter =
            new AdvancedCustomArrayAdapter(this, presidents, imageIDs);
        setListAdapter(adapter);
    }
```

If you debug this application using Eclipse, Figure 3-12 shows the first few rows that are displayed.
Observe that the first few visible rows are newly created (see the output in the LogCat window).

FIGURE 3-12

As you scroll the list upward, more rows are displayed. As shown in Figure 3-13, these rows have been recycled.

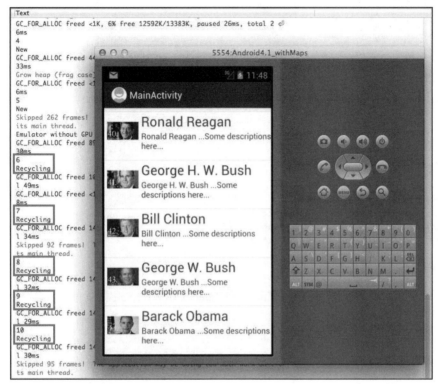

FIGURE 3-13

RECIPE 3.6 DISPLAYING A LIST OF ITEMS USING THE SPINNER VIEW

Android Versions
Level 1 and above

Permissions
None

Source Code to Download from Wrox.com
Spinner.zip

In addition to using the `ListView` to display a list of items, you can also use the `Spinner` view. The `Spinner` behaves like the drop-down listbox that is popular in the Windows OS. This recipe demonstrates how to use the `Spinner`.

Solution

For this recipe, let's use the `Spinner` view to display a list of names, specifically a list of US presidents.

To use the `Spinner`, add the `<Spinner>` element to the UI, such as the `activity_main.xml` file:

```
<RelativeLayout xmlns:android="http://schemas.android.com/apk/res/android"
    xmlns:tools="http://schemas.android.com/tools"
    android:layout_width="match_parent"
    android:layout_height="match_parent" >

    <Spinner
        android:id="@+id/spinner1"
        android:layout_width="wrap_content"
        android:layout_height="wrap_content"
        android:drawSelectorOnTop="true" />

</RelativeLayout>
```

In the activity, obtain a reference to the `Spinner` in your UI and assign it to an `ArrayAdapter` object:

```
package net.learn2develop.spinner;

import android.app.Activity;
import android.os.Bundle;
import android.view.View;
import android.widget.AdapterView;
import android.widget.AdapterView.OnItemSelectedListener;
import android.widget.ArrayAdapter;
import android.widget.Spinner;
import android.widget.Toast;

public class MainActivity extends Activity {
    Spinner s1;
    String[] presidents = {
            "Dwight D. Eisenhower",
            "John F. Kennedy",
            "Lyndon B. Johnson",
            "Richard Nixon",
            "Gerald Ford",
            "Jimmy Carter",
            "Ronald Reagan",
            "George H. W. Bush",
            "Bill Clinton",
            "George W. Bush",
            "Barack Obama"
    };
```

```
@Override
public void onCreate(Bundle savedInstanceState) {
    super.onCreate(savedInstanceState);
    setContentView(R.layout.activity_main);

    //---Spinner View---
    s1 = (Spinner) findViewById(R.id.spinner1);
    ArrayAdapter<String> adapter = new ArrayAdapter<String>(
        this, android.R.layout.simple_spinner_item, presidents);
    s1.setAdapter(adapter);

    s1.setOnItemSelectedListener(new OnItemSelectedListener() {
        public void onItemSelected(AdapterView<?> arg0, View arg1,
        int arg2, long arg3) {
            int index = s1.getSelectedItemPosition();
            Toast.makeText(getBaseContext(),
                "You have selected item : " + presidents[index],
                Toast.LENGTH_SHORT).show();
        }

        public void onNothingSelected(AdapterView<?> arg0) {
        }
    });
}

}
```

In the preceding example, the `ArrayAdapter` object loads a list of values from a `String` array:

```
ArrayAdapter<String> adapter = new ArrayAdapter<String>(
    this, android.R.layout.simple_spinner_item, presidents);
```

You then assign the `ArrayAdapter` object to the `Spinner` view:

```
s1.setAdapter(adapter);
```

You also call the `setOnItemSelectedListener()` method to assign an instance of the `OnItemSelectedListen` class so that you can handle the event when the user selects an item in the `Spinner`:

```
s1.setOnItemSelectedListener(new OnItemSelectedListener() {
    public void onItemSelected(AdapterView<?> arg0, View arg1,
    int arg2, long arg3) {
        int index = s1.getSelectedItemPosition();
        Toast.makeText(getBaseContext(),
            "You have selected item : " + presidents[index],
            Toast.LENGTH_SHORT).show();
    }

    public void onNothingSelected(AdapterView<?> arg0) {
    }
});
```

When the user selects an item in the `Spinner` view, the `onItemSelected()` method is fired.

Figure 3-14 shows the `Spinner` displaying a list of items when the user clicks on it.

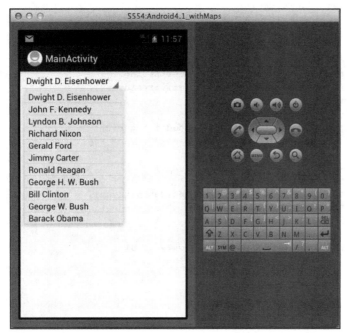

FIGURE 3-14

RECIPE 3.7 DISPLAYING A LIST OF IMAGES

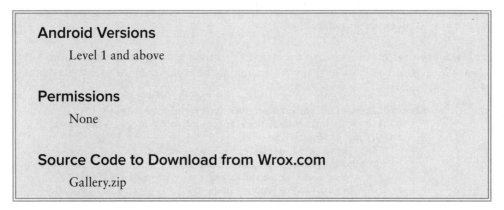

Android Versions
Level 1 and above

Permissions
None

Source Code to Download from Wrox.com
Gallery.zip

So far, all the recipes covered involve displaying mainly text and occasionally images. If you want to display a series of images to the user, you can make use of the `Gallery`. The `Gallery` is a view that shows items (such as images) in a center-locked, horizontal scrolling list. This recipe shows you how to use it.

Solution

For this recipe, assume you have some images stored in the `res/drawable-mdpi` folder of your project (see Figure 3-15).

Create an XML file named `attrs.xml` and store it in the `res/values` folder (see Figure 3-16).

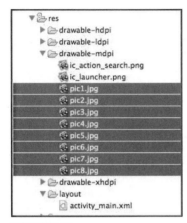

FIGURE 3-15   **FIGURE 3-16**

The content of the `attrs.xml` looks like this:

```
<resources>
    <declare-styleable name="MyGallery">
        <attr name="android:galleryItemBackground" />
    </declare-styleable>
</resources>
```

To use the `Gallery`, add the `<Gallery>` element in your UI, such as the `activity_main.xml` file:

```
<LinearLayout
    xmlns:android="http://schemas.android.com/apk/res/android"
    android:layout_width="fill_parent"
    android:layout_height="fill_parent"
    android:orientation="vertical">

    <Gallery
        android:id="@+id/gallery1"
        android:layout_width="fill_parent"
        android:layout_height="wrap_content" />

    <ImageView
        android:id="@+id/image1"
        android:layout_width="fill_parent"
        android:layout_height="250dp"
        android:scaleType="fitXY" />

</LinearLayout>
```

In the activity, add the following lines of code:

```java
package net.learn2develop.gallery;

import android.app.Activity;
import android.content.Context;
import android.content.res.TypedArray;
import android.os.Bundle;
import android.view.View;
import android.view.ViewGroup;
import android.widget.AdapterView;
import android.widget.AdapterView.OnItemClickListener;
import android.widget.BaseAdapter;
import android.widget.Gallery;
import android.widget.ImageView;
import android.widget.Toast;

//---The Gallery view is deprecated in Android 4.1;
// however it is still a useful view
// The following statement suppresses the compiler warning---
@SuppressWarnings("deprecation")
public class MainActivity extends Activity {
    //---the images to display---
    Integer[] imageIDs = {
            R.drawable.pic1,
            R.drawable.pic2,
            R.drawable.pic3,
            R.drawable.pic4,
            R.drawable.pic5,
            R.drawable.pic6,
            R.drawable.pic7
    };

    @Override
    public void onCreate(Bundle savedInstanceState) {
        super.onCreate(savedInstanceState);
        setContentView(R.layout.activity_main);

        //---Note that Gallery view is deprecated in Android 4.1---
        Gallery gallery = (Gallery) findViewById(R.id.gallery1);
        gallery.setAdapter(new ImageAdapter(this));
        gallery.setOnItemClickListener(new OnItemClickListener() {
            public void onItemClick(AdapterView<?> parent, View v, int position,
            long id)
            {
                Toast.makeText(getBaseContext(),
                        "pic" + (position + 1) + " selected",
                        Toast.LENGTH_SHORT).show();

                //---display the images selected---
                ImageView imageView = (ImageView) findViewById(R.id.image1);
                imageView.setImageResource(imageIDs[position]);
            }
        });

    }
```

```java
public class ImageAdapter extends BaseAdapter {
    private Context context;
    private int itemBackground;
    public ImageAdapter(Context c)
    {
        context = c;

        //---sets a grey background; wraps around the images
        TypedArray a =
            obtainStyledAttributes(R.styleable.MyGallery);
        itemBackground = a.getResourceId(
            R.styleable.MyGallery_android_galleryItemBackground, 0);
        a.recycle();
    }

    //---returns the number of images---
    public int getCount() {
        return imageIDs.length;
    }

    //---returns the ID of an item---
    public Object getItem(int position) {
        return position;
    }

    //---returns the ID of an item---
    public long getItemId(int position) {
        return position;
    }

    //---returns an ImageView view---
    public View getView(int position, View convertView, ViewGroup parent) {
        ImageView imageView = new ImageView(context);
        imageView.setImageResource(imageIDs[position]);
        imageView.setScaleType(ImageView.ScaleType.FIT_XY);
        imageView.setLayoutParams(new Gallery.LayoutParams(150, 120));
        imageView.setBackgroundResource(itemBackground);
        return imageView;
    }
}
```

}

First, you create the ImageAdapter class (which extends the BaseAdapter class) so that it can bind to the Gallery view with a series of ImageView views. The BaseAdapter class acts as a bridge between an AdapterView and the data source that feeds data into it. Examples of AdapterViews are as follows:

➤ ListView

➤ GridView

➤ Spinner

➤ Gallery

There are several subclasses of the `BaseAdapter` class in Android:

➤ `ListAdapter`

➤ `ArrayAdapter`

➤ `CursorAdapter`

➤ `SpinnerAdapter`

For the `ImageAdapter` class, you implemented the following methods:

➤ `getCount()`

➤ `getItem()`

➤ `getItemId()`

➤ `getView()`

In particular, the `getView()` method returns a `View` at the specified position. In this case, you returned an `ImageView` object.

When an image in the `Gallery` view is selected (i.e., clicked), the selected image's position (0 for the first image, 1 for the second image, and so on) is displayed and the image is displayed in the `ImageView`.

Figure 3-17 shows the `Gallery` in action.

FIGURE 3-17

RECIPE 3.8 ANIMATING THE CHANGING OF IMAGES USING THE IMAGESWITCHER

Android Versions

Level 1 and above

Permissions

None

Source Code to Download from Wrox.com

ImageSwitcher.zip

The previous recipe demonstrated how to use the `Gallery` together with an `ImageView` to display a series of thumbnail images so that when one is selected, it is displayed in the `ImageView`. However, rather than have an image appear abruptly when the user selects it in the `Gallery`, you might, for example, want to apply some animation to the images so that they can transition smoothly from one image to another. In this case, you need to use the `ImageSwitcher` together with the `Gallery`.

Solution

Like the previous recipe, this example assumes you have a series of images in the `res/drawable-mdpi` folder (see Figure 3-18).

Create an XML file named `attrs.xml` and store it in the `res/values` folder (see Figure 3-19).

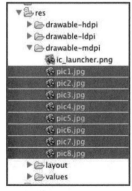

FIGURE 3-18

FIGURE 3-19

The content of the `attrs.xml` file is as follows:

```xml
<resources>
    <declare-styleable name="MyGallery">
        <attr name="android:galleryItemBackground" />
    </declare-styleable>
</resources>
```

Add the `<ImageSwitcher>` and `<Gallery>` elements to the UI, such as the `activity_main.xml` file:

```xml
<RelativeLayout
    xmlns:android="http://schemas.android.com/apk/res/android"
    android:layout_width="fill_parent"
    android:layout_height="fill_parent"
    android:background="#ff000000"
    android:orientation="vertical" >

    <ImageSwitcher
        android:id="@+id/switcher1"
        android:layout_width="fill_parent"
        android:layout_height="fill_parent"
        android:layout_alignParentBottom="true"
        android:layout_alignParentLeft="true"
        android:layout_alignParentRight="true" />

    <Gallery
        android:id="@+id/gallery1"
        android:layout_width="fill_parent"
        android:layout_height="wrap_content" />

</RelativeLayout>
```

Add the following code to the activity:

```java
package net.learn2develop.imageswitcher;

import android.app.Activity;
import android.content.Context;
import android.content.res.TypedArray;
import android.os.Bundle;
import android.view.View;
import android.view.ViewGroup;
import android.view.ViewGroup.LayoutParams;
import android.view.animation.AnimationUtils;
import android.widget.AdapterView;
import android.widget.AdapterView.OnItemClickListener;
import android.widget.BaseAdapter;
import android.widget.Gallery;
import android.widget.ImageSwitcher;
import android.widget.ImageView;
import android.widget.ViewSwitcher.ViewFactory;
```

```java
@SuppressWarnings("deprecation")
public class MainActivity extends Activity implements ViewFactory {
    //---the images to display---
    Integer[] imageIDs = {
            R.drawable.pic1,
            R.drawable.pic2,
            R.drawable.pic3,
            R.drawable.pic4,
            R.drawable.pic5,
            R.drawable.pic6,
            R.drawable.pic7
    };

    private ImageSwitcher imageSwitcher;

    /** Called when the activity is first created. */
    @Override
    public void onCreate(Bundle savedInstanceState) {
        super.onCreate(savedInstanceState);
        setContentView(R.layout.activity_main);

        imageSwitcher = (ImageSwitcher) findViewById(R.id.switcher1);
        imageSwitcher.setFactory(this);

        imageSwitcher.setInAnimation(
            AnimationUtils.loadAnimation(this, android.R.anim.fade_in));
        imageSwitcher.setOutAnimation( AnimationUtils.loadAnimation(this,
            android.R.anim.fade_out));

        Gallery gallery = (Gallery) findViewById(R.id.gallery1);
        gallery.setAdapter(new ImageAdapter(this));
        gallery.setOnItemClickListener(new OnItemClickListener() {
            public void onItemClick(AdapterView<?> parent,
            View v, int position, long id)
            {
                imageSwitcher.setImageResource(imageIDs[position]);
            }
        });
    }

    @Override
    public View makeView() {
        ImageView imageView = new ImageView(this);
        imageView.setBackgroundColor(0xFF000000);
        imageView.setScaleType(
            ImageView.ScaleType.FIT_CENTER);
        imageView.setLayoutParams(new
            ImageSwitcher.LayoutParams(
                LayoutParams.MATCH_PARENT,
                LayoutParams.MATCH_PARENT)
        );
        return imageView;
    }
```

```java
public class ImageAdapter extends BaseAdapter {
    private Context context;
    private int itemBackground;

    public ImageAdapter(Context c)
    {
        context = c;
        //---sets a grey background; wraps around the images
        TypedArray a =
            obtainStyledAttributes(R.styleable.MyGallery);
        itemBackground = a.getResourceId(
            R.styleable.MyGallery_android_galleryItemBackground, 0);
        a.recycle();
    }

    //---returns the number of images---
    public int getCount()
    {
        return imageIDs.length;
    }

    //---returns the ID of an item---
    public Object getItem(int position)
    {
        return position;
    }

    public long getItemId(int position)
    {
        return position;
    }

    //---returns an ImageView view---
    public View getView(int position, View convertView, ViewGroup parent)
    {
        ImageView imageView = new ImageView(context);
        imageView.setImageResource(imageIDs[position]);
        imageView.setScaleType(ImageView.ScaleType.FIT_XY);
        imageView.setLayoutParams(new Gallery.LayoutParams(
            150, 120)); imageView.setBackgroundResource(itemBackground);
        return imageView;
    }
}
}
```

The first thing to note in this example is that the ImageSwitcherActivity not only extends the Activity base class, but also implements the ViewFactory. To use the ImageSwitcher view, you need to implement the ViewFactory interface, which creates the views for use with the ImageSwitcher view. To enable this, implement the makeView() method:

```java
@Override
public View makeView() {
    ImageView imageView = new ImageView(this);
    imageView.setBackgroundColor(0xFF000000);
```

```
        imageView.setScaleType(
            ImageView.ScaleType.FIT_CENTER);
        imageView.setLayoutParams(new
            ImageSwitcher.LayoutParams(
                LayoutParams.MATCH_PARENT,
                LayoutParams.MATCH_PARENT)
        );
        return imageView;
    }
```

This method creates a new `View` to be added in the `ImageSwitcher` view, which in this case is an `ImageView`.

Like the `Gallery` example in the previous recipe, you also implemented an `ImageAdapter` class so that it can bind to the `Gallery` view with a series of `ImageView` views.

In the `onCreate()` method, you get a reference to the `ImageSwitcher` view and set the animation, specifying how images should fade in and out of the view. Finally, when an image is selected from the `Gallery` view, the image is displayed in the `ImageSwitcher` view (see Figure 3-20).

FIGURE 3-20

In this example, when an image is selected in the `Gallery`, it appears by fading in. When the next image is selected, the current image fades out. If you instead want the image to slide in from the left and slide out to the right when another image is selected, try the following animation:

```
        imageSwitcher.setInAnimation(AnimationUtils.loadAnimation(this,
            android.R.anim.slide_in_left));
```

```
imageSwitcher.setOutAnimation(AnimationUtils.loadAnimation(this,
    android.R.anim.slide_out_right));
```

RECIPE 3.9 DISPLAYING IMAGES USING THE GRIDVIEW

Android Versions

Level 1 and above

Permissions

None

Source Code to Download from Wrox.com

Grid.zip

The `GridView` shows items in a two-dimensional scrolling grid. You can use the `GridView` together with an `ImageView` to display a series of images. The following recipe demonstrates how.

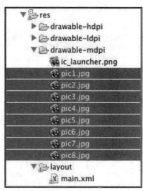

Solution

Like the previous recipe, this example assumes you have a series of images in the `res/drawable-mdpi` folder (see Figure 3-21).

To use the `GridView`, add the `<GridView>` element to your UI, such as the `activity_main.xml` file, as follows:

FIGURE 3-21

```xml
<RelativeLayout xmlns:android="http://schemas.android.com/apk/res/android"
    xmlns:tools="http://schemas.android.com/tools"
    android:layout_width="match_parent"
    android:layout_height="match_parent" >

    <GridView
        android:id="@+id/gridview"
        android:layout_width="fill_parent"
        android:layout_height="fill_parent"
        android:columnWidth="90dp"
        android:gravity="center"
        android:horizontalSpacing="10dp"
```

```
                android:numColumns="auto_fit"
                android:stretchMode="columnWidth"
                android:verticalSpacing="10dp" />

    </RelativeLayout>
```

Code the activity as follows:

```java
package net.learn2develop.grid;

import android.app.Activity;
import android.content.Context;
import android.os.Bundle;
import android.view.View;
import android.view.ViewGroup;
import android.widget.AdapterView;
import android.widget.AdapterView.OnItemClickListener;
import android.widget.BaseAdapter;
import android.widget.GridView;
import android.widget.ImageView;
import android.widget.Toast;

public class MainActivity extends Activity {
    //---the images to display---
    Integer[] imageIDs = {
            R.drawable.pic1,
            R.drawable.pic2,
            R.drawable.pic3,
            R.drawable.pic4,
            R.drawable.pic5,
            R.drawable.pic6,
            R.drawable.pic7
    };

    @Override
    public void onCreate(Bundle savedInstanceState) {
        super.onCreate(savedInstanceState);
        setContentView(R.layout.activity_main);

        GridView gridView = (GridView) findViewById(R.id.gridview);
        gridView.setAdapter(new ImageAdapter(this));

        gridView.setOnItemClickListener(new OnItemClickListener()
        {
            public void onItemClick(AdapterView<?> parent,
            View v, int position, long id) {
                Toast.makeText(getBaseContext(),
                    "pic" + (position + 1) + " selected",
                    Toast.LENGTH_SHORT).show();
            }
        });
    }
```

```java
public class ImageAdapter extends BaseAdapter
{
    private Context context;

    public ImageAdapter(Context c)
    {
        context = c;
    }

    //---returns the number of images---
    public int getCount() {
        return imageIDs.length;
    }

    //---returns the item---
    public Object getItem(int position) {
        return position;
    }

    //---returns the ID of an item---
    public long getItemId(int position) {
        return position;
    }

    //---returns an ImageView view---
    public View getView(int position, View convertView,
            ViewGroup parent)
    {
        ImageView imageView;
        if (convertView == null) {
            imageView = new ImageView(context);
            imageView.setLayoutParams(new
                    GridView.LayoutParams(85, 85));
            imageView.setScaleType(
                    ImageView.ScaleType.CENTER_CROP);
            imageView.setPadding(5, 5, 5, 5);
        } else {
            imageView = (ImageView) convertView;
        }
        imageView.setImageResource(imageIDs[position]);
        return imageView;
    }
}
```

As in the previous recipe, you create the `ImageAdapter` class (which extends the `BaseAdapter` class) so that it can bind to the `GridView` with a series of `ImageView` views.

When you run the application, you will see the `GridView` as shown in Figure 3-22.

FIGURE 3-22

RECIPE 3.10   BUILDING A MASTER-DETAIL USER INTERFACE

Android Versions

Level 1 and above

Permissions

None

Source Code to Download from Wrox.com

FragmentExample.zip

Beginning with Android 3.0, you can use fragments to populate your activity so that you have greater flexibility in customizing your application's UI for the various device screen sizes. One popular UI that people commonly use is the Master-Detail relationship. Figure 3-23 shows a good example, which you will build in this recipe. When the application is running on a device in landscape mode (or on a tablet), you will see two panels — the left panel displays a list of items and the right panel displays details about the item selected in the left panel.

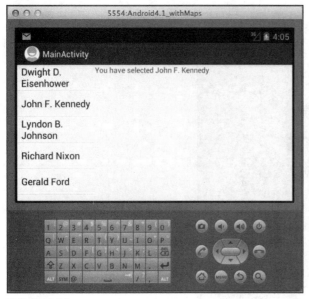

FIGURE 3-23

If the application is running on a device that displays it in portrait mode (or is running on a small-screen device, such as a smartphone), the left panel containing the list of items will occupy the entire screen (see Figure 3-24).

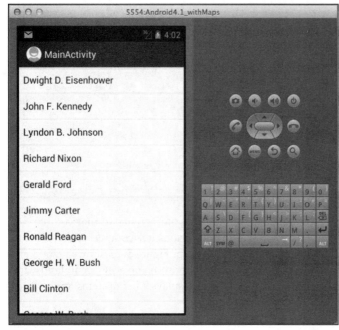

FIGURE 3-24

Selecting an item from the list will result in another activity loading details about the item selected (see Figure 3-25).

FIGURE 3-25

This recipe demonstrates how you can build this type of UI using fragments.

Solution

As shown in Figure 3-26, your res/layout folder will contain three XML files.

The uses of each file are as follows:

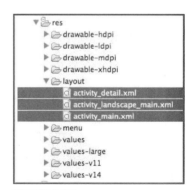

FIGURE 3-26

> ➤ activity_detail.xml — Contains the UI that shows details about the item selected.

> ➤ activity_landscape_main.xml — Contains the UI that holds two fragments, one for the list of items, and another to show details about the item selected. This UI is displayed when the device is in landscape orientation.

> ➤ activity_main.xml — Contains the UI that shows the list of items. This UI is displayed when the device is in portrait orientation.

The content of the `activity_main.xml` file is as follows:

```xml
<LinearLayout  xmlns:android="http://schemas.android.com/apk/res/android"
    xmlns:tools="http://schemas.android.com/tools"
    android:layout_width="match_parent"
    android:layout_height="match_parent" >

    <fragment
        android:id="@+id/masterFragment"
        android:name="net.learn2develop.fragmentexample.MasterFragment"
        android:layout_width="match_parent"
        android:layout_height="match_parent" />

</LinearLayout >
```

The content of the `activity_landscape_main.xml` file is as follows:

```xml
<LinearLayout xmlns:android="http://schemas.android.com/apk/res/android"
    android:layout_width="fill_parent"
    android:layout_height="fill_parent"
    android:orientation="horizontal" >

    <fragment
        android:id="@+id/masterFragment"
        android:name="net.learn2develop.fragmentexample.MasterFragment"
        android:layout_width="150dp"
        android:layout_height="match_parent" />

    <fragment
        android:id="@+id/detailFragment"
        android:name="net.learn2develop.fragmentexample.DetailFragment"
        android:layout_width="match_parent"
        android:layout_height="match_parent" />

</LinearLayout>
```

The content of the `activity_detail.xml` file is as follows:

```xml
<LinearLayout xmlns:android="http://schemas.android.com/apk/res/android"
    android:layout_width="fill_parent"
    android:layout_height="fill_parent"
    android:orientation="vertical" >

    <TextView
        android:id="@+id/txtSelectedPresident"
        android:layout_width="fill_parent"
        android:layout_height="wrap_content"
        android:text="" />

</LinearLayout>
```

As shown in Figure 3-27, the src folder of your application will contain three additional JAVA classes in addition to the MainActivity class that is already present:

➤ MasterFragment.java — The fragment that contains the list of items.

➤ DetailFragment.java — The fragment that contains details about the item selected. It will load the UI from activity_detail.xml.

FIGURE 3-27

➤ DetailActivity.java — The activity that is displayed when the device is in portrait orientation. It will load the UI from activity_detail.xml.

➤ MainActivity.java — The main activity that is called when your application is run. This activity loads the MasterFragment.java and DetailFragment.java classes when it is in landscape orientation. It loads the MasterFragment.java class when it is in portrait orientation.

Code the MainActivity.java file as follows:

```
package net.learn2develop.fragmentexample;

import android.content.res.Configuration;
import android.os.Bundle;
import android.support.v4.app.FragmentActivity;
import android.view.Menu;

public class MainActivity extends FragmentActivity {

    @Override
    public void onCreate(Bundle savedInstanceState) {
        super.onCreate(savedInstanceState);
        //setContentView(R.layout.activity_main);

        if (getResources().getConfiguration().orientation ==
                Configuration.ORIENTATION_LANDSCAPE) {
            //---landscape mode---
            setContentView(R.layout.activity_landscape_main);
        } else {
            //---portrait mode---
            setContentView(R.layout.activity_main);
        }
    }

    @Override
    public boolean onCreateOptionsMenu(Menu menu) {
        getMenuInflater().inflate(R.menu.activity_main, menu);
        return true;
    }

}
```

The `MainActivity` class detects during runtime whether the device is in landscape orientation. If it is, it loads the UI from `activity_landscape_main.xml`. Otherwise, it loads the UI from `activity_main.xml`.

> **NOTE** *Note the use of the* `android.support.v4.app.Fragment` *package name in the import statement. This is to ensure compatibility with earlier versions of the Android OS.*

Next, code the `DetailFragment.java` file as follows:

```java
package net.learn2develop.fragmentexample;

import android.os.Bundle;
import android.view.LayoutInflater;
import android.view.View;
import android.view.ViewGroup;
import android.widget.TextView;
import android.support.v4.app.Fragment;

public class DetailFragment extends Fragment {
    @Override
    public void onActivityCreated(Bundle savedInstanceState) {
        super.onActivityCreated(savedInstanceState);
    }

    @Override
    public void onCreate(Bundle savedInstanceState) {
        super.onCreate(savedInstanceState);
    }

    @Override
    public View onCreateView(LayoutInflater inflater, ViewGroup container,
            Bundle savedInstanceState) {
        View view = inflater.inflate(
            R.layout.activity_detail, container, false);
        return view;
    }

    public void setSelectedPresident(String name) {
        TextView view = (TextView)
            getView().findViewById(R.id.txtSelectedPresident);
        view.setText("You have selected " + name);
    }
}
```

The `DetailFragment` class extends the `Fragment` class. It loads its UI from the `activity_detail.xml` file. In this class, you expose a method named `setSelectedPresident()` to enable the `MasterFragment` class to pass it the name of the selected president.

Next, code the `MasterFragment.java` file as follows:

```java
package net.learn2develop.fragmentexample;

import android.content.Intent;
import android.os.Bundle;
import android.view.View;
import android.widget.ArrayAdapter;
import android.widget.ListView;
import android.widget.Toast;
import android.support.v4.app.ListFragment;

public class MasterFragment extends ListFragment {
    String[] presidents = {
            "Dwight D. Eisenhower",
            "John F. Kennedy",
            "Lyndon B. Johnson",
            "Richard Nixon",
            "Gerald Ford",
            "Jimmy Carter",
            "Ronald Reagan",
            "George H. W. Bush",
            "Bill Clinton",
            "George W. Bush",
            "Barack Obama"
    };

    /** Called when the activity is first created. */
    @Override
    public void onCreate(Bundle savedInstanceState) {
        super.onCreate(savedInstanceState);
        setListAdapter(new ArrayAdapter<String>(getActivity(),
                android.R.layout.simple_list_item_1,
                presidents));
    }

    public void onListItemClick(ListView parent,
    View v, int position, long id) {
        Toast.makeText(getActivity(),
            "You have selected " + presidents[position],
            Toast.LENGTH_SHORT).show();
        String selectedPresident = presidents[position];

        DetailFragment detailFragment = (DetailFragment)
            getFragmentManager().findFragmentById(R.id.detailFragment);

        //---if the detail fragment is not in the current activity as myself---
        if (detailFragment != null && detailFragment.isInLayout()) {
            //---the detail fragment is in the same activity as the master---
            detailFragment.setSelectedPresident(selectedPresident);
        } else {
```

```
                         //---the detail fragment is in its own activity---
                         Intent intent = new Intent(getActivity(), DetailActivity.class);
                         intent.putExtra("president", selectedPresident);
                         startActivity(intent);
                     }
                 }
             }
```

Observe that the `MasterFragment` class extends the `ListFragment` class. When an item is selected from the `ListView`, you need to get a reference to the `DetailFragment` class to determine whether it is also in the current layout as the `MasterFragment`. If it is, then you simply call the `setSelectedPresident()` method (which you define in the `DetailFragment` class) to pass it the name of the selected president. If it is not, you have to use an `Intent` object to start the `DetailActivity` and then use it to pass the name of the selected president.

Next, code the `DetailActivity.java` file as follows:

```
    package net.learn2develop.fragmentexample;

    import android.app.Activity;
    import android.content.res.Configuration;
    import android.os.Bundle;
    import android.widget.TextView;

    public class DetailActivity extends Activity {
        /** Called when the activity is first created. */
        @Override
        public void onCreate(Bundle savedInstanceState) {
            super.onCreate(savedInstanceState);
            setContentView(R.layout.activity_detail);

            //---if the user switches to landscape mode; destroy the activity---
            if (getResources().getConfiguration().orientation ==
                    Configuration.ORIENTATION_LANDSCAPE) {
                finish();
                return;
            }

            //---get the data passed from the master fragment---
            String name = getIntent().getStringExtra("president");
            TextView view = (TextView) findViewById(R.id.txtSelectedPresident);
            view.setText("You have selected " + name);
        }
    }
```

The `DetailActivity` class extends the `Activity` base class and it detects during run time if it is in landscape orientation. If so, it destroys itself so that the `MasterFragment` can load. If it is not (which means it is called by an intent from the `MasterFragment`), it retrieves the `Intent` object to obtain the name of the selected president and display in the `TextView`.

Finally, because you have more than one additional activity in your project, remember to declare it in the `AndroidManifest.xml` file:

```xml
<manifest xmlns:android="http://schemas.android.com/apk/res/android"
    package="net.learn2develop.fragmentexample"
    android:versionCode="1"
    android:versionName="1.0" >

    <uses-sdk
        android:minSdkVersion="8"
        android:targetSdkVersion="15" />

    <application
        android:icon="@drawable/ic_launcher"
        android:label="@string/app_name"
        android:theme="@style/AppTheme" >
        <activity
            android:name=".MainActivity"
            android:label="@string/title_activity_main" >
            <intent-filter>
                <action android:name="android.intent.action.MAIN" />

                <category android:name="android.intent.category.LAUNCHER" />
            </intent-filter>
        </activity>

        <activity
            android:name=".DetailActivity"
            android:label="@string/app_name" >
            <intent-filter>
                <action android:name=
                    "net.learn2develop.fragmentexample.DetailActivity" />

                <category android:name="android.intent.category.DEFAULT" />
            </intent-filter>
        </activity>

    </application>
</manifest>
```

When you run the application on a device in portrait orientation, you will see a list of items. Select an item and the details about the selected item will be displayed in another activity. Rotate the device to landscape orientation and observe that both fragments are now displayed. Selecting an item in the left panel will display the details of the selected name in the right panel.

Telephony

In this chapter, you will learn some of the cool recipes related to the phone functionality on Android devices. These recipes range from the simple, such as making calls programmatically from your application, to the interesting, such as blocking outgoing calls, auto-answering incoming calls, and more. You will also learn how to programmatically turn on Bluetooth, as well as switch the phone to Airplane mode. Finally, you will also learn how to obtain the phone number and ID for your SIM card.

RECIPE 4.1 CALLING FROM YOUR APPLICATION

Android Versions

Level 1 and above

Permissions

android.permission.CALL_PHONE

Source Code Download from Wrox.com

MakeCalls.zip

If you are developing an application for a business that provides phone support, why not build that capability directly into the application? For example, suppose the user is currently using your application and needs to make a call to the company for help; in this case, your application can directly dial the phone number. This recipe shows you how.

Solution

To enable users to dial a phone number directly from your application, you can use an `Intent` object by passing it the `ACTION_DIAL` action, together with the URI in the following format: `tel:<phone_number>`:

```
package net.learn2develop.makecalls;

import android.app.Activity;
import android.content.Intent;
import android.net.Uri;
import android.os.Bundle;

public class MainActivity extends Activity {

    @Override
    public void onCreate(Bundle savedInstanceState) {
        super.onCreate(savedInstanceState);
        setContentView(R.layout.activity_main);

        String phoneNumber = "+13175723496";
        Intent i = new
                Intent(android.content.Intent.ACTION_DIAL,
                        Uri.parse("tel:+" + phoneNumber));
        startActivity(i);
    }

}
```

The preceding code snippet causes the Phone application to dial the specified number (see Figure 4-1). To place the call, the user needs to physically press the call button.

FIGURE 4-1

If you want the Phone application to directly place the call for users without waiting for them to press the call button, you can instead use the ACTION_CALL action:

```
Intent i = new
        Intent(android.content.Intent.ACTION_CALL,
               Uri.parse("tel:+" + phoneNumber));
startActivity(i);
```

Note that if your application is placing a call directly, you need to add the CALL_PHONE permission to your AndroidManifest.xml file:

```
<uses-permission android:name="android.permission.CALL_PHONE"/>
```

> **NOTE** *Please see the section "A Note About Permissions" in this book's introduction for more information on using permissions with the recipes in this book.*

RECIPE 4.2 MONITORING THE STATE OF THE PHONE

> **Android Versions**
>   Level 1 and above
>
> **Permissions**
>   android.permission.READ_PHONE_STATE
>
> **Source Code Download from Wrox.com**
>   Phone.zip

The phone on the Android device is always in one of the three states: idle (when it is not engaged in any calls), ringing (when there is an incoming call), or off hook (when the user answers the call). The capability to monitor the states of the phone enables you to write some interesting applications. For example, if there were an incoming call when you were driving, you may want to automatically send an SMS message to the caller to inform them that you are busy and cannot answer the call. This recipe shows you how to monitor the state of your phone.

Solution

To monitor for changes to the state of the phone, you need to create a class that extends the PhoneStateListener base class:

```
package net.learn2develop.phone;

import android.content.Context;
```

```
import android.telephony.PhoneStateListener;
import android.telephony.TelephonyManager;
import android.widget.Toast;

public class PhoneReceiver extends PhoneStateListener {
    Context context;
    public PhoneReceiver(Context context) {
        this.context = context;
    }

    @Override
    public void onCallStateChanged(int state,
            String incomingNumber) {
        super.onCallStateChanged(state, incomingNumber);

        Toast.makeText(context, "onCallStateChanged state=" +
                state + "incomingNumber=" + incomingNumber,
                Toast.LENGTH_LONG).show();

        switch (state) {
        case TelephonyManager.CALL_STATE_IDLE:
            Toast.makeText(context, "idle",
                    Toast.LENGTH_LONG).show();
            break;
        case TelephonyManager.CALL_STATE_RINGING:
            Toast.makeText(context, "ringing",
                    Toast.LENGTH_LONG).show();
            break;
        case TelephonyManager.CALL_STATE_OFFHOOK:
            Toast.makeText(context, "offhook",
                    Toast.LENGTH_LONG).show();
            break;
        }
    }
}
```

The constructor for this class takes a Context argument. You override the onCallStateChanged() method so that when there is a change to the phone state (such as the phone ringing or the user answering the phone or ending a call), you can handle the change. In the preceding example, you simply use the Toast class to display a message. More important, you can obtain the phone number of the caller, perhaps to send an SMS message back and so on.

To be notified of changes to the phone state, you first need to create an instance of the TelephonyManager class and the PhoneReceiver class:

```
package net.learn2develop.phone;

import android.app.Activity;
import android.content.Context;
import android.os.Bundle;
import android.telephony.TelephonyManager;
```

```
public class MainActivity extends Activity {
    TelephonyManager manager;
    PhoneReceiver myPhoneStateListener;

    @Override
    public void onCreate(Bundle savedInstanceState) {
        super.onCreate(savedInstanceState);
        setContentView(R.layout.activity_main);

        myPhoneStateListener = new PhoneReceiver(this);
        manager = ((TelephonyManager)
                getSystemService(Context.TELEPHONY_SERVICE));
    }
}
```

In the onResume() method, you can start listening to the changes using the listen() method of the TelephonyManager class, passing it an instance of the PhoneReceiver class as well as the constant LISTEN_CALL_STATE:

```
import android.telephony.PhoneStateListener;
...

    @Override
    public void onResume() {
        super.onResume();
        manager.listen(myPhoneStateListener,
                PhoneStateListener.LISTEN_CALL_STATE);
    }
```

In the onPause() method, you remove the listener by using the same listen() method and the LISTEN_NONE constant:

```
    @Override
    public void onPause() {
        super.onPause();
        manager.listen(myPhoneStateListener,
                PhoneStateListener.LISTEN_NONE);
    }
```

Finally, you need to add the READ_PHONE_STATE permission in the AndroidManifest.xml file:

```
<uses-permission
        android:name="android.permission.READ_PHONE_STATE" />
```

> **NOTE** *Be sure to unregister the listener in the* onPause() *event when your activity is sent to the background. Otherwise, when the activity returns to the foreground, the activity will register the listener again. If that happens, your* onCallStateChanged *will be called multiple times.*

▉ RECIPE 4.3 ▉ MONITORING PHONE STATE IN THE BACKGROUND

Android Versions

Level 1 and above

Permissions

android.permission.READ_PHONE_STATE

Source Code Download from Wrox.com

Phone.zip

The previous recipe showed you how to monitor your phone state using the `PhoneStateListener` class. However, if your application is not running, you will not be able to monitor for changes in phone state. A better way, therefore, is to declare a `BroadcastReceiver` object in the `AndroidManifest.xml` file; that way, as long as your application is installed on the device (even if the application is not running), you will be able to monitor for changes to the phone state.

Solution

To ensure that your application continues to monitor for changes to the phone state, you need to create a class that extends the `BroadcastReceiver` base class. Within this class, you create an inner class that implements the `PhoneStateListener` class (see the previous recipe for details on how it works). Then you override the `onReceive()` method of the `BroadcastReceiver` class so that you can call the `listen()` method of the `TelephonyManager` class to monitor for phone state changes using an instance of the `PhoneStateListener` class. You need to ensure that you do not register the listener more than once.

The following example shows how to code the steps just outlined:

```
package net.learn2develop.phone;

import android.content.BroadcastReceiver;
import android.content.Context;
import android.content.Intent;
import android.telephony.PhoneStateListener;
import android.telephony.TelephonyManager;
import android.widget.Toast;

public class PhoneStateReceiver extends BroadcastReceiver {
    TelephonyManager manager;
    PhoneReceiver myPhoneStateListener;
    static boolean alreadyListening = false;

    @Override
```

```java
        public void onReceive(Context context, Intent intent) {
            myPhoneStateListener = new PhoneReceiver(context);
            manager = ((TelephonyManager) context
                    .getSystemService(Context.TELEPHONY_SERVICE));

            //---do not add the listener more than once---
            if (!alreadyListening) {
                manager.listen(myPhoneStateListener,
                        PhoneStateListener.LISTEN_CALL_STATE);
                alreadyListening = true;
            }
        }

        public class PhoneReceiver extends PhoneStateListener {
            Context context;
            public PhoneReceiver(Context context) {
                this.context = context;
            }

            @Override
            public void onCallStateChanged(int state,
                    String incomingNumber) {
                super.onCallStateChanged(state, incomingNumber);
                switch (state) {
                case TelephonyManager.CALL_STATE_IDLE:
                    Toast.makeText(context, "Idle",
                            Toast.LENGTH_LONG).show();
                    break;
                case TelephonyManager.CALL_STATE_RINGING:
                    Toast.makeText(context, "Ringing: " + incomingNumber,
                            Toast.LENGTH_LONG).show();
                    break;
                case TelephonyManager.CALL_STATE_OFFHOOK:
                    Toast.makeText(context, "Offhook",
                            Toast.LENGTH_LONG).show();
                    break;
                }
            }
        }
    }
}
```

In the `AndroidManifest.xml` file, you need to add the `<receiver>` element so that it can monitor for changes to the phone state:

```xml
<manifest xmlns:android="http://schemas.android.com/apk/res/android"
    package="net.learn2develop.phone"
    android:versionCode="1"
    android:versionName="1.0" >

    <uses-sdk
        android:minSdkVersion="8"
        android:targetSdkVersion="15" />

    <uses-permission
        android:name="android.permission.READ_PHONE_STATE" />
```

```
<application
    android:icon="@drawable/ic_launcher"
    android:label="@string/app_name"
    android:theme="@style/AppTheme" >
    <activity
        android:name=".MainActivity"
        android:label="@string/title_activity_main" >
        <intent-filter>
            <action android:name="android.intent.action.MAIN" />

            <category android:name="android.intent.category.LAUNCHER" />
        </intent-filter>
    </activity>

    <!-- put this here so that even if the app is not running,
    your app can be woken up if there is a change in phone
    state -->
    <receiver android:name=".PhoneStateReceiver">
        <intent-filter>
            <action
                android:name=
                    "android.intent.action.PHONE_STATE" />
        </intent-filter>
    </receiver>
</application>

</manifest>
```

That's all there is to it. There is no need for you to register the listener in your activity. Once the application is installed on the device, the BroadcastReceiver will automatically be fired whenever there is a change in phone state.

RECIPE 4.4 BLOCKING OUTGOING CALLS

Android Versions

Level 1 and above

Permissions

android.permission.PROCESS_OUTGOING_CALLS

Source Code Download from Wrox.com

BlockOutgoingCall.zip

If you are writing a parental control application, you might want to block the user from making calls to certain numbers. For example, you might not want your children to call specific numbers, such as premium-rate phone numbers offered by service providers for online dating, online quizzes, and so on.

In this recipe, you will learn how to block a specific outgoing call.

Solution

To block an outgoing call, create a `BroadcastReceiver` class and override its `onReceive()` method. When an outgoing call is made, the `onReceive()` method is called. To prevent the phone from calling, you simply need to call the `setResultData()` method by passing it a `null` argument. This will prevent the device from making the call. Of course, you may want to block only certain numbers, and hence in this method you can retrieve the phone number that the user is trying to call. Using this, you can selectively block outgoing calls. The following code snippet shows the `BroadcastReceiver` class:

```
package net.learn2develop.blockoutgoingcall;

import android.content.BroadcastReceiver;
import android.content.Context;
import android.content.Intent;
import android.widget.Toast;

public class OutgoingCallsReceiver extends BroadcastReceiver {

    @Override
    public void onReceive(Context context, Intent intent) {
        String outgoingNumber =
            intent.getStringExtra(Intent.EXTRA_PHONE_NUMBER).toString();
        if (outgoingNumber.contentEquals("1234567")) {
            setResultData(null);
            Toast.makeText(context, "This call is not allowed!",
                Toast.LENGTH_LONG).show();
        }
    }
}
```

In order for the `BroadcastReceiver` class to be fired when an outgoing call is made, you need to add the `PROCESS_OUTGOING_CALLS` permission, as well as declare the receiver in the `AndroidManifest.xml` file:

```
<manifest xmlns:android="http://schemas.android.com/apk/res/android"
    package="net.learn2develop.blockoutgoingcall"
    android:versionCode="1"
    android:versionName="1.0" >

    <uses-sdk
        android:minSdkVersion="8"
        android:targetSdkVersion="15" />

    <uses-permission android:name="android.permission.PROCESS_OUTGOING_CALLS"/>

    <application
        android:icon="@drawable/ic_launcher"
        android:label="@string/app_name"
        android:theme="@style/AppTheme" >
```

```
    <activity
        android:name=".MainActivity"
        android:label="@string/title_activity_main" >
        <intent-filter>
            <action android:name="android.intent.action.MAIN" />

            <category android:name="android.intent.category.LAUNCHER" />
        </intent-filter>
    </activity>

    <receiver android:name=".OutgoingCallsReceiver" >
        <intent-filter android:priority="0">
            <action android:name=
                "android.intent.action.NEW_OUTGOING_CALL" />
        </intent-filter>
    </receiver>
</application>

</manifest>
```

That's it! If the user tries to call a number that is defined in your `BroadcastReceiver` class, the call will not be successful.

RECIPE 4.5 AUTO-ANSWERING AN INCOMING CALL

Android Versions

> Level 1 and above

Permissions

> android.permission.READ_PHONE_STATE

Source Code Download from Wrox.com

> AutoCalls.zip

Recipe 4.3 showed you how to monitor the state of the phone to detect whether it is ringing, off hook, or idle. Another useful behavior is answering a call automatically when the phone rings. For example, you might want to write an application that allows the user to automatically answer a call (only for some specific phone numbers) when the user is busy (such as when he is driving). This recipe demonstrates how to do that.

Solution

To programmatically answer an incoming call, your application simply needs to emulate the device with a Bluetooth headset attached. When an incoming call is detected, you fire an `Intent` object to simulate the user pressing the button on the Bluetooth headset.

First, to detect an incoming call, you need a `BroadcastReceiver` class to monitor for changes in phone state (as discussed in Recipe 4.3). The following `IncomingCallsReceiver` class is a subclass of the `BroadcastReceiver` class:

```
package net.learn2develop.autocalls;

import android.content.BroadcastReceiver;
import android.content.Context;
import android.content.Intent;
import android.telephony.TelephonyManager;
import android.view.KeyEvent;

public class IncomingCallsReceiver extends BroadcastReceiver {
    @Override
    public void onReceive(Context context, Intent intent) {
        if (!intent.getAction().equals(
            "android.intent.action.PHONE_STATE")) return;
        String extraState =
            intent.getStringExtra(TelephonyManager.EXTRA_STATE);

        if (extraState.equals(TelephonyManager.EXTRA_STATE_RINGING)) {
            String incomingNumber =
                intent.getStringExtra(TelephonyManager.EXTRA_INCOMING_NUMBER);

            if (incomingNumber.contentEquals("1234567")) {
                //---answer the call---
                Intent i = new Intent(Intent.ACTION_MEDIA_BUTTON);
                i.putExtra(Intent.EXTRA_KEY_EVENT,
                        new KeyEvent(KeyEvent.ACTION_UP,
                        KeyEvent.KEYCODE_HEADSETHOOK));
                context.sendOrderedBroadcast(i, null);
            }
        }
        return;
    }
};
```

When a change in phone state is detected, you first check if it is the phone ringing using the `EXTRA_STATE` constant. If it is (`EXTRA_STATE_RINGING`), you obtain the incoming phone number using the `EXTRA_INCOMING_NUMBER` constant. Using this information, you can determine if the application should automatically answer the call. You do that using an `Intent` object with the `ACTION_MEDIA_BUTTON` action, passing it an extra `KeyEvent` object. Finally, you send the broadcast using the `sendOrderedBroadcast()` method. This enables the phone to automatically answer an incoming call based on the phone number you set in your code.

To monitor changes to phone state, you need to add the `READ_PHONE_STATE` permission to the `AndroidManifest.xml` file. You also need to declare the `BroadcastReceiver` class:

```
<manifest xmlns:android="http://schemas.android.com/apk/res/android"
    package="net.learn2develop.autocalls"
    android:versionCode="1"
    android:versionName="1.0" >
```

```
<uses-sdk
    android:minSdkVersion="8"
    android:targetSdkVersion="15" />

<uses-permission android:name="android.permission.READ_PHONE_STATE" />

<application
    android:icon="@drawable/ic_launcher"
    android:label="@string/app_name"
    android:theme="@style/AppTheme" >
    <activity
        android:name=".MainActivity"
        android:label="@string/title_activity_main" >
        <intent-filter>
            <action android:name="android.intent.action.MAIN" />

            <category android:name="android.intent.category.LAUNCHER" />
        </intent-filter>
    </activity>

    <receiver android:name=".IncomingCallsReceiver" >
        <intent-filter>
            <action android:name="android.intent.action.PHONE_STATE" />
        </intent-filter>
    </receiver>

</application>

</manifest>
```

While you can answer the incoming call programmatically, you cannot terminate a call using the same approach. You might assume you could use the following code snippet to programmatically reject an incoming call:

```
//---hang up the call---
//---the following code needs CALL_PRIVILEGED permission,
// which is not available to third-party apps
// hence won't work---
Intent i = new Intent(Intent.ACTION_MEDIA_BUTTON);
i.putExtra(Intent.EXTRA_KEY_EVENT,
        new KeyEvent(KeyEvent.ACTION_DOWN,
        KeyEvent.KEYCODE_HEADSETHOOK));
context.sendOrderedBroadcast(i,
    "android.permission.CALL_PRIVILEGED");
```

However, the preceding code will not work, as it requires the CALL_PRIVILEGED permission; but even if you add this permission to the AndroidManifest.xml file, it still won't work. It is not available to third-party apps; it is only available to the system.

RECIPE 4.6 SWITCHING TO AIRPLANE MODE

Android Versions

Level 1 and above

Permissions

android.permission.WRITE_SETTINGS

Source Code Download from Wrox.com

AirplaneMode.zip

If you want to turn off all the wireless connectivity on an Android device, you can programmatically enable Airplane mode on the device. This recipe shows you how.

Solution

To enable Airplane mode, use the putInt() method from the Settings.System class and pass in an ContentResolver object, together with the AIRPLANE_MODE_ON constant, and a value indicating whether to turn Airplane mode on (1) or off (0). You then utilize the Intent object's extras bundle by adding state and setting its value to either true (to turn on Airplane mode) or false (to turn off Airplane mode). Finally, you send a broadcast using the Intent object:

```
package net.learn2develop.airplanemode;

import android.app.Activity;
import android.content.Intent;
import android.os.Bundle;
import android.provider.Settings;

public class MainActivity extends Activity {

    @Override
    public void onCreate(Bundle savedInstanceState) {
        super.onCreate(savedInstanceState);
        setContentView(R.layout.activity_main);
    }

    private void SetAirplaneMode(boolean enabled){
        //---toggle Airplane mode---
        Settings.System.putInt(
            getContentResolver(),
            Settings.System.AIRPLANE_MODE_ON, enabled ? 1 : 0);
```

```
            Intent i = new Intent(Intent.ACTION_AIRPLANE_MODE_CHANGED);
            i.putExtra("state", enabled);
            sendBroadcast(i);
        }

    }
```

To enable your application to turn on the Airplane mode, you need to add the WRITE_SETTINGS permission to the AndroidManifest.xml file:

```
<uses-permission android:name="android.permission.WRITE_SETTINGS"/>
```

To check whether a device is in Airplane mode, you can use the following code snippet:

```
    public boolean isAirplaneModeOn(){
        return Settings.System.getInt(
                getContentResolver(),
                Settings.System.AIRPLANE_MODE_ON, 0) != 0;
    }
```

If you need to monitor for changes to the Airplane mode, you can create a BroadcastReceiver class, like this:

```
package net.learn2develop.airplanemode;

import android.content.BroadcastReceiver;
import android.content.Context;
import android.content.Intent;
import android.widget.Toast;

public class AirplaneModeReceiver extends BroadcastReceiver {
    @Override
    public void onReceive(Context context, Intent intent) {
        Toast.makeText(context, "Service state changed",
                Toast.LENGTH_LONG).show();
    }
}
```

Whenever the phone or Wi-Fi is turned on or off, the onReceive() method will fire.

You would also need to register the BroadcastReceiver class in your AndroidManifest.xml file, with the action SERVICE_STATE:

```
<manifest xmlns:android="http://schemas.android.com/apk/res/android"
    package="net.learn2develop.airplanemode"
    android:versionCode="1"
    android:versionName="1.0" >

    <uses-sdk
        android:minSdkVersion="8"
        android:targetSdkVersion="15" />

    <uses-permission android:name="android.permission.WRITE_SETTINGS"/>
```

```
<application
    android:icon="@drawable/ic_launcher"
    android:label="@string/app_name"
    android:theme="@style/AppTheme" >
    <activity
        android:name=".MainActivity"
        android:label="@string/title_activity_main" >
        <intent-filter>
            <action android:name="android.intent.action.MAIN" />

            <category android:name="android.intent.category.LAUNCHER" />
        </intent-filter>
    </activity>

    <receiver
        android:name=".AirplaneModeReceiver"
        android:enabled="true" >
        <intent-filter>
            <action android:name="android.intent.action.SERVICE_STATE" />
        </intent-filter>
    </receiver>
</application>

</manifest>
```

The SERVICE_STATE action enables you to monitor changes to the Airplane mode (including individual changes to Wi-Fi). The change in service state is also fired when the phone is shut down, as well as when it is starting up.

RECIPE 4.7 GETTING THE PHONE NUMBER, IMEI, AND SIM CARD ID

Android Versions

Level 1 and above

Permissions

android.permission.READ_PHONE_STATE

Source Code Download from Wrox.com

SIMCardID.zip

If you are writing a security application, you might want to know whether the user has changed the SIM card on the phone. For example, the first time your application is run on the device, you can obtain the SIM card ID of the device and store it in your application. Every time the phone switches from `AirplaneModeON` to `AirplaneModeOFF` (see previous recipe for how to detect this), you would then check the SIM card ID with the one that you previously recorded. If you detect that the SIM ID has changed, you might want to programmatically send an SMS message to another phone so that you can be notified. This scenario is common when your phone is stolen. Usually, thieves will swap out the current SIM card with their own. In this case, when the phone is restarted after putting in a new SIM card, your application will obtain the SIM card ID and compare it against its previously recorded SIM ID. Besides the SIM card ID, another piece of useful information about the phone is the IMEI — International Mobile Equipment Identity. An IMEI number is a number that is used to uniquely identify a mobile device. Knowing the IMEI of a device allows it to be identified when it is recovered. This recipe shows you how to obtain all this information.

Solution

To get the details about your phone, you need to obtain an instance of the `TelephonyManager` class:

```
package net.learn2develop.simcardid;

import android.app.Activity;
import android.content.Context;
import android.os.Bundle;
import android.telephony.TelephonyManager;
import android.widget.Toast;

public class MainActivity extends Activity {

    @Override
    public void onCreate(Bundle savedInstanceState) {
        super.onCreate(savedInstanceState);
        setContentView(R.layout.activity_main);

        TelephonyManager tm = (TelephonyManager)
                getSystemService(Context.TELEPHONY_SERVICE);
    }

}
```

To get the ID of your SIM card, use the `getSimSerialNumber()` method of the `TelephonyManager` object:

```
//---get the SIM card ID---
String simID = tm.getSimSerialNumber();
if (simID != null)
    Toast.makeText(this, "SIM card ID: " + simID,
    Toast.LENGTH_LONG).show();
```

To get the phone number of your phone, use the `getLine1Number()` method of the `TelephonyManager` object:

```
//---get the phone number---
String telNumber = tm.getLine1Number();
if (telNumber != null)
    Toast.makeText(this, "Phone number: " + telNumber,
    Toast.LENGTH_LONG).show();
```

To get the IMEI number of the phone, use the `getDeviceId()` method of the `TelephonyManager` object:

```
//---get the IMEI number---
String IMEI = tm.getDeviceId();
if (IMEI != null)
    Toast.makeText(this, "IMEI number: " + IMEI,
    Toast.LENGTH_LONG).show();
```

In order to obtain the SIM card ID, phone number, and device ID, you need to add the `READ_PHONE_STATE` permission to the `AndroidManifest.xml` file:

```
<uses-permission android:name="android.permission.READ_PHONE_STATE"/>
```

RECIPE 4.8 ENABLING BLUETOOTH

Android Versions

Level 1 and above

Permissions

android.permission.BLUETOOTH

android.permission.BLUETOOTH_ADMIN

Source Code Download from Wrox.com

Bluetooth.zip

If you are writing a Bluetooth application, you can programmatically enable the Bluetooth radio on the device. This recipe shows you two ways to accomplish this.

Solution

Before attempting to use the Bluetooth radio on the device, it is recommended that you first check whether Bluetooth is available on it. This recipe will show you how to:

➤ Check if the Bluetooth radio is available on the device

➤ Enable the Bluetooth radio if it is available

➤ Monitor the state of the Bluetooth radio on the device

Checking for Bluetooth Availability

To check for Bluetooth availability on the device, you create a variable of type `BluetoothAdapter`. To instantiate the `BluetoothAdapter` class, you call the `BluetoothAdapter.getDefaultAdapter()`

method. If Bluetooth is not available on the device, then the `BluetoothAdapter.getDefaultAdapter()` method will return a `null`. The following code snippet illustrates this:

```
package net.learn2develop.bluetooth;

import android.app.Activity;
import android.bluetooth.BluetoothAdapter;
import android.os.Bundle;
import android.widget.Toast;

public class MainActivity extends Activity {
    BluetoothAdapter bluetoothAdapter;

    //---check if bluetooth is available on the device---
    private boolean BluetoothAvailable()
    {
        if (bluetoothAdapter == null)
            return false;
        else
            return true;
    }

    /** Called when the activity is first created. */
    @Override
    public void onCreate(Bundle savedInstanceState) {
        super.onCreate(savedInstanceState);
        setContentView(R.layout.activity_main);

        bluetoothAdapter = BluetoothAdapter.getDefaultAdapter();
        Toast.makeText(this, "Bluetooth available: " + BluetoothAvailable(),
                Toast.LENGTH_LONG).show();
    }

}
```

Enabling Bluetooth

If Bluetooth is available, you should next check whether it is enabled. You can do that using the `isEnabled()` method of the `BluetoothAdapter` object. If it is not enabled, you can enable it using an `Intent` object, as shown in the following code snippet:

```
package net.learn2develop.bluetooth;

import android.app.Activity;
import android.bluetooth.BluetoothAdapter;
import android.content.Intent;
import android.os.Bundle;
import android.widget.Toast;

public class MainActivity extends Activity {
    BluetoothAdapter bluetoothAdapter;
    static final int REQUEST_ENABLE_BT = 0;
```

```
//---check if bluetooth is available on the device---
private boolean BluetoothAvailable()
{
    if (bluetoothAdapter == null)
        return false;
    else
        return true;
}

//---enable bluetooth on the device---
private void EnableBluetooth() {
    if (BluetoothAvailable() && !bluetoothAdapter.isEnabled()) {
        Intent i = new Intent(
                BluetoothAdapter.ACTION_REQUEST_ENABLE);
        startActivityForResult(i,
                REQUEST_ENABLE_BT);
    }
}

public void onActivityResult(int requestCode,
        int resultCode, Intent data) {
    if (requestCode == REQUEST_ENABLE_BT) {
        if (resultCode == RESULT_OK)
        {
            Toast.makeText(this, "Bluetooth turned on!",
                    Toast.LENGTH_SHORT).show();
        }
    }
}

/** Called when the activity is first created. */
@Override
public void onCreate(Bundle savedInstanceState) {
    super.onCreate(savedInstanceState);
    setContentView(R.layout.activity_main);

    bluetoothAdapter = BluetoothAdapter.getDefaultAdapter();
    Toast.makeText(this, "Bluetooth available: " + BluetoothAvailable(),
            Toast.LENGTH_LONG).show();

    if (BluetoothAvailable())
        EnableBluetooth();
}

}
```

Note that you should use an `Intent` object to ask the OS to display a dialog prompting the user to turn on Bluetooth (see Figure 4-2). To determine whether the user has done so after the prompt, you start the `Intent` object using the `startActivityForResult()` method. By overriding the `onActivityResult()` method, you will know whether the user has enabled Bluetooth.

FIGURE 4-2

To enable Bluetooth for the user, you need to add the BLUETOOTH and BLUETOOTH_ADMIN permissions:

```
<uses-permission android:name="android.permission.BLUETOOTH"/>
<uses-permission android:name="android.permission.BLUETOOTH_ADMIN"/>
```

Monitoring the State of Bluetooth

If you want to monitor the state of Bluetooth on the device, you can use a BroadcastReceiver class. The following code snippet shows how to use a BroadcastReceiver class together with an IntentFilter object to listen for changes in the state of the Bluetooth radio:

```
package net.learn2develop.bluetooth;

import android.app.Activity;
import android.bluetooth.BluetoothAdapter;
```

```
import android.content.BroadcastReceiver;
import android.content.Context;
import android.content.Intent;
import android.content.IntentFilter;
import android.os.Bundle;
import android.widget.Toast;

public class MainActivity extends Activity {
    BluetoothAdapter bluetoothAdapter;
    static final int REQUEST_ENABLE_BT = 0;

    //---check if bluetooth is available on the device---
    private boolean BluetoothAvailable()
    {
        if (bluetoothAdapter == null)
            return false;
        else
            return true;
    }

    //---enable bluetooth on the device---
    private void EnableBluetooth() {
        if (BluetoothAvailable() && !bluetoothAdapter.isEnabled()) {
            Intent i = new Intent(
                    BluetoothAdapter.ACTION_REQUEST_ENABLE);
            startActivityForResult(i,
                    REQUEST_ENABLE_BT);
        }
    }

    public void onActivityResult(int requestCode,
            int resultCode, Intent data) {
        if (requestCode == REQUEST_ENABLE_BT) {
            if (resultCode == RESULT_OK)
            {
                Toast.makeText(this, "Bluetooth turned on!",
                        Toast.LENGTH_SHORT).show();
            }
        }
    }

    /** Called when the activity is first created. */
    @Override
    public void onCreate(Bundle savedInstanceState) {
        super.onCreate(savedInstanceState);
        setContentView(R.layout.activity_main);

        bluetoothAdapter = BluetoothAdapter.getDefaultAdapter();
        Toast.makeText(this, "Bluetooth available: " + BluetoothAvailable(),
                Toast.LENGTH_LONG).show();

        if (BluetoothAvailable())
            EnableBluetooth();
```

```
            MyBTBroadcastReceiver mReceiver = new MyBTBroadcastReceiver();

            IntentFilter intentFilter = new
                IntentFilter("android.bluetooth.adapter.action.STATE_CHANGED");
            registerReceiver(mReceiver, intentFilter);
        }

    public class MyBTBroadcastReceiver extends BroadcastReceiver {
        @Override
        public void onReceive(Context context, Intent intent) {
            int state = intent.getExtras().getInt(BluetoothAdapter.EXTRA_STATE);
            switch (state) {
            case BluetoothAdapter.STATE_OFF:
                Toast.makeText(context, "Off", Toast.LENGTH_SHORT).show();
                break;
            case BluetoothAdapter.STATE_TURNING_OFF:
                Toast.makeText(context, "Turning Off",
                    Toast.LENGTH_SHORT).show();
                break;
            case BluetoothAdapter.STATE_ON:
                Toast.makeText(context, "On", Toast.LENGTH_SHORT).show();
                break;
            case BluetoothAdapter.STATE_TURNING_ON:
                Toast.makeText(context, "Turning On",
                    Toast.LENGTH_SHORT).show();
                break;
            }
        }
    }

    }
```

Your `IntentFilter` object listens for the `android.bluetooth.adapter.action.STATE_CHANGED` action. Whenever the Bluetooth on the device changes state, it will invoke your `BroadcastReceiver` class. In it, you check the state to deduce the current state of the Bluetooth adapter.

If you want to programmatically enable Bluetooth on the device without the user's knowledge, you can use the `enable()` method of the `BluetoothAdapter` object:

```
        //---disable Bluetooth---
        bluetoothAdapter.enable();
```

> **NOTE** *You should not programmatically enable Bluetooth without the user's explicit consent.*

To disable Bluetooth, use the `disable()` method:

```
        //---enable Bluetooth---
        bluetoothAdapter.disable();
```

RECIPE 4.9 DISPLAYING THE CALL LOG

Android Versions

Level 1 and above

Permissions

android.permission.READ_CONTACTS

Source Code Download from Wrox.com

CallLogs.zip

All the call activities on your phone are logged in the call_log content provider. Therefore, if you want details about all the incoming, outgoing, or missed calls, you can query the content provider to get them. This recipe shows you how easy it is.

Solution

To get the call log details, query the call_log content provider, iterating through the results by using a Cursor object. The following code snippet retrieves all the call details and sorts them by date. It then prints out the details of each call — ID, phone number, date of call, type of call, and whether the call has been acknowledged:

```
package net.learn2develop.calllogs;

import android.app.Activity;
import android.database.Cursor;
import android.net.Uri;
import android.os.Bundle;
import android.util.Log;

public class MainActivity extends Activity {

    @Override
    public void onCreate(Bundle savedInstanceState) {
        super.onCreate(savedInstanceState);
        setContentView(R.layout.activity_main);

        GetCallLogs();
    }

    private void GetCallLogs() {
        final String[] projection = null;
        final String selection = null;
        final String[] selectionArgs = null;
        final String sortOrder = android.provider.CallLog.Calls.DATE + " DESC";
        Cursor cursor = null;
        try{
```

```
                cursor = this.getContentResolver().query(
                        Uri.parse("content://call_log/calls"),
                        projection,
                        selection,
                        selectionArgs,
                        sortOrder);
                while (cursor.moveToNext()) {
                    //---id---
                    String callLogID = cursor.getString(cursor.getColumnIndex(
                                        android.provider.CallLog.Calls._ID));

                    //---phone number---
                    String callNumber = cursor.getString(cursor.getColumnIndex(
                                        android.provider.CallLog.Calls.NUMBER));

                    //---date of call---
                    String callDate = cursor.getString(cursor.getColumnIndex(
                                        android.provider.CallLog.Calls.DATE));

                    //---1-incoming; 2-outgoing; 3-missed---
                    String callType = cursor.getString(cursor.getColumnIndex(
                                        android.provider.CallLog.Calls.TYPE));

                    //---0-call has been acknowledged; 1-call
                    // has not been acknowledge---
                    String isCallNew = cursor.getString(cursor.getColumnIndex(
                                        android.provider.CallLog.Calls.NEW));

                    Log.d("", "callLogID: " + callLogID);
                    Log.d("", "callNumber: " + callNumber);
                    Log.d("", "callDate: " + callDate);
                    Log.d("", "callType: " + callType);
                    Log.d("", "isCallNew: " + isCallNew);

                    //---check for missed call that has not been acknowledged---
                    if (Integer.parseInt(callType) ==
                            android.provider.CallLog.Calls.MISSED_TYPE &&
                            Integer.parseInt(isCallNew) > 0) {
                        Log.d("", "Missed Call Found: " + callNumber);
                    }
                }
            } catch (Exception ex){
                Log.d("", "ERROR: " + ex.toString());
            } finally{
                cursor.close();
            }
        }

    }
```

In the preceding code snippet, you check for missed calls that have not been acknowledged (i.e., that you have not called back) and print out their phone numbers.

In order to query the call_log content provider, you need to add the READ_CONTACTS permission to the AndroidManifest.xml file:

```
<uses-permission android:name="android.permission.READ_CONTACTS"/>
```

Messaging

SMS messaging has always been one of the most popular features available on all mobile phones, from the early mobile phones to the latest and greatest smartphones in use today. The infrastructure for sending and receiving SMS messages is nearly universally available, making SMS a ubiquitous communication solution. Moreover, your application can send and receive SMS messages using Android programmatically without restrictions, thereby making it a very attractive option for communication use.

RECIPE 5.1 SENDING SMS MESSAGES THROUGH THE BUILT-IN MESSAGING APPLICATION

Android Versions

Level 1 and above

Permissions

None

Source Code to Download from Wrox.com

MessagingApp.zip

In this recipe, you learn how to send SMS messages using the built-in Messaging application installed on all Android phones. Using this approach enables you to "send and forget" — all you need to do is invoke the Messaging application using an `Intent` object and pass it the necessary pieces of information, such as the recipient's phone number and the message. Users see the familiar user interface of the Messaging application on their device, saving you the need to create a separate UI for entering the phone number, message, and so on.

Solution

To invoke the built-in Messaging application on your Android device to send an SMS message, you need to use an `Intent` object together with the `startActivity()` method. The following code shows how to invoke the built-in Messaging app:

```
package net.learn2develop.messagingapp;

import android.app.Activity;
import android.content.Intent;
import android.os.Bundle;

public class MainActivity extends Activity {

    @Override
    public void onCreate(Bundle savedInstanceState) {
        super.onCreate(savedInstanceState);
        setContentView(R.layout.activity_main);

        Intent i = new Intent(android.content.Intent.ACTION_VIEW);
        i.putExtra("address", "5556; 5558; 5560");
        i.putExtra("sms_body", "Greetings!");
        i.setType("vnd.android-dir/mms-sms");
        startActivity(i);
    }

}
```

Take note of the following:

➤ You use an action of type `android.content.Intent.Action_View`.

➤ You need to set the MIME type of the `Intent` object to `"vnd.android-dir/mms-sms"`.

➤ You specify the recipient phone numbers using the `address` key. If you have multiple recipients, use the ";" to delimit the phone numbers. In the preceding example, there are three recipients: 5556, 5558, and 5560.

➤ You specify the message body using the `sms_body` key.

Figure 5-1 shows the Messaging app populated with the phone numbers of the recipients, as well as the message body.

> **NOTE** *The phone numbers used in this example are for testing with the Android emulators (AVDs). Each AVD has a port number, beginning with 5554 for the first, 5556 for the second, and so on (they are not consecutive; they increase by two). These port numbers also serve as the phone number of the AVDs. Hence, you can send SMS messages to these AVDs using their port number.*

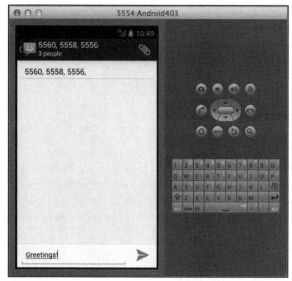

FIGURE 5-1

As shown in the preceding code snippet, you use the semicolon (;) character to delimit the phone numbers:

```
i.putExtra("address", "5556; 5558; 5560");
```

However, the semicolon may not work on devices of some brands. For these devices, replacing it with the comma (,) often works. The important point here is that you need to test this on real devices to see what works. You can use the following code snippet to programmatically detect the type of devices your application is running on and then decide to use either ; or , as the delimiter:

```
String manufacturer = android.os.Build.MANUFACTURER;  //---level 4---
String model = android.os.Build.MODEL;

Toast.makeText(this, manufacturer + ", " +
                model, Toast.LENGTH_LONG).show();
```

You should also prefix your phone numbers with the plus sign (+) and the country code to ensure that your application works globally.

RECIPE 5.2 SENDING SMS MESSAGES PROGRAMMATICALLY IN YOUR ANDROID APPLICATION

Android Versions
Level 4 and above

Permissions
android.permission.SEND_SMS

Source Code to Download from Wrox.com
SendSMS.zip

The previous recipe showed sending SMS messages using the built-in Messaging application. That is useful if you want to present users with a familiar UI to a message. However, in some situations you might want to programmatically send SMS messages in your Android application. For example, your application might monitor the current location of a user and automatically send an SMS message to a predefined phone number, which would be very helpful if you were building an application to ensure someone's safety, such as children or the elderly at home.

Solution

To send an SMS message programmatically from within your Android application, use the SmsManager class, available from the android.telephony.SmsManager package. The following code snippet shows how to send an SMS message to another device (emulator 5556) with the message "Greetings!":

> **NOTE** *To enable sending SMS messages programmatically from your application, be sure to add the* android.permission.SEND_SMS *permission; otherwise, your application will crash.*

```
package net.learndevelop.sendsms;

import android.app.Activity;
import android.os.Bundle;
import android.telephony.SmsManager;

public class MainActivity extends Activity {

    @Override
    public void onCreate(Bundle savedInstanceState) {
        super.onCreate(savedInstanceState);
        setContentView(R.layout.activity_main);
```

```
        SmsManager sms = SmsManager.getDefault();
        sms.sendTextMessage("5556", null, "Greetings!",
                            null, null);
    }

  }
```

You first create an instance of the `SmsManager` class using the `SmsManager.getDefault()` method, and then call the `sendTextMessages()` method to send an SMS message.

The `sendTextMessages()` method takes five arguments:

➤   `destinationAddress` — Phone number of the recipient

➤   `scAddress` — Service center address; use `null` for default SMSC

➤   `text` — Content of the SMS message

➤   `sentIntent` — Pending intent to invoke when the message is sent (discussed in more detail in the next recipe)

➤   `deliveryIntent` — Pending intent to invoke when the message has been delivered (discussed in more detail in the next recipe)

> **NOTE** *If you send an SMS message programmatically using the* `SmsManager` *class, the sent message will not appear in the built-in Messaging application.*

RECIPE 5.3   MONITORING THE STATUS OF SENT SMS MESSAGES PROGRAMMATICALLY

Android Versions

Level 4 and above

Permissions

android.permission.SEND_SMS

Source Code to Download from Wrox.com

SendSMSWithFeedback.zip

When sending SMS messages programmatically, you might want to monitor the sending status to ensure that the messages are sent and delivered correctly.

Solution

To monitor the status of the SMS message sending, you need to make use of two PendingIntent objects: one for tracking when the message is sent, and another one for tracking whether the message is delivered correctly. You also need two BroadcastReceiver objects, so that you can listen for intents when the SMS message has been sent and delivered:

```
package net.learn2develop.sendsmswithfeedback;

import android.app.Activity;
import android.app.PendingIntent;
import android.content.BroadcastReceiver;
import android.os.Bundle;

public class MainActivity extends Activity {
    String SENT = "SMS_SENT";
    String DELIVERED = "SMS_DELIVERED";
    PendingIntent sentPI, deliveredPI;
    BroadcastReceiver smsSentReceiver, smsDeliveredReceiver;

    @Override
    public void onCreate(Bundle savedInstanceState) {
        super.onCreate(savedInstanceState);
        setContentView(R.layout.activity_main);
    }

}
```

> **NOTE** *What is the difference between a sent message versus a delivered message? A sent message means that the message has been sent successfully from the sender's phone; but it may or may not be delivered to the recipient. For example, a message is not delivered if the recipient's phone is switched off, or for some reason the carrier is not able to deliver the message to the recipient. A message is not sent successfully if the phone number is not valid (such as specifying the phone number in the wrong format).*

In the onCreate() method of the activity, you call the getBroadcast() method of the PendingIntent class to retrieve a PendingIntent object that will perform a broadcast. You do this twice — once for the sent PendingIntent object and once for the delivered PendingIntent object:

```
package net.learn2develop.sendsmswithfeedback;

import android.app.Activity;
import android.app.PendingIntent;
import android.content.BroadcastReceiver;
import android.content.Intent;
import android.os.Bundle;

public class MainActivity extends Activity {
    String SENT = "SMS_SENT";
    String DELIVERED = "SMS_DELIVERED";
```

```
PendingIntent sentPI, deliveredPI;
BroadcastReceiver smsSentReceiver, smsDeliveredReceiver;

@Override
public void onCreate(Bundle savedInstanceState) {
    super.onCreate(savedInstanceState);
    setContentView(R.layout.activity_main);

    sentPI = PendingIntent.getBroadcast(this, 0,
            new Intent(SENT), 0);

    deliveredPI = PendingIntent.getBroadcast(this, 0,
            new Intent(DELIVERED), 0);

}

}
```

In the onResume() method of the activity, you create two BroadcastReceiver objects and implement their onReceive() methods. The first BroadcastReceiver object checks whether the message is sent successfully, while the second BroadcastReceiver object checks whether the message is delivered successfully:

```
package net.learn2develop.sendsmswithfeedback;

import android.app.Activity;
import android.app.PendingIntent;
import android.content.BroadcastReceiver;
import android.content.Context;
import android.content.Intent;
import android.content.IntentFilter;
import android.os.Bundle;
import android.telephony.SmsManager;
import android.widget.Toast;

public class MainActivity extends Activity {
    String SENT = "SMS_SENT";
    String DELIVERED = "SMS_DELIVERED";
    PendingIntent sentPI, deliveredPI;
    BroadcastReceiver smsSentReceiver, smsDeliveredReceiver;

    @Override
    public void onCreate(Bundle savedInstanceState) {
        super.onCreate(savedInstanceState);
        setContentView(R.layout.activity_main);

        sentPI = PendingIntent.getBroadcast(this, 0,
                new Intent(SENT), 0);

        deliveredPI = PendingIntent.getBroadcast(this, 0,
                new Intent(DELIVERED), 0);
    }

    @Override
    public void onResume() {
```

```java
        super.onResume();

        //---create the BroadcastReceiver when the SMS is sent---
        smsSentReceiver = new BroadcastReceiver(){
            @Override
            public void onReceive(Context arg0, Intent arg1) {
                switch (getResultCode())
                {
                case Activity.RESULT_OK:
                    Toast.makeText(getBaseContext(), "SMS sent",
                            Toast.LENGTH_SHORT).show();
                    break;
                case SmsManager.RESULT_ERROR_GENERIC_FAILURE:
                    Toast.makeText(getBaseContext(), "Generic failure",
                            Toast.LENGTH_SHORT).show();
                    break;
                case SmsManager.RESULT_ERROR_NO_SERVICE:
                    Toast.makeText(getBaseContext(), "No service",
                            Toast.LENGTH_SHORT).show();
                    break;
                case SmsManager.RESULT_ERROR_NULL_PDU:
                    Toast.makeText(getBaseContext(), "Null PDU",
                            Toast.LENGTH_SHORT).show();
                    break;
                case SmsManager.RESULT_ERROR_RADIO_OFF:
                    Toast.makeText(getBaseContext(), "Radio off",
                            Toast.LENGTH_SHORT).show();
                    break;
                }
            }
        };

        //---create the BroadcastReceiver when the SMS is delivered---
        smsDeliveredReceiver = new BroadcastReceiver(){
            @Override
            public void onReceive(Context arg0, Intent arg1) {
                switch (getResultCode())
                {
                case Activity.RESULT_OK:
                    Toast.makeText(getBaseContext(), "SMS delivered",
                            Toast.LENGTH_SHORT).show();
                    break;
                case Activity.RESULT_CANCELED:
                    Toast.makeText(getBaseContext(), "SMS not delivered",
                            Toast.LENGTH_SHORT).show();
                    break;
                }
            }
        };

        //---register the two BroadcastReceivers---
        registerReceiver(smsSentReceiver, new IntentFilter(SENT));
        registerReceiver(smsDeliveredReceiver, new IntentFilter(DELIVERED));

        //---send a SMS message---
        SmsManager sms = SmsManager.getDefault();
```

```
sms.sendTextMessage("5556", null, "Greetings!",
                        sentPI, deliveredPI);
    }

}
```

After creating the two `BroadcastReceiver` objects, you register them using the `registerReceiver()` method. You do so by passing it an `IntentFilter` object, which takes a string constructor containing the action to match.

Finally, you send the SMS message using the `SmsManager` class.

When the activity goes into the background, you need to unregister the two `BroadcastReceiver` objects in the `onPause()` method of the activity:

```
@Override
public void onPause() {
    super.onPause();
    //---unregister the two BroadcastReceivers---
    unregisterReceiver(smsSentReceiver);
    unregisterReceiver(smsDeliveredReceiver);
}
```

When the message is successfully sent and delivered, the `Toast` class displays its status.

> **NOTE** *When you send SMS messages using the Android emulator, only the* `sentPI` PendingIntent *object is fired; the* `deliveredPI` PendingIntent *object is not fired.*

RECIPE 5.4 MONITORING OUTGOING SMS MESSAGES

Android Versions

Level 1 and above

Permissions

android.permission.READ_SMS

Source Code to Download from Wrox.com

DetectOutgoingSMS.zip

You want your application to monitor all the outgoing SMS messages sent by the user using the built-in Messaging application.

Solution

If you want to monitor user-sent SMS messages through the built-in Messaging application, you need to look out for changes to the SMS content provider used by the Messaging app. All messages received and sent by the Messaging app are stored in the content provider located at content://sms. Hence, if a user sends a message, that message will be stored in this content provider. To monitor for changes in this content provider, you need to use two classes: ContentResolver and ContentObserver:

```java
package net.learn2develop.detectoutgoingsms;

import android.app.Activity;
import android.content.ContentResolver;
import android.database.ContentObserver;
import android.os.Bundle;

public class MainActivity extends Activity {
    ContentResolver contentResolver;
    ContentObserver smsContentObserver;

    @Override
    public void onCreate(Bundle savedInstanceState) {
        super.onCreate(savedInstanceState);
        setContentView(R.layout.activity_main);

    }

}
```

A ContentResolver object enables you to access a content provider, while a ContentObserver object enables you to register a callback when there is a change to the content of a content provider.

To instantiate the ContentResolver object, use the getContentResolver() method:

```java
    @Override
    public void onCreate(Bundle savedInstanceState) {
        super.onCreate(savedInstanceState);
        setContentView(R.layout.activity_main);

        contentResolver = getContentResolver();
    }
```

To instantiate the ContentObserver object, create a new instance of it and override two methods: onChange() and deliverSelfNotifications():

```java
package net.learn2develop.detectoutgoingsms;

import android.app.Activity;
import android.content.ContentResolver;
import android.database.ContentObserver;
import android.database.Cursor;
import android.net.Uri;
import android.os.Bundle;
```

```java
import android.os.Handler;
import android.util.Log;

public class MainActivity extends Activity {
    ContentResolver contentResolver;
    ContentObserver smsContentObserver;

    @Override
    public void onCreate(Bundle savedInstanceState) {
        super.onCreate(savedInstanceState);
        setContentView(R.layout.activity_main);

        contentResolver = getContentResolver();
    }

    @Override
    public void onResume() {
        super.onResume();

        smsContentObserver = new ContentObserver(new Handler()) {
            @Override
            public void onChange(boolean selfChange) {
                Uri smsURI = Uri.parse("content://sms/sent");
                Cursor c = getContentResolver().query(smsURI,
                    new String[] { "address", "date", "body", "type" },
                                    null, null, null);

                String[] columns = new String[] {
                    "address", "date", "body","type" };

                //---go to the first row; which is the most recently
                // sent message---
                c.moveToNext();

                //---get the various properties of the SMS message---
                String recipient = c.getString(c.getColumnIndex(columns[0]));
                String date = c.getString(c.getColumnIndex(columns[1]));
                String message = c.getString(c.getColumnIndex(columns[2]));
                String type = c.getString(c.getColumnIndex(columns[3]));

                //---print out the details of the message---
                Log.d("DetectOutoingSMS", recipient + ", " + date + ", " +
                    message + ", " + type);
            }

            @Override
            public boolean deliverSelfNotifications() {
                return true;
            }
        };
```

```
contentResolver.registerContentObserver(
    Uri.parse("content://sms"), true, smsContentObserver);
}

}
```

In the preceding code snippet, you register the `ContentObserver` object with the `ContentResolver` object using the `registerContentObserver()` method. You monitor for changes made to the `content://sms` content provider. When they occur, the `onChange()` method is fired. Here, you use a `Cursor` object to retrieve all the messages sent using the Messaging app. To retrieve the latest sent message, simply move the cursor to the next record and print out the details.

Note that when a message is sent using the Messaging app, the `onChange()` method is fired three times.

The first two times the `onChange()` method is fired are for the previous message that was sent. The third time will correctly display the latest message that is sent by the user. Details of the SMS include recipient phone number, time sent, message content, and message type, as shown here:

```
DetectOutgoingSMS (674): 555-6, 1333418700156, Hello!, 2
```

> **NOTE** *You might be wondering why, instead of looking for changes in* `content://sms`, *you can't just monitor the changes in* `content://sms/sent` *instead, like this:*
>
> ```
> contentResolver.registerContentObserver(
>     Uri.parse("content://sms/sent"), true,
>     smsContentObserver);
> ```
>
> *However, doing so will not trigger the* `ContentObserver` *object.*

When you are done monitoring the changes, it is important to unregister the `ContentObserver` object. You do this using the `unregisterContentObserver()` method:

```
@Override
public void onDestroy() {
    super.onDestroy();
    contentResolver.unregisterContentObserver(
        smsContentObserver);
}
```

Remember to add the `android.permission.READ_SMS` permission to the `AndroidManifest.xml` file in order to programmatically read the content of the SMS content provider.

RECIPE 5.5 INTERCEPTING INCOMING SMS MESSAGES

Android Versions

Level 1 and above

Permissions

android.permission.RECEIVE_SMS

Source Code to Download from Wrox.com

InterceptSMSMessages.zip

You want to intercept all incoming SMS messages so that only your application can receive them.

Solution

To receive SMS messages from within your Android application, you need to add a new Java class to your package. This class needs to extend the `BroadcastReceiver` base class, like this:

```java
package net.learn2develop.interceptsmsmessages;

import android.content.BroadcastReceiver;
import android.content.Context;
import android.content.Intent;
import android.os.Bundle;
import android.telephony.SmsMessage;
import android.util.Log;
import android.widget.Toast;

public class SMSReceiver extends BroadcastReceiver
{
    @Override
    public void onReceive(Context context, Intent intent)
    {
        //---get the SMS message passed in---
        Bundle bundle = intent.getExtras();
        SmsMessage[] msgs = null;
        String str = "SMS from ";
        if (bundle != null)
        {
            //---retrieve the SMS message received---
            Object[] pdus = (Object[]) bundle.get("pdus");
            msgs = new SmsMessage[pdus.length];
            for (int i=0; i<msgs.length; i++){
                msgs[i] = SmsMessage.createFromPdu((byte[])pdus[i]);
                if (i==0) {
```

```
                    //---get the sender address/phone number---
                    str += msgs[i].getOriginatingAddress();
                    str += ": ";
                }
                //---get the message body---
                str += msgs[i].getMessageBody().toString();
            }
            //---display the new SMS message---
            Toast.makeText(context, str, Toast.LENGTH_SHORT).show();

            //---prevent this SMS message from being broadcasted---
            abortBroadcast();
            Log.d("SMSReceiver", str);
        }
    }
}
```

The `BroadcastReceiver` class enables your application to receive intents sent by other applications using the `sendBroadcast()` method (in this case the Android OS will do that when it receives an incoming SMS message). When an intent is received, the `onReceive()` method is called; hence, you need to override this method.

When an incoming SMS message is received, the `onReceive()` method is fired. The SMS message is contained in the `Intent` object (`intent`; the second parameter in the `onReceive()` method) via a `Bundle` object. Note that each SMS message received will invoke the `onReceive()` method. If your device receives five SMS messages, then the `onReceive()` method will be called five times.

Each SMS message is stored in an `Object` array in the PDU format. If the SMS message contains fewer than 160 characters, then the array will have one element. If an SMS message contains more than 160 characters, then the message will be split into multiple smaller messages and stored as multiple elements in the array.

To extract the content of each message, you use the static `createFromPdu()` method from the `SmsMessage` class. The phone number of the sender is obtained via the `getOriginatingAddress()` method. Therefore, if you need to send an autoreply to the sender, this is the method to obtain the sender's phone number. To extract the body of the message, you use the `getMessageBody()` method.

The `abortBroadcast()` method will prevent the current `Intent` object from being broadcasted further. Essentially, you want to prevent other applications from receiving this SMS message.

To ensure that your application will fire the `BroadcastReceiver` class when an incoming SMS message is received, you need to add a permission and register the class in the `AndroidManifest.xml` file:

```xml
<manifest xmlns:android="http://schemas.android.com/apk/res/android"
    package="net.learn2develop.interceptsmsmessages"
    android:versionCode="1"
    android:versionName="1.0" >

    <uses-sdk
        android:minSdkVersion="8"
        android:targetSdkVersion="15" />
```

```
<uses-permission android:name="android.permission.RECEIVE_SMS" />

<application
    android:icon="@drawable/ic_launcher"
    android:label="@string/app_name"
    android:theme="@style/AppTheme" >
    <activity
        android:name=".MainActivity"
        android:label="@string/title_activity_main" >
        <intent-filter>
            <action android:name="android.intent.action.MAIN" />

            <category android:name="android.intent.category.LAUNCHER" />
        </intent-filter>
    </activity>

    <receiver android:name=".SMSReceiver" >
        <intent-filter android:priority="100" >
            <action android:name=
                "android.provider.Telephony.SMS_RECEIVED" />
        </intent-filter>
    </receiver>
</application>

</manifest>
```

Setting the `android:priority` attribute to a high value gives your application a higher priority to receive the message. In essence, you want your application to receive the SMS before the built-in Messaging application does, so that you can intercept the message without the user realizing it.

> **NOTE** *Once you register your* `BroadcastReceiver` *class in the* `AndroidManifest`
> `.xml` *file, your application will continue to listen for incoming SMS messages even if it is not running; as long as the application is installed on the device, any incoming SMS messages will be received by the application.*

Network Programming

Unless you are writing a Hello World application, chances are good your application needs to connect to the outside world. In this chapter, you will learn how to connect your Android applications to the outside world using a variety of techniques. In particular, you will learn how to do the following:

➤ Connect to web servers using HTTP

➤ Consume XML web services

➤ Consume JSON web services

➤ Communicate using sockets

➤ Communicate using Bluetooth

RECIPE 6.1 CONNECTING TO SERVERS USING HTTP GET

Android Versions

Level 1 and above

Permissions

android.permission.INTERNET

Source Code to Download at Wrox.com

HTTP.zip

One very common way for your application to talk to the outside world is to connect to web servers. As you are probably aware, web servers use the stateless Hyper Text Transfer Protocol (HTTP) to communicate with web clients. Two main advantages of HTTP are that it is lightweight and widely deployed.

In this recipe, you learn how to connect your Android application to a web server using HTTP and download data directly from it.

Solution

To connect to a server using HTTP, you can use two methods: GET and POST. Using GET, any data (known as a query string) that you want to pass to the server is appended to the URL. The following OpenHttpGetConnection() method shows how you can open a connection to a server using the HttpClient and HttpResponse classes:

```
// ---Connects using HTTP GET---
public static InputStream OpenHttpGETConnection(String url) {
    InputStream inputStream = null;
    try {
        HttpClient httpclient = new DefaultHttpClient();
        HttpResponse httpResponse = httpclient.execute(new HttpGet(url));
        inputStream = httpResponse.getEntity().getContent();
    } catch (Exception e) {
        Log.d("InputStream", e.getLocalizedMessage());
    }
    return inputStream;
}
```

When the connection is established, the HttpResponse object returns an InputStream object. Using the InputStream object, you can read incoming data directly from the server.

For example, consider the currency convertor web service located at http://www.webservicex.net/CurrencyConvertor.asmx. The ConversionRate web method supports communicating with it using HTTP GET. Figure 6-1 shows the URL string that you need to pass to it (the top part) and the result that it returns (the bottom part).

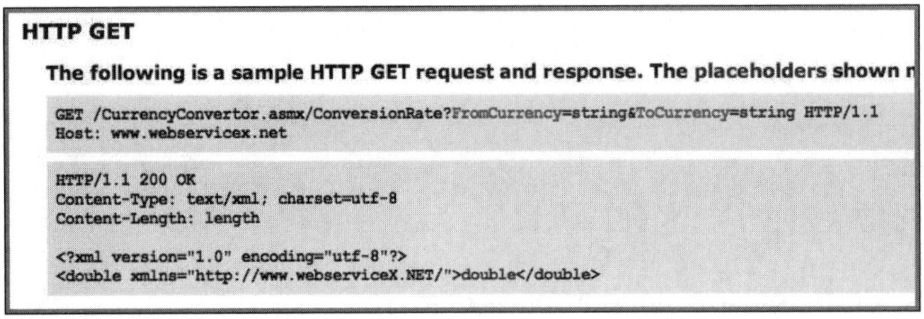

HTTP GET

The following is a sample HTTP GET request and response. The placeholders shown r

```
GET /CurrencyConvertor.asmx/ConversionRate?FromCurrency=string&ToCurrency=string HTTP/1.1
Host: www.webservicex.net
```

```
HTTP/1.1 200 OK
Content-Type: text/xml; charset=utf-8
Content-Length: length

<?xml version="1.0" encoding="utf-8"?>
<double xmlns="http://www.webserviceX.NET/">double</double>
```

FIGURE 6-1

To call the web service, you can create a method like the following, which
OpenHttpGETConnection() method and uses the InputStream object returned
download the result from the web service:

```
private String DownloadText(String URL) {
    int BUFFER_SIZE = 2000;
    InputStream in = null;
    try {
        in = OpenHttpGETConnection(URL);
    } catch (Exception e) {
        Log.d("DownloadText", e.getLocalizedMessage());
        return "";
    }

    InputStreamReader isr = new InputStreamReader(in);
    int charRead;
    String str = "";
    char[] inputBuffer = new char[BUFFER_SIZE];
    try {
        while ((charRead = isr.read(inputBuffer)) > 0) {
            // ---convert the chars to a String---
            String readString = String
                    .copyValueOf(inputBuffer, 0, charRead);
            str += readString;
            inputBuffer = new char[BUFFER_SIZE];
        }
        in.close();
    } catch (IOException e) {
        Log.d("DownloadText", e.getLocalizedMessage());
        return "";
    }
    return str;
}
```

Here, you use the InputStreamReader class to download the result (an XML string) from the
web service via the InputStream object.

Unfortunately, you cannot directly call the DownloadText() method in your activity, as this involves
network operations. Beginning with Android 3.0, network operations cannot be performed directly
from the UI thread of your Android application. To call the DownloadText() method, you need to
wrap the call using a subclass of the AsyncTask class, as shown here:

```
private class DownloadTextTask extends AsyncTask<String, Void, String> {
    protected String doInBackground(String... urls) {
        return DownloadText(urls[0]);
    }

    @Override
    protected void onPostExecute(String result) {
        Toast.makeText(getBaseContext(), result, Toast.LENGTH_LONG).show();
        Log.d("DownloadTextTask", result);
    }
}
```

The preceding class, `DownloadTextTask`, calls the `DownloadText()` method asynchronously, thereby preventing the UI thread from freezing due to network activity. To call the web service using the `DownloadTextTask` class, use the following statement:

```
new DownloadTextTask()
.execute("http://www.webservicex.net/
    CurrencyConvertor.asmx/ConversionRate?
    FromCurrency=EUR&ToCurrency=USD");
```

Note that the URL contains the information needed to be passed to the web service. Here, you are trying to find the exchange rate between the euro (EUR) and U.S. dollars (USD).

Figure 6-2 shows a typical result returned by the web service.

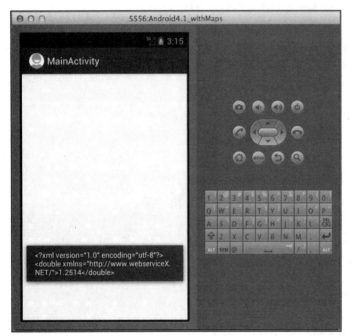

FIGURE 6-2

In order to connect to the server, you need to have the `INTERNET` permission in the `AndroidManifest.xml` file:

```
<uses-permission android:name="android.permission.INTERNET" />
```

> **NOTE** *This book assumes you are familiar with permissions in context. If you need more information, please see the section, "A Note About Permissions" in the book's Introduction.*

RECIPE 6.2 CONNECTING TO SERVERS USING HTTP POST

Android Versions

Level 1 and above

Permissions

android.permission.INTERNET

Source Code to Download at Wrox.com

HTTP.zip

The previous recipe showed how to connect to a server using HTTP GET, whereby the data to pass to the server is appended to the end of the URL. Instead of using HTTP GET, you can also use the alternative HTTP POST method. With HTTP GET, all the data passed to the server is contained in the URL, and it is typically constrained in size (typically less than 2,000 characters). With HTTP POST you can send the data separately to the server, essentially bypassing the data size limit. This recipe demonstrates how to connect to a web server using HTTP POST.

Solution

To connect to a server using HTTP POST, use the `HttpClient`, `HttpPost`, and `HttpResponse` classes, as shown here:

```
//---Connects using HTTP POST---
public InputStream OpenHttpPOSTConnection(String url) {
    InputStream inputStream = null;
    try {
        HttpClient httpclient = new DefaultHttpClient();
        HttpPost httpPost = new HttpPost(url);

        //---set the headers---
        httpPost.addHeader("Host", "www.webservicex.net");
        httpPost.addHeader("Content-Type",
                "application/x-www-form-urlencoded");

        //---the key/value pairs to post to the server---
        List<NameValuePair> nameValuePairs = new ArrayList<NameValuePair>(2);
        nameValuePairs.add(new BasicNameValuePair("FromCurrency", "USD"));
        nameValuePairs.add(new BasicNameValuePair("ToCurrency", "SGD"));
        httpPost.setEntity(new UrlEncodedFormEntity(nameValuePairs));

        HttpResponse httpResponse = httpclient.execute(httpPost);
        inputStream = httpResponse.getEntity().getContent();
```

```
        } catch (Exception e) {
            Log.d("OpenHttpPOSTConnection", e.getLocalizedMessage());
        }
        return inputStream;
    }
```

As in the previous recipe, you connect to the currency exchange web service using HTTP POST. Figure 6-3 shows the headers and data that you need to send to the server (the top part) and the result returned by it (the bottom part).

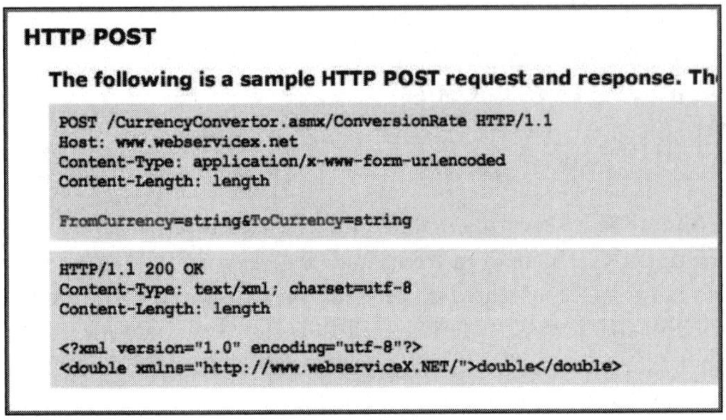

HTTP POST

The following is a sample HTTP POST request and response. Th

```
POST /CurrencyConvertor.asmx/ConversionRate HTTP/1.1
Host: www.webservicex.net
Content-Type: application/x-www-form-urlencoded
Content-Length: length

FromCurrency=string&ToCurrency=string

HTTP/1.1 200 OK
Content-Type: text/xml; charset=utf-8
Content-Length: length

<?xml version="1.0" encoding="utf-8"?>
<double xmlns="http://www.webserviceX.NET/">double</double>
```

FIGURE 6-3

In the OpenHttpPOSTConnection() method, you make use of the HttpPost class to add headers that you need to send to the server. In particular, you need to set the HOST and Content-Type headers. You also need to send the currency information using the setEntity() method of the HttpPost object. Here, the data (FromCurrency and ToCurrency) is passed in as a list of NameValuePair objects.

As in the previous recipe, you call the OpenHttpPOSTConnection() method in the DownloadText() method so that it can download the returned result:

```
private String DownloadText(String URL) {
    int BUFFER_SIZE = 2000;
    InputStream in = null;
    try {
        in = OpenHttpPOSTConnection(URL);
    } catch (Exception e) {
        Log.d("Networking", e.getLocalizedMessage());
        return "";
    }

    InputStreamReader isr = new InputStreamReader(in);
    int charRead;
    String str = "";
```

```
char[] inputBuffer = new char[BUFFER_SIZE];
try {
    while ((charRead = isr.read(inputBuffer)) > 0) {
        // ---convert the chars to a String---
        String readString = String
                    .copyValueOf(inputBuffer, 0, charRead);
        str += readString;
        inputBuffer = new char[BUFFER_SIZE];
    }
    in.close();
} catch (IOException e) {
    Log.d("DownloadText", e.getLocalizedMessage());
    return "";
}
return str;
}
```

You also need to call the `DownloadText()` method in a separate thread, so wrap it using a subclass of the `AsyncTask` class:

```
private class DownloadTextTask extends AsyncTask<String, Void, String> {
    protected String doInBackground(String... urls) {
        return DownloadText(urls[0]);
    }

    @Override
    protected void onPostExecute(String result) {
        Toast.makeText(getBaseContext(), result, Toast.LENGTH_LONG).show();
        Log.d("DownloadTextTask", result);
    }
}
```

Finally, call the web service using the `DownloadTextTask` class using the following statement:

```
//---using HTTP POST---
new DownloadTextTask().execute("http://www.webservicex.net/
    CurrencyConvertor.asmx/ConversionRate");
```

> **NOTE** *Remember that you need to have the* INTERNET *permission in the* `AndroidManifest.xml` *file.*

Figure 6-4 shows the result returned by the web service.

FIGURE 6-4

RECIPE 6.3 DOWNLOADING BINARY DATA USING HTTP

Android Versions

Level 1 and above

Permissions

android.permission.INTERNET

Source Code to Download at Wrox.com

HTTP.zip

The first two recipes in this chapter showed how to connect to web servers using the HTTP GET and POST methods. Both examples showed how to download text content from the server. In this recipe, you will learn how to download binary content. In particular, this recipe shows how to download an image from the server and display it in an ImageView.

Solution

First, to display an image in your activity, you need an `ImageView` element in your UI, such as
`activity_main.xml`:

```
<RelativeLayout xmlns:android="http://schemas.android.com/apk/res/android"
    xmlns:tools="http://schemas.android.com/tools"
    android:layout_width="match_parent"
    android:layout_height="match_parent" >

    <ImageView
        android:id="@+id/img"
        android:layout_width="wrap_content"
        android:layout_height="wrap_content"
        android:layout_gravity="center" />

</RelativeLayout>
```

To download an image from a web service, you can use the `OpenHttpGETConnection()` method
shown in the first recipe in this chapter.

To download the image, define the following method, which connects to the server and decodes the
data in the `InputStream` object using the `decodeStream()` method of the `BitmapFactory` class:

```
private Bitmap DownloadImage(String URL)
{
    Bitmap bitmap = null;
    InputStream in = null;
    try {
        in = OpenHttpGETConnection(URL);
        bitmap = BitmapFactory.decodeStream(in);
        in.close();
    } catch (Exception e) {
        Log.d("DownloadImage", e.getLocalizedMessage());
    }
    return bitmap;
}
```

As is in the previous recipes, you need to call the `DownloadImage()` method inside a subclass of the
`AsyncTask` class; therefore, define the following class:

```
private class DownloadImageTask extends AsyncTask
<String, Void, Bitmap> {
    protected Bitmap doInBackground(String... urls) {
        return DownloadImage(urls[0]);
    }

    protected void onPostExecute(Bitmap result) {
        ImageView img = (ImageView) findViewById(R.id.img);
        img.setImageBitmap(result);
    }
}
```

As shown in Figure 6-5, you set the `ImageView` to display the image downloaded.

FIGURE 6-5

NOTE *Remember that you need to have the* INTERNET *permission in the* AndroidManifest.xml *file.*

RECIPE 6.4 CONSUMING XML WEB SERVICES

Android Versions

Level 1 and above

Permissions

android.permission.INTERNET

Source Code to Download at Wrox.com

HTTP.zip

Most web services developed in the past few years have been written to return the result using XML representation. XML, being an extensible language, has been the language of choice for many developers as it is ubiquitous and is supported by almost all computing platforms. This recipe shows you how to parse the XML result and extract the information you need.

Solution

To illustrate how you can connect to a web service and then parse its XML result, this example uses the Dictionary web service at `http://services.aonaware.com/DictService/DictService.asmx`. This web service enables you to check word definitions. For this example, you use the `Define` method to check the meaning of a specified word. This web service supports the following methods of access: SOAP 1.1, SOAP 1.2, HTTP `GET`, and HTTP `POST`. For simplicity, this example uses the HTTP `GET` method.

Figure 6-6 shows the information you need to send (top part) to the server and the result (bottom part) returned from the server.

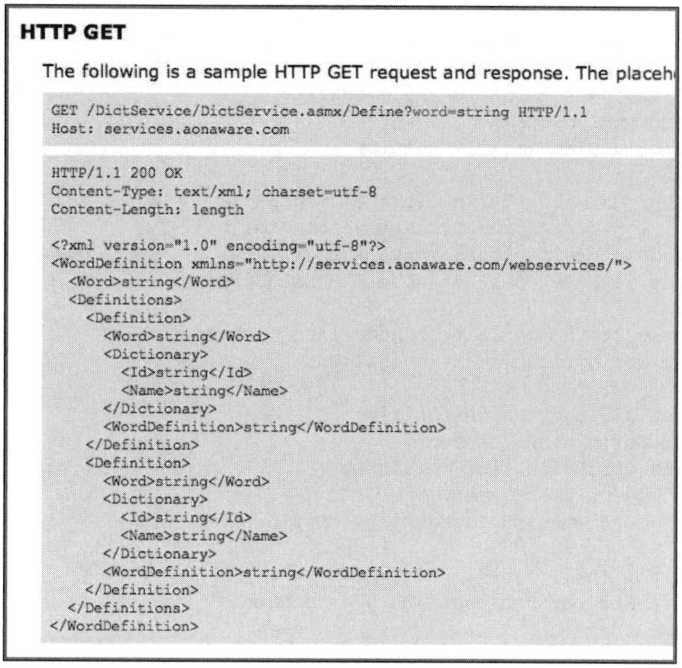

```
HTTP GET

The following is a sample HTTP GET request and response. The placeh

GET /DictService/DictService.asmx/Define?word=string HTTP/1.1
Host: services.aonaware.com

HTTP/1.1 200 OK
Content-Type: text/xml; charset=utf-8
Content-Length: length

<?xml version="1.0" encoding="utf-8"?>
<WordDefinition xmlns="http://services.aonaware.com/webservices/">
  <Word>string</Word>
  <Definitions>
    <Definition>
      <Word>string</Word>
      <Dictionary>
        <Id>string</Id>
        <Name>string</Name>
      </Dictionary>
      <WordDefinition>string</WordDefinition>
    </Definition>
    <Definition>
      <Word>string</Word>
      <Dictionary>
        <Id>string</Id>
        <Name>string</Name>
      </Dictionary>
      <WordDefinition>string</WordDefinition>
    </Definition>
  </Definitions>
</WordDefinition>
```

FIGURE 6-6

As you can see, the web service returns an XML string containing the result of the service call. In particular, the definitions of a word are contained within the various `<WordDefinition>` elements. Hence, your task is to retrieve the contents of the various `<WordDefinition>` elements.

To do so, define the following `WordDefinition()` method:

```
private String WordDefinition(String word) {
    InputStream in = null;
    String strDefinition = "";
    try {
        in = OpenHttpGETConnection(
            "http://services.aonaware.com/DictService/" +
            "DictService.asmx/Define?word=" + word);
        Document doc = null;
        DocumentBuilderFactory dbf =
            DocumentBuilderFactory.newInstance();
        DocumentBuilder db;
        try {
            db = dbf.newDocumentBuilder();
            doc = db.parse(in);
        } catch (ParserConfigurationException e) {
            e.printStackTrace();
        } catch (Exception e) {
            e.printStackTrace();
        }
        doc.getDocumentElement().normalize();

        //---retrieve all the <Definition> elements---
        NodeList definitionElements =
            doc.getElementsByTagName("Definition");

        //---iterate through each <Definition> elements---
        for (int i = 0; i < definitionElements.getLength(); i++) {
            Node itemNode = definitionElements.item(i);
            if (itemNode.getNodeType() == Node.ELEMENT_NODE)
            {
                //---convert the Definition node into an Element---
                Element definitionElement = (Element) itemNode;

                //---get all the <WordDefinition> elements under
                // the <Definition> element---
                NodeList wordDefinitionElements =
                        definitionElement.
                        getElementsByTagName("WordDefinition");

                strDefinition = "";
                //---iterate through each <WordDefinition>
                // elements---
                for (int j = 0; j <
                wordDefinitionElements.getLength(); j++) {
                    //---get all the child nodes under the
                    // <WordDefinition> element---
```

```
                    NodeList textNodes =
                        (wordDefinitionElements.item(j)).
                        getChildNodes();
                    strDefinition +=
                        ((Node)
                        textNodes.item(0)).getNodeValue() +
                        ". \n";
                }
            }
        }
    } catch (Exception e) {
        Log.d("NetworkingActivity", e.getLocalizedMessage());
    }
    //---return the definitions of the word---
    return strDefinition;
}
```

This method calls the OpenHttpGETConnection() method (discussed in Recipe 6.1) to connect to the web service using HTTP GET. It then loads the result from the web service into a Document object through the use of the DocumentBuilderFactory and DocumentBuilder classes. The Document object represents an XML document using the Document Object Model (DOM). You then parse through the XML result by iterating through the elements and locating the contents of the <WordDefinition> elements.

As in all network operations, you need to call the WordDefinition() method inside a subclass of the AsyncTask class:

```
private class AccessWebServiceTask extends AsyncTask
<String, Void, String> {
    protected String doInBackground(String... urls) {
        return WordDefinition(urls[0]);
    }

    protected void onPostExecute(String result) {
        Toast.makeText(getBaseContext(), result,
        Toast.LENGTH_LONG).show();
    }
}
```

Finally, use the following statement to access the web service:

```
//---access a Web Service using GET---
new AccessWebServiceTask().execute("cool");
```

Figure 6-7 shows the result returned by the web service.

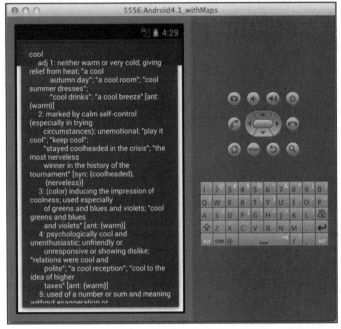

FIGURE 6-7

> **NOTE** *Remember that you need to have the* INTERNET *permission in the* AndroidManifest.xml *file.*

RECIPE 6.5 CONSUMING JSON WEB SERVICES

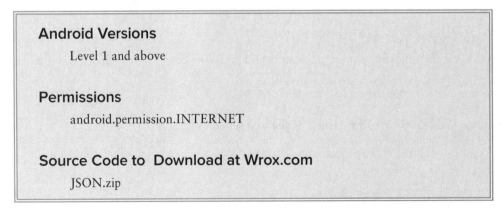

Android Versions

Level 1 and above

Permissions

android.permission.INTERNET

Source Code to Download at Wrox.com

JSON.zip

Apart from XML web services, another type of web service that is gaining popularity is JSON (JavaScript Object Notation). JSON is a lightweight data interchange format that is designed to be easy to be processed by both humans and machines. Instead of using tags (such as <title> and

`</title>`) to represent the meaning of data in an XML document, JSON uses braces ("{", "}"), colons (":"), and brackets ("[", "]") to organize data in name/value pairs and arrays.

This recipe shows you how to consume JSON web services in your Android application.

Solution

For this recipe, you will consume two JSON web services:

➤ GeoNames JSON web service — Offers a service that returns the weather for a given location. The result is returned as a JSON string.

➤ GeoNames Postal Code Search — Offers a service that returns a list of city names matching a given postal code.

> **NOTE** *This example depends on a third-party web service to work properly. This example, under the acceptable use policy of geonames.org (*`http://www.geonames.org/export/`*) uses the demo account. As with all accounts, the demo account is limited in how many queries it will service in each 24-hour period. If you find yourself getting unexplained errors when attempting this recipe, the demo account may have reached that limit. You can avoid this problem if you register with the site for your own personal demo account. Registration and additional info is available at* `http://www.geonames.org/login.`

To connect to the web services and obtain the returning JSON string, simply connect to the server using HTTP GET or POST (for simplicity, this example uses HTTP GET; see the Recipe 6.1), and then obtain the returning string (which is in JSON format). The following `readJSONFeed()` method does just that:

```java
public String readJSONFeed(String URL) {
    StringBuilder stringBuilder = new StringBuilder();
    HttpClient httpClient = new DefaultHttpClient();
    HttpGet httpGet = new HttpGet(URL);
    try {
        HttpResponse response = httpClient.execute(httpGet);
        StatusLine statusLine = response.getStatusLine();
        int statusCode = statusLine.getStatusCode();
        if (statusCode == 200) {
            HttpEntity entity = response.getEntity();
            InputStream inputStream = entity.getContent();
            BufferedReader reader = new BufferedReader(
                    new InputStreamReader(inputStream));
            String line;
            while ((line = reader.readLine()) != null) {
                stringBuilder.append(line);
            }
            inputStream.close();
        } else {
            Log.d("readJSONFeed", "Failed to download file");
        }
    } catch (Exception e) {
```

```
                Log.d("readJSONFeed", e.getLocalizedMessage());
        }
    return stringBuilder.toString();
}
```

The only remaining challenge with consuming a JSON web service is parsing the returning JSON string. Let's take a detailed look at how this can be done. For the first service that you will be using, you pass a pair of latitude and longitude values and it returns the weather information for that location. An example result looks like this (formatted for clarity):

```
{
    "weatherObservation": {
        "clouds":"scattered clouds",
        "weatherCondition":"n/a",
        "observation":"KCFV 090852Z AUTO 06005KT 10SM
         SCT090 SCT110 24/20 A3000 RMK AO2 SLP148 T02390200
         53002",
        "windDirection":60,
        "ICAO":"KCFV",
        "seaLevelPressure":1014.8,
        "elevation":225,
        "countryCode":"US",
        "lng":-95.56666666666666,
        "temperature":"23.9",
        "dewPoint":"20",
        "windSpeed":"05",
        "humidity":78,
        "stationName":"Coffeyville, Coffeyville Municipal
                       Airport",
        "datetime":"2012-07-09 08:52:00",
        "lat":37.083333333333336
    }
}
```

To connect to the web service and parse the JSON result, you can create the following class:

```
private class ReadWeatherJSONFeedTask extends AsyncTask
<String, Void, String> {
    protected String doInBackground(String... urls) {
        return readJSONFeed(urls[0]);
    }

    protected void onPostExecute(String result) {
        try {
            JSONObject jsonObject = new JSONObject(result);
            JSONObject weatherObservationItems = new
                JSONObject(jsonObject.getString("weatherObservation"));

            Toast.makeText(getBaseContext(),
                    weatherObservationItems.getString("clouds") +
                    " - " + weatherObservationItems.getString("stationName"),
                    Toast.LENGTH_SHORT).show();
```

```
        } catch (Exception e) {
            Log.d("ReadWeatherJSONFeedTask", e.getLocalizedMessage());
        }
    }
}
```

The important things to note here are as follows:

➤ You use the JSONObject class to convert the JSON string into a JSON object with key/value mappings.

➤ The getString() method of the JSONObject class returns the value specified by the key. In this example, it returns the value of the key "weatherObservation". The returning result is then converted into another JSON object.

➤ You can now retrieve the value of each individual key inside the JSON object, such as clouds, stationName, etc.

To use the ReadWeatherJSONFeedTask class, you use the following statement:

```
new ReadWeatherJSONFeedTask().execute(
    "http://ws.geonames.org/findNearByWeatherJSON?lat=" +
    txtLat.getEditableText().toString() + "&lng=" +
    txtLong.getText().toString());
```

Figure 6-8 shows the result returned by the web service.

FIGURE 6-8

Let's look at another example. The second web service returns a list of city names based on a specified postal code. The result from that web service looks like this:

```
{
    "postalCodes": [
        {
            "adminCode3":"3203",
            "adminName2":"Wahlkreis St. Gallen",
            "adminName3":"St. Gallen",
            "adminCode2":"1721",
            "adminCode1":"SG",
            "postalCode":"9011",
            "countryCode":"CH",
            "lng":9.399858534040646,
            "placeName":"St. Gallen",
            "lat":47.414775328611945,
            "adminName1":"Kanton St. Gallen"
        },
        {
            "adminCode1":"GS",
            "postalCode":"9011",
            "countryCode":"HU",
            "lng":17.781944437499998,
            "placeName":"Gyor",
            "lat":47.607638900000005,
            "adminName1":"Gyor-Moson-Sopron"
        },
        {
            "adminName2":"Tromsø",
            "adminCode2":"1902",
            "adminCode1":"19",
            "postalCode":"9011",
            "countryCode":"NO",
            "lng":18.95508,
            "placeName":"Troms",
            "lat":69.6489,
            "adminName1":"Troms"
        },
        {
            ...
            ...
        }
    ]
}
```

To use the web service, you can create the following class:

```
private class ReadPlacesFeedTask extends AsyncTask
<String, Void, String> {
```

```
protected String doInBackground(String... urls) {
    return readJSONFeed(urls[0]);
}

protected void onPostExecute(String result) {
    try {
        JSONObject jsonObject = new JSONObject(result);
        JSONArray postalCodesItems = new
            JSONArray(jsonObject.getString("postalCodes"));

        //---print out the content of the json feed---
        for (int i = 0; i < postalCodesItems.length(); i++) {
            JSONObject postalCodesItem =
                postalCodesItems.getJSONObject(i);
            Toast.makeText(getBaseContext(),
                    postalCodesItem.getString("postalCode") + " - " +
                postalCodesItem.getString("placeName") + ", " +
                postalCodesItem.getString("countryCode"),
                Toast.LENGTH_SHORT).show();
        }
    } catch (Exception e) {
        Log.d("ReadPlacesFeedTask", e.getLocalizedMessage());
    }
}
}
```

The important things to note here are as follows:

➤ You use the JSONObject class to convert the JSON string into a JSON object with key/value mappings.

➤ The getString() method of the JSONObject class returns the value specified by the key. In this example, it returns the value of the key "postalCodes". The returning result is then converted into a JSONArray object, which contains an array of JSON objects.

➤ You then iterate through the JSONArray and for each JSON object extract the value of the individual keys, such as postalCode, placeName, countryCode, etc.

To use the ReadPlacesFeedTask class, you use the following statement:

```
new ReadPlacesFeedTask().execute(
    "http://api.geonames.org/postalCodeSearchJSON?postalcode=" +
    txtPostalCode.getEditableText().toString() +
    "&maxRows=10&username=demo");
```

Figure 6-9 shows a snapshot of the result returned by the web service.

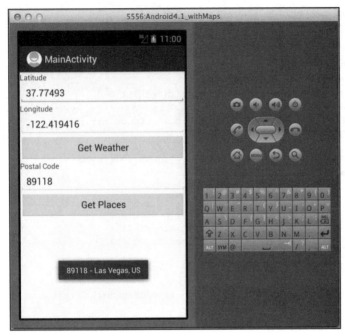

FIGURE 6-9

> **NOTE** *Remember that you need to have the* INTERNET *permission in the* AndroidManifest.xml *file.*

RECIPE 6.6 GETTING THE IP ADDRESS OF THE DEVICE

Android Versions

Level 1 and above

Permissions

android.permission.INTERNET

Source Code to Download at Wrox.com

IPAddress.zip

One of the things your application needs to know when performing network operations is its own IP address. This recipe shows you how to obtain the IPv4 and IPv6 addresses of your device.

Solution

The following `getLocalIpv4Address()` method shows how you can obtain the IPv4 address of your Android device:

```
public String getLocalIpv4Address() {
    try {
        for (Enumeration<NetworkInterface> networkInterfaceEnum =
            NetworkInterface.getNetworkInterfaces();
            networkInterfaceEnum.hasMoreElements();) {
            NetworkInterface networkInterface =
                networkInterfaceEnum.nextElement();
            for (Enumeration<InetAddress> ipAddressEnum = networkInterface
                    .getInetAddresses(); ipAddressEnum.hasMoreElements();) {
                InetAddress inetAddress = (InetAddress) ipAddressEnum
                        .nextElement();
                //---check that it is not a loopback address and
                // it is IPv4---
                if (!inetAddress.isLoopbackAddress()
                        && InetAddressUtils.isIPv4Address(inetAddress
                                .getHostAddress())) {
                    return inetAddress.getHostAddress();
                }
            }
        }
    } catch (SocketException ex) {
        Log.e("getLocalIpv4Address", ex.toString());
    }
    return null;
}
```

The preceding code iterates over all the network interfaces on your device and returns the IPv4 version address of the interface address by using the `getHostAddress()` method of an `InetAddress` object. It also verifies that it only returns the IPv4 version of the address and that the address is not a loopback address (127.0.01).

The following `getLocalIpv6Address()` method shows how you can obtain the IPv6 address of your Android device:

```
public String getLocalIpv6Address() {
    try {
        for (Enumeration<NetworkInterface> networkInterfaceEnum =
            NetworkInterface.getNetworkInterfaces();
            networkInterfaceEnum.hasMoreElements();) {
            NetworkInterface networkInterface =
                networkInterfaceEnum.nextElement();
            for (Enumeration<InetAddress> ipAddressEnum = networkInterface
                    .getInetAddresses(); ipAddressEnum.hasMoreElements();) {
                InetAddress inetAddress = (InetAddress) ipAddressEnum
                        .nextElement();
                //---check that it is not a loopback address and
                // it is not IPv4---
```

```
                            if (!inetAddress.isLoopbackAddress()
                                    && !InetAddressUtils.isIPv4Address(inetAddress
                                        .getHostAddress())) {
                                return inetAddress.getHostAddress().toString();
                            }
                        }
                    }
            } catch (SocketException ex) {
                Log.e("getLocalIpv6Address", ex.toString());
            }
            return null;
        }
```

The preceding code is similar to the earlier example, but in this case you confirm that the IP address is neither the loopback address nor the IPv4 version.

> **NOTE** *Remember that you need to have the* INTERNET *permission in the* AndroidManifest.xml *file.*

RECIPE 6.7 CREATING A SOCKET SERVER

Android Versions

Level 1 and above

Permissions

android.permission.INTERNET

Source Code to Download at Wrox.com

SocketServer.zip

A socket is an endpoint of an application participating in a two-way communication across the network. A socket is comprised of an IP address and a port number. Using sockets, applications can efficiently transfer data across the network. In this recipe, you will learn how to create a socket server that listens for incoming connections. Then, Recipe 6.8 shows you how to develop a socket client that connects to the server.

Solution

To create a socket server, first declare four objects as follows:

```
static String SERVER_IP;
static final int SERVER_PORT = 5000;
```

```
Handler handler = new Handler();
ServerSocket serverSocket;
```

The first object holds the IP address of the device, which will act as a socket server. The second object holds the port number on which the server is listening. In theory, you can use any port number from 0 to 65,535, but in the real world port numbers from 0 to 1,023 are typically reserved for running privileged server processes. Hence, your port number can be from 1,024 to 65,535, as long as it does not conflict with another application running on the device with the same port number that you have chosen.

The `Handler` object is used to update your UI. Typically, you need to do this if you are currently executing on a separate thread other than the UI and you need to update the UI. This is important because network operations are not allowed to be called directly from the UI thread. Hence, any updates that you need to reflect on the UI from the network thread need to make use of a Handler object.

The `ServerSocket` is a thread that you will define later to listen for incoming socket connections.

For simplicity, you will implement the socket server using the device's IPv4 address. The following `getLocalIpv4Address()` method returns the IPv4 address of the Android device on which it is running:

```
//---get the local IPv4 address---
public String getLocalIpv4Address() {
    try {
        for (Enumeration<NetworkInterface> networkInterfaceEnum =
            NetworkInterface.getNetworkInterfaces();
            networkInterfaceEnum.hasMoreElements();) {
            NetworkInterface networkInterface = networkInterfaceEnum
                .nextElement();
            for (Enumeration<InetAddress> ipAddressEnum = networkInterface
                .getInetAddresses(); ipAddressEnum.hasMoreElements();) {
                InetAddress inetAddress = (InetAddress) ipAddressEnum
                    .nextElement();
                // ---check that it is not a loopback address and
                // it is IPv4---
                if (!inetAddress.isLoopbackAddress()
                        && InetAddressUtils.isIPv4Address(inetAddress
                            .getHostAddress())) {
                    return inetAddress.getHostAddress();
                }
            }
        }
    } catch (SocketException ex) {
        Log.e("IPAddress", ex.toString());
    }
    return null;
}
```

NOTE *Details about this method are discussed in the previous recipe.*

To implement a socket server, create the `ServerThread` class that implements the `Runnable` interface, like this:

```
public class ServerThread implements Runnable {
    public void run() {
        try {
            if (SERVER_IP != null) {
                handler.post(new Runnable() {
                    @Override
                    public void run() {
                        textView1.setText(textView1.getText()
                                + "Server listening on IP: " + SERVER_IP
                                + "\n");
                    }
                });

                //---create an instance of the server socket---
                serverSocket = new ServerSocket(SERVER_PORT);

                while (true) {
                    //---wait for incoming clients---
                    Socket client = serverSocket.accept();

                    //---the above code is a blocking call;
                    // i.e. it will block until a client connects---

                    //---client has connected---
                    handler.post(new Runnable() {
                        @Override
                        public void run() {
                            textView1.setText(textView1.getText()
                                    + "Connected to client." + "\n");
                        }
                    });

                    try {
                        //---get an InputStream object to read from the
                        // socket---
                        BufferedReader br = new BufferedReader(
                                new InputStreamReader(
                                        client.getInputStream()));

                        OutputStream outputStream =
                                client.getOutputStream();

                        //---read all incoming data terminated with a \n
                        // char---
                        String line = null;
                        while ((line = br.readLine()) != null) {
                            final String strReceived = line;

                            //---send whatever you received back to the
                            // client---
```

```
                            String s = line + "\n";
                            outputStream.write(s.getBytes());

                            handler.post(new Runnable() {
                                @Override
                                public void run() {
                                    textView1.setText(textView1.getText()
                                            + strReceived + "\n");
                                }
                            });
                        }

                        //---client has disconnected from the server---
                        handler.post(new Runnable() {
                            @Override
                            public void run() {
                                textView1.setText(textView1.getText()
                                        + "Client disconnected." + "\n");
                            }
                        });

                    } catch (Exception e) {
                        final String error = e.getLocalizedMessage();
                        handler.post(new Runnable() {
                            @Override
                            public void run() {
                                textView1.setText(textView1.getText()
                                        + error);
                            }
                        });
                    }
                }
            } else {
                handler.post(new Runnable() {
                    @Override
                    public void run() {
                        textView1.setText(textView1.getText()
                                + "No internet connection on device."
                                + "\n");
                    }
                });
            }
        } catch (Exception e) {
            final String error = e.getLocalizedMessage();
            handler.post(new Runnable() {
                @Override
                public void run() {
                    textView1.setText(textView1.getText() + error + "\n");
                }
            });
        }
```

```
            handler.post(new Runnable() {
                @Override
                public void run() {
                    textView1.setText(textView1.getText() + "\n" + "Server exited"
                        + "\n");
                }
            });
        }
    }
```

The `ServerThread` class does the following:

➤ It creates a server socket using the `ServerSocket` class, passing it the port number at which it should listen.

➤ It listens for an incoming socket connection using the `accept()` method of the socket object. This is a blocking call, and execution continues only after a client has connected.

➤ Once a client has connected, you get the `InputStream` object from the client so that you can read from the client. To read from the client, you use a `BufferedReader` object. You also obtain an `OutputStream` object from the client so that you can write back to the client. In this example, you send back to the client whatever you have received from it.

➤ The server waits for the client to send data to it (the data needs to be terminated with a newline character ("\n")). It runs this indefinitely until the client disconnects.

➤ You use the `Handler` object to update the UI thread.

To start the socket server, you can use the `onStart()` method of the activity (when the activity comes to the foreground):

```
@Override
protected void onStart() {
    super.onStart();
    //---get the IP address of itself---
    SERVER_IP = getLocalIpv4Address();

    //---start the server---
    Thread serverThread = new Thread(new ServerThread());
    serverThread.start();
}
```

When the activity goes into the background, you close the socket server in the `onStop()` method of the activity:

```
@Override
protected void onStop() {
    super.onStop();
    try {
        serverSocket.close();
    } catch (IOException e) {
        e.printStackTrace();
    }
}
```

For all socket connections, you need the INTERNET permission in the AndroidManifest.xml file:

```
<uses-permission android:name="android.permission.INTERNET"/>
```

When you deploy this application onto a real Android device, you should see something like what is shown in Figure 6-10.

FIGURE 6-10

> **NOTE** *If you deploy the application onto an Android emulator, you will see a fixed IP address of 10.0.2.15. Even with several Android emulators running, each will have this same fixed IP address. Therefore, be sure to test the server on a real Android device.*

The next recipe demonstrates how to build a socket client that connects to this server.

RECIPE 6.8 CREATING A SOCKET CLIENT

Android Versions

Level 1 and above

Permissions

android.permission.INTERNET

Source Code to Download at Wrox.com

SocketClient.zip

The previous recipe implemented a socket server that listens at port 5000. This recipe shows how to implement a socket client that connects to it and sends it some data. In the real world, knowing how to implement a socket client will allow you to create very compelling applications. For example, you may build a cinema ticket reservation system where the socket server will listen for incoming connections from users (the socket clients) who want to reserve seats and book cinema tickets. When a user reserves a seat, all the other connected users will receive a notification informing them that a seat has been taken and is no longer available. That way, users are always looking at the updated seating plan of the cinema.

Solution

First, create the following objects:

```
static final String SERVER_IP = "192.168.1.13";
static final int SERVER_PORT = 5000;

Handler handler = new Handler();
static Socket socket;

PrintWriter printWriter;
```

The first two objects set the IP address and port number of the socket server (based on the example in the previous recipe). As usual, the `Handler` object is used to update your UI in a thread-safe manner. The `Socket` object is used to connect to the socket server. The `PrintWriter` object is a convenience method to write data to the server through an `OutputStream` object.

To connect to the socket server, you create the `ClientThread` that implements the `Runnable` interface:

```
public class ClientThread implements Runnable {
    public void run() {
        try {
            InetAddress serverAddr = InetAddress.getByName(SERVER_IP);
```

```java
    handler.post(new Runnable() {
        @Override
        public void run() {
            textView1.setText(textView1.getText()
                    + "Connecting to the server");
        }
    });

socket = new Socket(serverAddr, SERVER_PORT);
try {
    printWriter = new PrintWriter(new BufferedWriter(
            new OutputStreamWriter(socket.getOutputStream())),
            true);

    //---get an InputStream object to read from the server---
    BufferedReader br = new BufferedReader(
            new InputStreamReader(socket.getInputStream()));

    try {
        //---read all incoming data terminated with a \n
        // char---
        String line = null;
        while ((line = br.readLine()) != null) {
            final String strReceived = line;

            handler.post(new Runnable() {
                @Override
                public void run() {
                    textView1.setText(textView1.getText()
                            + "\n" + strReceived);
                }
            });
        }

        //---disconnected from the server---
        handler.post(new Runnable() {
            @Override
            public void run() {
                textView1.setText(textView1.getText()
                        + "\n" + "Client disconnected");
            }
        });

    } catch (Exception e) {
        final String error = e.getLocalizedMessage();
        handler.post(new Runnable() {
            @Override
            public void run() {
                textView1.setText(textView1.getText() + "\n" +
                error);
            }
        });
    }
```

```
                    } catch (Exception e) {
                        final String error = e.getLocalizedMessage();
                        handler.post(new Runnable() {
                            @Override
                            public void run() {
                                textView1.setText(textView1.getText() + "\n" +
                                error);
                            }
                        });
                    }

                    handler.post(new Runnable() {
                        @Override
                        public void run() {
                            textView1.setText(textView1.getText()
                                    + "\n" + "Connection closed.");
                        }
                    });

                } catch (Exception e) {
                    final String error = e.getLocalizedMessage();
                    handler.post(new Runnable() {
                        @Override
                        public void run() {
                            textView1.setText(textView1.getText() + "\n" + error);
                        }
                    });
                }
            }
        }
    }
```

The `ClientThread` class does the following:

➤ Connects to the socket server using the `Socket` class, passing it the IP address and port number of the server

➤ Creates a `BufferReader` object from the socket's `InputStream` object so that it can read data from the server

➤ Loops indefinitely while waiting for the server to send data to it

To connect to the socket server, you can start it in the `onStart()` method of your activity:

```
@Override
protected void onStart() {
    super.onStart();
    Thread clientThread = new Thread(new ClientThread());
    clientThread.start();
}
```

When the activity goes into the background, you can disconnect from the server in the `onStop()` method of your activity:

```
@Override
protected void onStop() {
    super.onStop();
```

```
        try {
            socket.shutdownInput();
            socket.close();
        } catch (IOException e) {
            e.printStackTrace();
        }
    }
```

Note that calling the `close()` method of the `Socket` object is not enough to disconnect. Because you have a separate thread looping indefinitely while waiting for incoming data from the server, calling the `close()` method will not disconnect the socket. Instead, you need to first call the `shutdownInput()` method of the `Socket` object so that it can close the input stream of the socket.

To send data to the socket server, use the `PrintWriter` object's `println()` method:

```
public void onClick(View view) {
    handler.post(new Runnable() {
        @Override
        public void run() {
            printWriter.println(editText1.getText().toString());
        }
    });
}
```

Note that the `println()` method automatically appends a newline character ("\n") to the end of the string that you are sending to the socket server.

Deploy the application onto another Android device. You can also deploy onto an Android emulator. Figure 6-11 shows the emulator sending a message to the server and getting a reply.

FIGURE 6-11

RECIPE 6.9 CHECKING FOR THE AVAILABILITY OF BLUETOOTH

Android Versions

Level 1 and above

Permissions

android.permission.BLUETOOTH

android.permission.BLUETOOTH_ADMIN

Source Code to Download at Wrox.com

TurnOnBluetooth.zip

Most Android devices on the market today support Bluetooth connectivity. Bluetooth is useful for short-range communication when you need to exchange small packets of data between devices. In the following few recipes, you will learn how to develop Android applications that communicate over Bluetooth. This recipe shows how to determine whether the Bluetooth radio is available on the target device.

Solution

To use the Bluetooth functionality in your application, you need to add the following two permissions in your `AndroidManifest.xml` file:

```
<uses-permission android:name="android.permission.BLUETOOTH"/>
    <uses-permission android:name="android.permission.BLUETOOTH_ADMIN"/>
```

Then, declare the following objects:

```
BluetoothAdapter bluetoothAdapter;
static final int REQUEST_ENABLE_BT = 0;
```

The `BluetoothAdapter` object is used to represent the Bluetooth adapter on your device. Once you have this object instantiated, you can get the list of pair devices on your device, create a listening socket, and so on.

To instantiate the `BluetoothAdapter` object, use the `getDefaultAdapter()` method of the `BluetoothAdapter` class:

```
bluetoothAdapter = BluetoothAdapter.getDefaultAdapter();
```

To determine whether Bluetooth is available on your device, simply check whether the
`BluetoothAdapter` object is null:

```
//---check if bluetooth is available on the device---
private boolean IsBluetoothAvailable() {
    if (bluetoothAdapter == null)
        return false;
    else
        return true;
}
```

If Bluetooth is available, you need to confirm that it is turned on using the `isEnabled()` method:

```
if (IsBluetoothAvailable()) {
    if (!bluetoothAdapter.isEnabled()) {
        // ---you can also use this; but do not use without explicit user
        // permission---
        // bluetoothAdapter.enable();

        Intent i = new Intent(BluetoothAdapter.ACTION_REQUEST_ENABLE);
        startActivityForResult(i, REQUEST_ENABLE_BT);
    } else {
        bluetoothAdapter.disable();
    }
}
```

To programmatically turn on the Bluetooth radio on your device, create an `Intent` object using the
`ACTION_REQUEST_ENABLE` action. To turn off the Bluetooth radio, simple call the `disable()` method
of the `BluetoothAdapter` object. When you turn on the Bluetooth radio using an `Intent` object,
you will see a prompt on the device (see Figure 6-12).

> **NOTE** *You can also programmatically turn on the Bluetooth radio using the*
> `enable()` *method of the* `BluetoothAdapter` *object. However, doing so automatically turns on the radio without user intervention. You should not do this without explicitly asking the user's permission.*

The user can tap Yes to turn on the Bluetooth radio, or No to keep it turned off. Programmatically,
you can determine whether the Bluetooth radio is turned on or off via the `onActivityResult()`
method (which is the callback method when you use the `startActivityForResult()` method to
invoke an intent):

```
protected void onActivityResult(int requestCode, int resultCode,
        Intent data) {
    if (requestCode == REQUEST_ENABLE_BT) {
        if (resultCode == RESULT_OK) {
            Log.d("onActivityResult","Bluetooth turned on.");
        } else {
            Log.d("onActivityResult","Bluetooth failed to
                turn on.");                        }
    }
}
```

FIGURE 6-12

RECIPE 6.10 MONITORING THE STATE OF BLUETOOTH

Android Versions

Level 1 and above

Permissions

android.permission.BLUETOOTH

android.permission.BLUETOOTH_ADMIN

Source Code to Download at Wrox.com

TurnOnBluetooth.zip

If your application uses Bluetooth connectivity, it is useful to know whether the user has just turned on Bluetooth, or just turned it off. This recipe shows how to monitor the state of Bluetooth on the device. For example, if you are writing a service that uses Bluetooth in the background, you need to closely monitor the state of the Bluetooth and start or stop your service appropriately.

Solution

To monitor the state of Bluetooth, create a Java class that extends the `BroadcastReceiver` base class, like this:

```java
package net.learn2develop.turnonbluetooth;

import android.bluetooth.BluetoothAdapter;
import android.content.BroadcastReceiver;
import android.content.Context;
import android.content.Intent;
import android.widget.Toast;

public class MyBTBroadcastReceiver extends BroadcastReceiver {
    @Override
    public void onReceive(Context context, Intent intent) {
        int state = intent.getExtras().getInt(BluetoothAdapter.EXTRA_STATE);
        switch (state) {
        case BluetoothAdapter.STATE_OFF:
            Toast.makeText(context, "Off", Toast.LENGTH_SHORT).show();
            break;
        case BluetoothAdapter.STATE_TURNING_OFF:
            Toast.makeText(context, "Turning Off", Toast.LENGTH_SHORT).show();
            break;
        case BluetoothAdapter.STATE_ON:
            Toast.makeText(context, "On", Toast.LENGTH_SHORT).show();
            break;
        case BluetoothAdapter.STATE_TURNING_ON:
            Toast.makeText(context, "Turning On", Toast.LENGTH_SHORT).show();
            break;
        }
    }
}
```

The `onReceive()` method is fired whenever there is a change in Bluetooth state. Here, you can monitor four states of Bluetooth: turned off, in the process of turning off, turned on, and in the process of turning on.

Remember to register the broadcast receiver in the `AndroidManifest.xml` file:

```xml
<manifest xmlns:android="http://schemas.android.com/apk/res/android"
    package="net.learn2develop.turnonbluetooth"
    android:versionCode="1"
    android:versionName="1.0" >

    <uses-sdk
        android:minSdkVersion="8"
        android:targetSdkVersion="15" />
```

```
<uses-permission android:name="android.permission.BLUETOOTH" />
<uses-permission android:name="android.permission.BLUETOOTH_ADMIN" />

<application
    android:icon="@drawable/ic_launcher"
    android:label="@string/app_name"
    android:theme="@style/AppTheme" >
    <activity
        android:name=".MainActivity"
        android:label="@string/title_activity_main" >
        <intent-filter>
            <action android:name="android.intent.action.MAIN" />

            <category android:name="android.intent.category.LAUNCHER" />
        </intent-filter>
    </activity>

    <receiver android:name=".MyBTBroadcastReceiver" >
        <intent-filter>
            <action android:name=
                "android.bluetooth.adapter.action.STATE_CHANGED" />
        </intent-filter>
    </receiver>

</application>

</manifest>
```

Once this is done, your application will be able to determine whenever there is a change in the state of the Bluetooth radio.

RECIPE 6.11 CREATING A BLUETOOTH CHAT APPLICATION

Android Versions

    Level 1 and above

Permissions

    android.permission.BLUETOOTH

    android.permission.BLUETOOTH_ADMIN

Source Code to Download at Wrox.com

    UsingBluetooth.zip

In this recipe, you will build a Bluetooth Android application. This application acts as a server as well as a client: It will run as a server so that other Bluetooth devices can connect and communicate with it; and at the same time, it will have the capability to connect to other devices through Bluetooth.

Solution

In this recipe's solution, you will create an application that:

➤ Makes itself discoverable to other Bluetooth devices running the same application

➤ Discovers other devices running the same application

➤ Runs a Bluetooth socket server that listens for incoming Bluetooth socket connection

➤ Connects to other Bluetooth devices using a socket client

> **NOTE** *You need two Bluetooth devices in order to test the application discussed in this recipe.*

Creating the Project

Create a new Android Application project and name it `UsingBluetooth`.

Add the required permission in your `AndroidManifest.xml` file:

```
<uses-permission android:name="android.permission.BLUETOOTH" />
<uses-permission android:name="android.permission.BLUETOOTH_ADMIN" />
```

Creating the User Interface

Populate the `activity_main.xml` file, located in the `res/layout` folder, as follows:

```
<ScrollView xmlns:android="http://schemas.android.com/apk/res/android"
    android:layout_width="fill_parent"
    android:layout_height="fill_parent" >

    <LinearLayout
        xmlns:android="http://schemas.android.com/apk/res/android"
        android:layout_width="match_parent"
        android:layout_height="match_parent"
        android:orientation="vertical"
        android:focusable="true"
        android:focusableInTouchMode="true" >

        <Button
            android:layout_width="fill_parent"
            android:layout_height="wrap_content"
```

```
        android:onClick="MakeDiscoverable"
        android:text="Make Discoverable" />

    <Button
        android:layout_width="fill_parent"
        android:layout_height="wrap_content"
        android:onClick="DiscoverDevices"
        android:text="Discover Devices" />

    <TextView
        android:layout_width="fill_parent"
        android:layout_height="wrap_content"
        android:text="Devices discovered (tap to connect)" />

    <ListView
        android:id="@id/android:list"
        android:layout_width="fill_parent"
        android:layout_height="120dp" />

    <TextView
        android:layout_width="fill_parent"
        android:layout_height="wrap_content"
        android:text="Enter message here" />

    <Button
        android:layout_width="fill_parent"
        android:layout_height="wrap_content"
        android:onClick="SendMessage"
        android:text="Send Message" />

    <EditText
        android:id="@+id/txtMessage"
        android:layout_width="fill_parent"
        android:layout_height="wrap_content"
        android:hint="Message to send to the selected device" />

    <TextView
        android:layout_width="fill_parent"
        android:layout_height="wrap_content"
        android:text="Messages Received" />

    <TextView
        android:id="@+id/txtData"
        android:layout_width="fill_parent"
        android:layout_height="wrap_content" />
</LinearLayout>

</ScrollView>
```

This will create the UI shown in Figure 6-13.

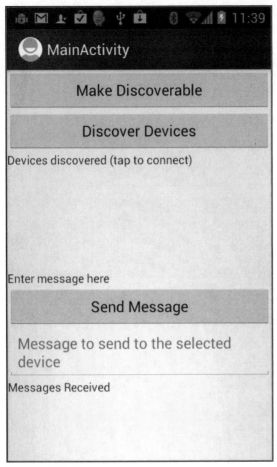

FIGURE 6-13

Adding New Classes

You need to create several threads for listening as well as connecting to other Bluetooth devices. Hence, create the Java classes as highlighted in Figure 6-14.

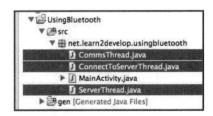

FIGURE 6-14

Importing the Packages Used

In the `MainActivity.java` file, import the following packages:

```
import java.io.IOException;
import java.util.ArrayList;
import android.app.ListActivity;
import android.bluetooth.BluetoothAdapter;
import android.bluetooth.BluetoothDevice;
```

```
import android.content.BroadcastReceiver;
import android.content.Context;
import android.content.Intent;
import android.content.IntentFilter;
import android.os.AsyncTask;
import android.os.Bundle;
import android.os.Handler;
import android.os.Message;
import android.util.Log;
import android.view.Menu;
import android.view.View;
import android.widget.ArrayAdapter;
import android.widget.EditText;
import android.widget.ListView;
import android.widget.TextView;
import android.widget.Toast;
```

Declaring the Objects

In the `MainActivity.java` file, declare the following objects:

```
public class MainActivity extends ListActivity {

    public final static String UUID = "3606f360-e4df-11e0-9572-0800200c9a66";

    BluetoothAdapter bluetoothAdapter;
    BroadcastReceiver discoverDevicesReceiver;
    BroadcastReceiver discoveryFinishedReceiver;

    //---store all the discovered devices---
    ArrayList<BluetoothDevice> discoveredDevices;
    ArrayList<String> discoveredDevicesNames;

    static TextView txtData;
    EditText txtMessage;

    //---thread for running the server socket---
    ServerThread serverThread;

    //---thread for connecting to the client socket---
    ConnectToServerThread connectToServerThread;
```

Note that because the activity contains a `ListView`, you need to make this activity a subclass of the `ListActivity` base class.

In the `onCreate()` method, initialize the following objects:

```
@Override
public void onCreate(Bundle savedInstanceState) {
    super.onCreate(savedInstanceState);
    setContentView(R.layout.activity_main);

    //---init the ArrayList objects and bluetooth adapter---
    discoveredDevices = new ArrayList<BluetoothDevice>();
    discoveredDevicesNames = new ArrayList<String>();

    bluetoothAdapter = BluetoothAdapter.getDefaultAdapter();

    //---for displaying the messages received---
    txtData = (TextView) findViewById(R.id.txtData);
    txtMessage = (EditText) findViewById(R.id.txtMessage);
}
```

The `discoveredDevices` object will store the list of discovered Bluetooth devices. Each device is represented as a `BluetoothDevice` object. The `discoveredDevicesNames` object stores the user-friendly names of the corresponding devices in the `discoveredDevices` object.

Making Your Device Discoverable

Add the following method to the `MainActivity.java` file:

```
//---make yourself discoverable---
public void MakeDiscoverable(View view)
{
    Intent i = new Intent(
        BluetoothAdapter.ACTION_REQUEST_DISCOVERABLE);
    i.putExtra(
        BluetoothAdapter.EXTRA_DISCOVERABLE_DURATION, 300);
    startActivity(i);
}
```

The preceding code makes your Android device discoverable by Bluetooth for 300 seconds (five minutes).

Figure 6-15 shows the prompt that users see when you want to make your device discoverable.

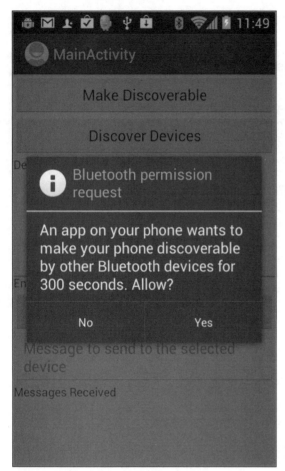

FIGURE 6-15

Discovering Other Devices

To discover other Bluetooth devices, add the following methods to the MainActivity.java file:

```
//---used to discover other bluetooth devices---
private void DiscoveringDevices() {
    if (discoverDevicesReceiver == null) {
        discoverDevicesReceiver = new BroadcastReceiver() {
            //---fired when a new device is discovered---
            @Override
            public void onReceive(Context context, Intent intent) {
                String action = intent.getAction();

                //---a device is discovered---
                if (BluetoothDevice.ACTION_FOUND.equals(action)) {
                    //---get the BluetoothDevice object from
                    // the Intent---
```

```
                    BluetoothDevice device =
                        intent.getParcelableExtra(
                            BluetoothDevice.EXTRA_DEVICE);

                    //---add the name and address to an array
                    // adapter to show in a ListView---
                    //---only add if the device is not already
                    // in the list---
                    if (!discoveredDevices.contains(device)) {
                        //---add the device---
                        discoveredDevices.add(device);

                        //---add the name of the device; used for
                        // ListView---
                        discoveredDevicesNames.add(device.getName());

                        //---display the items in the ListView---
                        setListAdapter(new
                            ArrayAdapter<String>(getBaseContext(),
                            android.R.layout.simple_list_item_1,
                            discoveredDevicesNames));
                    }
                }
            }
        };
    }

    if (discoveryFinishedReceiver==null) {
        discoveryFinishedReceiver = new BroadcastReceiver() {
            //---fired when the discovery is done---
            @Override
            public void onReceive(Context context, Intent intent) {
                //---enable the listview when discovery is over;
                // about 12 seconds---
                getListView().setEnabled(true);
                Toast.makeText(getBaseContext(),
                        "Discovery completed. Select a device to " +
                        "start chatting.",
                        Toast.LENGTH_LONG).show();
                unregisterReceiver(discoveryFinishedReceiver);
            }
        };
    }

    //---register the broadcast receivers---
    IntentFilter filter1 = new
        IntentFilter(BluetoothDevice.ACTION_FOUND);
    IntentFilter filter2 = new
        IntentFilter(BluetoothAdapter.ACTION_DISCOVERY_FINISHED);

    registerReceiver(discoverDevicesReceiver, filter1);
    registerReceiver(discoveryFinishedReceiver, filter2);
```

```
        //---disable the listview when discover is in progress---
        getListView().setEnabled(false);
        Toast.makeText(getBaseContext(),
                "Discovery in progress...please wait...",
                Toast.LENGTH_LONG).show();
        bluetoothAdapter.startDiscovery();
    }

    //---discover other bluetooth devices---
    public void DiscoverDevices(View view)
    {
        //---discover other devices---
        DiscoveringDevices();
    }
```

Basically, you created two inner broadcast receiver classes — one for discovering other Bluetooth devices (discoverDevicesReceiver) and one for when the discovery process is completed (discoveryFinishedReceiver). You then registered them using the BluetoothDevice.ACTION_ FOUND and BluetoothAdapter.ACTION_DISCOVERY_FINISHED intent filters, respectively. When new devices are discovered, you add their device information (represented using a BluetoothDevice object) and their names to the two arrays so that you can use one of them to bind to the ListView. It is important to refrain from communicating with a found Bluetooth device until the discovery process is over; therefore, you need to disable the ListView when the discovery process is ongoing, and enable it again when the discovery is completed.

Creating a Thread for Communication

Add the following block of code to the MainActivity.java file:

```
//---used for updating the UI on the main activity---
static Handler UIupdater = new Handler() {
    @Override
    public void handleMessage(Message msg) {
        int numOfBytesReceived = msg.arg1;
        byte[] buffer = (byte[]) msg.obj;
        //---convert the entire byte array to string---
        String strReceived = new String(buffer);
        //---extract only the actual string received---
        strReceived = strReceived.substring(
            0, numOfBytesReceived);
        //---display the text received on the TextView---
        txtData.setText(txtData.getText().toString() +
            strReceived);
    }
};
```

The Handler object enables you to update the UI in a thread-safe manner.

Populate the CommsThread.java file that you have created earlier with the following:

```
package net.learn2develop.usingbluetooth;

import java.io.IOException;
```

```java
import java.io.InputStream;
import java.io.OutputStream;

import android.bluetooth.BluetoothSocket;
import android.util.Log;

public class CommsThread extends Thread {
    final BluetoothSocket bluetoothSocket;
    final InputStream inputStream;
    final OutputStream outputStream;

    public CommsThread(BluetoothSocket socket) {
        bluetoothSocket = socket;
        InputStream tmpIn = null;
        OutputStream tmpOut = null;
        try {
            //---creates the inputstream and outputstream objects
            // for reading and writing through the sockets---
            tmpIn = socket.getInputStream();
            tmpOut = socket.getOutputStream();
        } catch (IOException e) {
            Log.d("CommsThread", e.getLocalizedMessage());
        }
        inputStream = tmpIn;
        outputStream = tmpOut;
    }

    public void run() {
        //---buffer store for the stream---
        byte[] buffer = new byte[1024];

        //---bytes returned from read()---
        int bytes;

        //---keep listening to the InputStream until an
        // exception occurs---
        while (true) {
            try {
                //---read from the inputStream---
                bytes = inputStream.read(buffer);

                //---update the main activity UI---
                MainActivity.UIupdater.obtainMessage(0,bytes, -1,
                    buffer).sendToTarget();
            } catch (IOException e) {
                Log.d("CommsThread", e.getLocalizedMessage());
                break;
            }
        }
    }

    //---call this from the main Activity to
    // send data to the remote device---
```

```java
    public void write(String str) {
        try {
            outputStream.write(str.getBytes());
        } catch (IOException e) {
            Log.d("CommsThread", e.getLocalizedMessage());
        }
    }

    //---call this from the main Activity to
    // shutdown the connection---
    public void cancel() {
        try {
            bluetoothSocket.close();
        } catch (IOException e) {
            Log.d("CommsThread", e.getLocalizedMessage());
        }
    }
}
```

This class basically obtains the `InputStream` and `OutputStream` objects from a connected Bluetooth device so that it can listen for incoming data as well send data to the device. You perform all these operations in a thread so that it does not tie up the UI of your application. Moreover, Android 3.0 and above does not allow you to perform network operations from the UI thread of your application. The constructor of this class takes a `BluetoothSocket` object, which represents a connection between two Bluetooth devices.

Creating a Thread to Listen for Incoming Connections

Populate the `ServerThread.java` file you created earlier as follows:

```java
package net.learn2develop.usingbluetooth;

import java.io.IOException;
import java.util.UUID;

import android.bluetooth.BluetoothAdapter;
import android.bluetooth.BluetoothServerSocket;
import android.bluetooth.BluetoothSocket;
import android.util.Log;

public class ServerThread extends Thread {
    //---the server socket---
    private final BluetoothServerSocket bluetoothServerSocket;

    public ServerThread(BluetoothAdapter bluetoothAdapter) {
        BluetoothServerSocket tmp = null;
        try {
            //---UUID must be the same for both the client and
            // the server---
            tmp =
                bluetoothAdapter.listenUsingRfcommWithServiceRecord(
                    "BluetoothApp", UUID.fromString(MainActivity.UUID));
```

```
        } catch (IOException e) {
            Log.d("ServerThread", e.getLocalizedMessage());
        }
        bluetoothServerSocket = tmp;
    }

    public void run() {
        BluetoothSocket socket = null;

        //---keep listening until exception occurs
        // or a socket is returned---
        while (true) {
            try {
                socket = bluetoothServerSocket.accept();
            } catch (IOException e) {
                Log.d("ServerThread", e.getLocalizedMessage());
                break;
            }
            //---if a connection was accepted---
            if (socket != null) {
                //---create a separate thread to listen for
                // incoming data---
                CommsThread commsThread = new CommsThread(socket);
                commsThread.run();
            }
        }
    }

    public void cancel() {
        try {
            bluetoothServerSocket.close();
        } catch (IOException e) {
            Log.d("ServerThread", e.getLocalizedMessage());
        }
    }
}
```

This class listens for incoming Bluetooth connections and runs indefinitely.

The constructor for this class takes in a `BluetoothAdapter` object. To connect to the other Bluetooth device, you make use of the `BluetoothSocket` class. An instance of the `BluetoothServerSocket` class is obtained through the `listenUsingRfcommWithServiceRecord()` method of the `BluetoothAdapter` object. This method takes in a name for the connection as well as a UUID (universally unique identifier), which must be the same between two communicating Bluetooth devices. In this example, the UUID is defined in the `MainActivity` class:

```
public final static String UUID = "3606f360-e4df-11e0-9572-0800200c9a66";
```

When a connection is accepted, the `BluetoothServerSocket` object returns a `BluetoothSocket` object, which you use to start the `CommsThread` thread to start a communication channel between the two connected Bluetooth devices.

Creating a Thread to Connect to the Server

Populate the `ConnectToServerThread.java` file you created earlier as follows:

```java
package net.learn2develop.usingbluetooth;

import java.io.IOException;
import java.util.UUID;

import android.bluetooth.BluetoothAdapter;
import android.bluetooth.BluetoothDevice;
import android.bluetooth.BluetoothSocket;
import android.util.Log;

public class ConnectToServerThread extends Thread {
    public CommsThread commsThread;
    public BluetoothSocket bluetoothSocket;
    private BluetoothAdapter bluetoothAdapter;

    public ConnectToServerThread(BluetoothDevice device,
    BluetoothAdapter btAdapter) {
        BluetoothSocket tmp = null;
        bluetoothAdapter = btAdapter;
        //---get a BluetoothSocket to connect with the given
        // BluetoothDevice---
        try {
            //---UUID must be the same for both the client and
            // the server---
            tmp = device.createRfcommSocketToServiceRecord(
                UUID.fromString(MainActivity.UUID));
        } catch (IOException e) {
            Log.d("ConnectToServerThread", e.getLocalizedMessage());
        }
        bluetoothSocket = tmp;
    }

    public void run() {
        //---cancel discovery because it will slow down the
        // connection---
        bluetoothAdapter.cancelDiscovery();
        try {
            //---connect the device through the socket. This will
            // block until it succeeds or throws an exception---
            bluetoothSocket.connect();

            //---create a thread for the communication channel---
            commsThread = new CommsThread(
                bluetoothSocket);
            commsThread.start();
        } catch (IOException connectException) {
            //---unable to connect; close the socket and get out---
            try {
                bluetoothSocket.close();
            } catch (IOException closeException) {
                Log.d("ConnectToServerThread",
```

```
                      closeException.getLocalizedMessage());
            }
            return;
        }
    }

    public void cancel() {
        try {
            bluetoothSocket.close();
            if (commsThread!=null) commsThread.cancel();
        } catch (IOException e) {
            Log.d("ConnectToServerThread", e.getLocalizedMessage());
        }
    }
}
```

The purpose of this class is to connect to another Bluetooth device. The constructor for this class takes in a `BluetoothDevice` object (the device to which you want to connect) and a `BluetoothAdapter` object. To connect to the other Bluetooth device, you make use of the `BluetoothSocket` class. An instance of the `BluetoothSocket` class is obtained through the `createRfcommSocketToServiceRecord()` method of the `BluetoothDevice` object. This method takes in a UUID (universally unique identifier) argument, which must be the same between two communicating Bluetooth devices. In this example, the UUID is defined in the `MainActivity` class:

```
public final static String UUID = "3606f360-e4df-11e0-9572-0800200c9a66";
```

To connect to the server, you use the `connect()` method of the `BluetoothSocket` object. This is a blocking call and will only continue after it has successfully connected to the server. After connection is established, you run the `CommsThread` class to start the communication channel between the two devices.

> **NOTE** *If you are writing a client application that connects to a Bluetooth serial board, you should use the well-known SPP UUID - 00001101-0000-1000-8000-00805F9B34FB.*

Putting All the Pieces Together

Finally, you can now link up all the various classes that you have defined in the previous sections.

Override the `onResume()` method in the `MainActivity.java` file as follows:

```
@Override
public void onResume() {
    super.onResume();
    //---start the socket server---
    serverThread = new ServerThread(bluetoothAdapter);
    serverThread.start();
}
```

When the activity comes to the foreground, start the `ServerThread` class to start the Bluetooth socket server.

Override the `onPause()` method in the `MainActivity.java` file as follows:

```
@Override
public void onPause() {
    super.onPause();
    //---cancel discovery of other bluetooth devices
    bluetoothAdapter.cancelDiscovery();

    //---unregister the broadcast receiver for
    // discovering devices---
    if (discoverDevicesReceiver != null) {
        try {
            unregisterReceiver(discoverDevicesReceiver);
        } catch(Exception e) {

        }
    }

    //---if you are currently connected to someone...---
    if (connectToServerThread!=null) {
        try {
            //---close the connection---
            connectToServerThread.bluetoothSocket.close();
        } catch (IOException e) {
            Log.d("MainActivity", e.getLocalizedMessage());
        }
    }
    //---stop the thread running---
    if (serverThread!=null) serverThread.cancel();
}
```

Here, when the activity goes into the background, you cancel the discovery of Bluetooth devices and close the connection to other Bluetooth devices if there is one. Finally, you stop the `ServerThread` class.

Override the `onListItemClick ()` method in the `MainActivity.java` file as follows:

```
//---when a client is tapped in the ListView---
public void onListItemClick(ListView parent, View v,
int position, long id) {
    //---if you are already talking to someone...---
    if (connectToServerThread!=null) {
        try {
            //---close the connection first---
            connectToServerThread.bluetoothSocket.close();
        } catch (IOException e) {
            Log.d("MainActivity", e.getLocalizedMessage());
        }
    }

    //---connect to the selected Bluetooth device---
    BluetoothDevice deviceSelected =
```

```
        discoveredDevices.get(position);
    connectToServerThread = new
        ConnectToServerThread(deviceSelected, bluetoothAdapter);
    connectToServerThread.start();

    //---tell the user that he is connected to who---
    Toast.makeText(this, "You have connected to " +
            discoveredDevices.get(position).getName(),
            Toast.LENGTH_SHORT).show();
}
```

This method is fired whenever the user selects an item in the ListView. Because the ListView
contains the names of all discovered Bluetooth devices, tapping on an item in the ListView essentially connects to it using the ConnectToServerThread class.

To send some data to the server, you need to use the CommsThread instance in the
ConnectToServerThread instance and call its write() method. This call is asynchronous,
so you need to wrap this in a subclass of the AsyncTask class (put the following class in the
MainActivity.java file):

```
private class WriteTask extends AsyncTask<String, Void, Void> {
    protected Void doInBackground(String... args) {
        try {
            connectToServerThread.commsThread.write(args[0]);
        } catch (Exception e) {
            Log.d("MainActivity", e.getLocalizedMessage());
        }
        return null;
    }
}
```

To send a message, create an instance of the WriteTask class and call its execute() method:

```
//---send a message to the connected socket client---
public void SendMessage(View view)
{
    if (connectToServerThread!=null) {
        new WriteTask().execute(txtMessage.getText().toString());
    } else {
        Toast.makeText(this, "Select a client first",
            Toast.LENGTH_SHORT).show();
    }
}
```

Testing the Application

To test the application:

1. On each device, tap the Make Discoverable button to make the device discoverable by
   Bluetooth.

2. On each device, tap the Discover Devices button to discover the other device.

3. You should now see the discovered device in the ListView (see Figure 6-16).

4. Select the device that you want to talk to and type in a message in the `EditText` view.

5. Tap the Send Message button to send the message to the other device.

The other device should now see the message displayed at the bottom of the screen.

FIGURE 6-16

> **NOTE** *This example assumes that you have already enabled Bluetooth on both devices. For an example demonstrating how to turn on Bluetooth programmatically, check out Recipe 6.9.*

7

Using Google Maps

Google Maps is one of the many applications bundled with the Android platform. In addition to simply using the Maps application directly, you can also embed it into your own applications and make it do some very cool things. The Android SDK provides the `MapView` view, which displays a map (with data obtained from the Google Maps service).

This chapter contains various recipes on how to use Google Maps in your Android applications and programmatically perform the following:

➤ Display the Google Maps using the `MapView`

➤ Change the views of Google Maps

➤ Obtain the latitude and longitude of locations in Google Maps

➤ Perform geocoding and reverse geocoding (translating an address to latitude and longitude and vice versa)

➤ Add markers to Google Maps

RECIPE 7.1 DISPLAYING GOOGLE MAPS

Android Versions
Level 1 and above

Permissions
android.permission.INTERNET

Source Code to Download from Wrox.com
Maps-Basic.zip

You want to display Google Maps in your Android Application using the `MapView` view.

Solution

Beginning with the Android SDK release v1.0, you need to apply for a free Google Maps API key before you can integrate Google Maps into your Android application. When you apply for the key, you must also agree to Google's terms of use, so be sure to read them carefully. Once the key is obtained, you will need it to add it to your application so that the Google Maps will display correctly. The following sections walk you through this.

Applying for the Google Maps API Key

To apply for a key, follow the series of steps outlined next.

> **NOTE** *Google provides detailed documentation on applying for a Maps API key at* `http://code.google.com/android/add-ons/google-apis/mapkey.html`.

First, if you are testing the application on the Android emulator or an Android device directly connected to your development machine, locate the SDK debug certificate located in the default folder (`/Users/<username>/.android` for OS X users and `C:\Users\<username>\.android` for Windows 7 users). You can verify the existence of the debug certificate by going to Eclipse and selecting Eclipse ⇨ Preferences (for OS X) or Window ⇨ Preferences (for Windows). Expand the Android item and select Build (see Figure 7-1). On the right side of the window, you can see the debug certificate's location.

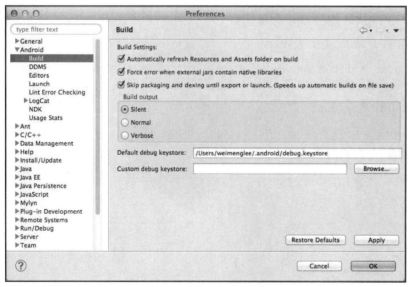

FIGURE 7-1

> **NOTE** *For Windows XP users, the default Android folder is* `C:\Documents and Settings\<username>\Local Settings\Application Data\Android`.

The filename of the debug keystore is `debug.keystore`. This is the certificate that Eclipse uses to sign your application so that it may be run on the Android emulator or devices. Using the debug keystore, you need to extract its MD5 fingerprint using the `Keytool` application included with your JDK installation. This fingerprint is needed to apply for the free Google Maps key. You can usually find the `keytool` application in the `C:\Program Files\Java\<JDK_version_number>\bin` folder (for Windows users).

Issue the following command (see also Figure 7-2; for Windows users, you can open the Command window and change the directory to where the `keytool` application is located and then type in the command as shown in the figure) to extract the MD5 fingerprint:

```
keytool -list -alias androiddebugkey -keystore
"C:\Users\<username>\.android\debug.keystore" -storepass android
-keypass android -v
```

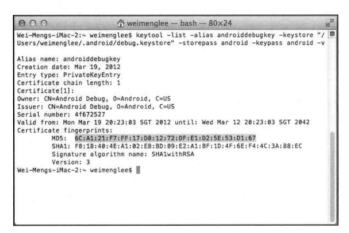

FIGURE 7-2

In this example, my MD5 fingerprint is `6C:A1:21:F7:FF:17:D8:12:72:DF:E1:D2:5E:53:D1:67`.

In the preceding command, the following arguments were used:

➤ `-list` — Shows details about the specified keystore

➤ `-alias` — Alias for the keystore, which is "`androiddebugkey`" for `debug.keystore`

➤ `-keystore` — Specifies the location of the keystore

➤ `-storepass` — Specifies the password for the keystore, which is "`android`" for `debug.keystore`

➤ `-keypass` — Specifies the password for the key in the keystore, which is "`android`" for `debug.keystore`

➤ `-v` — Specifies verbose mode, which displays all the different certificate fingerprints; in this case, MD5 and SHA1

> **NOTE** *Although you can use the MD5 fingerprint of the debug keystore to obtain the Maps API key for debugging your application on the Android emulator or devices, the key will not be valid if you try to export your Android application as an APK file. When you are ready to deploy your application to the Android Market (or other methods of distribution), you need to reapply for a Maps API key using the certificate that will be used to sign your application.*

Copy the MD5 certificate fingerprint and navigate your web browser to: `http://code.google.com/android/maps-api-signup.html`. Follow the instructions on the page to complete the application and obtain the Google Maps key. When you are done, you should see something similar to what is shown in Figure 7-3.

FIGURE 7-3

With the first step of the solution complete, it's time to move to the second step: Displaying the map.

Displaying the Map

With the Google Maps API key obtained, you are now ready to display Google Maps in your Android application. In order to display Google Maps in your application using the `MapView`, you need to add the `INTERNET` permission in your `AndroidManifest.xml` file. In addition, you need to reference the Maps library:

```
<manifest xmlns:android="http://schemas.android.com/apk/res/android"
    package="net.learn2develop.maps"
    android:versionCode="1"
```

```
        android:versionName="1.0" >

    <uses-sdk
        android:minSdkVersion="8"
        android:targetSdkVersion="15" />

    <uses-permission android:name="android.permission.INTERNET"/>

    <application
        android:icon="@drawable/ic_launcher"
        android:label="@string/app_name"
        android:theme="@style/AppTheme" >

        <uses-library android:name="com.google.android.maps" />

        <activity
            android:name=".MainActivity"
            android:label="@string/title_activity_main" >
            <intent-filter>
                <action android:name="android.intent.action.MAIN" />

                <category android:name="android.intent.category.LAUNCHER" />
            </intent-filter>
        </activity>
    </application>

</manifest>
```

> **NOTE** *In order to use the* `MapView` *view, your Android project must use the Google APIs as the target. You can verify this by checking Project Explorer in Eclipse and looking for the Google APIs folder (see Figure 7-4). When you expand the Google APIs folder, you should see the* `maps.jar` *file, which contains the* `MapView` *libraries.*

FIGURE 7-4

In the XML file (for example, `main.xml`) of your activity, you need to add the `<com.google.android.maps.MapView>` element:

```
<RelativeLayout xmlns:android="http://schemas.android.com/apk/res/android"
    xmlns:tools="http://schemas.android.com/tools"
    android:layout_width="match_parent"
    android:layout_height="match_parent" >

    <com.google.android.maps.MapView
        android:id="@+id/mapView"
        android:layout_width="fill_parent"
        android:layout_height="fill_parent"
        android:apiKey="014sCTTyRmXQPd37eZiwVQHX9rQD08yVGM2iqTQ"
        android:clickable="true"
        android:state_enabled="true" />

</RelativeLayout>
```

Replace the value of the `android:apiKey` attribute with that of the Maps API key you obtained earlier.

Finally, the activity that displays the Google Maps must extend the `MapActivity` base class:

```
import android.os.Bundle;

import com.google.android.maps.MapActivity;

public class MainActivity extends MapActivity {
    @Override
    public void onCreate(Bundle savedInstanceState) {
        super.onCreate(savedInstanceState);
        setContentView(R.layout.activity_main);
    }

    @Override
    protected boolean isRouteDisplayed() {
        return false;
    }

}
```

When extending the `MapActivity` base class, you need to also implement the `isRouteDisplayed()` method, which is used for Google's accounting purposes, and you should return `true` for this method if you are displaying routing information on the map. For most simple cases, you can simply return `false`.

When the application is run, you should see Google Maps as shown in Figure 7-5.

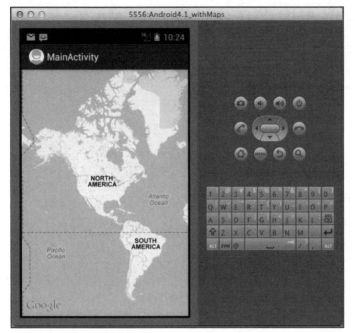

FIGURE 7-5

NOT SEEING THE MAP?

If instead of seeing Google Maps displayed you see an empty screen with grids, then most likely you are using the wrong API key in the main.xml file. It is also possible that you omitted the INTERNET permission in your AndroidManifest .xml file. Finally, ensure that you have Internet connectivity on your emulator/ devices.

If your program does not run (i.e., it crashes), then you probably forgot to add the following statement to the AndroidManifest.xml file:

```
<uses-library android:name="com.google.android.maps" />
```

Note its placement in the AndroidManifest.xml file; it should be within the <application> element but outside the <activity> element.

RECIPE 7.2 ZOOMING IN AND OUT OF GOOGLE MAPS

Android Versions

Level 1 and above

Permissions

android.permission.INTERNET

Source Code to Download from Wrox.com

Maps-Zoom.zip

You want to zoom in and out of Google Maps.

Solution

To zoom in and out of Google Maps, you have three options:

➤ Pinch the map directly on the device. This option is only available on real devices, as the Android emulator does not support multi-touch.

➤ Display the zoom controls on the map so that the user can tap (or click on the emulator) on the zoom controls to zoom in or out of the map.

➤ Programmatically zoom in or out of the map.

To display the zoom control, you first get an instance of the MapView on your activity's UI, like this:

```
package net.learn2develop.maps;

import android.os.Bundle;

import com.google.android.maps.MapActivity;
import com.google.android.maps.MapView;

public class MainActivity extends MapActivity {
    MapView mapView;
    @Override
    public void onCreate(Bundle savedInstanceState) {
        super.onCreate(savedInstanceState);
        setContentView(R.layout.activity_main);

        mapView = (MapView) findViewById(R.id.mapView);
        mapView.setBuiltInZoomControls(true);
    }
```

```
@Override
protected boolean isRouteDisplayed() {
    return false;
}

}
```

You then call its `setBuiltInZoomControls()` method to display the zoom controls for the map. Figure 7-6 shows what the zoom controls look like.

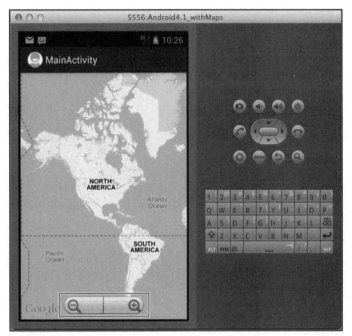

FIGURE 7-6

> **NOTE** *The zoom controls automatically hide themselves after a few seconds of inactivity on the map. To make them appear again, simply tap (or click on an emulator) on the map.*

To programmatically zoom in or out of the map, you can get an instance of the `MapView`'s `MapController` class, and then call its `zoomIn()` or `zoomOut()` methods, like this:

```
package net.learn2develop.maps;

import android.os.Bundle;
import android.view.KeyEvent;
```

```
import com.google.android.maps.MapActivity;
import com.google.android.maps.MapController;
import com.google.android.maps.MapView;

public class MainActivity extends MapActivity {
    MapView mapView;
    @Override
    public void onCreate(Bundle savedInstanceState) {
        super.onCreate(savedInstanceState);
        setContentView(R.layout.activity_main);

        mapView = (MapView) findViewById(R.id.mapView);
        mapView.setBuiltInZoomControls(true);
    }

    @Override
    protected boolean isRouteDisplayed() {
        return false;
    }

    public boolean onKeyDown(int keyCode, KeyEvent event)
    {
        MapController mc = mapView.getController();
        switch (keyCode)
        {
            case KeyEvent.KEYCODE_3:
                mc.zoomIn();
                break;
            case KeyEvent.KEYCODE_1:
                mc.zoomOut();
                break;
        }
        return super.onKeyDown(keyCode, event);
    }

}
```

In the preceding code snippet, pressing the 3 key on the hardware keyboard of the Android device (or emulator) will cause the map to zoom to the next level. Pressing 1 will cause the map to zoom out to the previous level.

You can also zoom the map to a specific level using the setZoom() method and passing it an integer value:

```
mc.setZoom(13);
```

The larger the value, the more zoomed in the map becomes.

RECIPE 7.3 CHANGING MAP MODES

> **Android Versions**
>   Level 1 and above
>
> **Permissions**
>   android.permission.INTERNET
>
> **Source Code to Download from Wrox.com**
>   Maps-Views.zip

You want to change the different view modes offered by the `MapView`. This recipe will show you how to display the `MapView` in satellite mode as well as show the traffic conditions.

Solution

By default, the `MapView` displays the Google Map in Map mode, which is simply a graphical rendering of the map (see Figure 7-7).

FIGURE 7-7

The MapView supports the satellite view, which is a combination of map view and satellite view (see Figure 7-8). To do so, use the setSatellite() method of the MapView class:

```
package net.learn2develop.maps;

import android.os.Bundle;

import com.google.android.maps.MapActivity;
import com.google.android.maps.MapView;

public class MainActivity extends MapActivity {
    MapView mapView;

    @Override
    public void onCreate(Bundle savedInstanceState) {
        super.onCreate(savedInstanceState);
        setContentView(R.layout.activity_main);

        mapView = (MapView) findViewById(R.id.mapView);
        mapView.setBuiltInZoomControls(true);

        mapView.setSatellite(true);
    }

    @Override
    protected boolean isRouteDisplayed() {
        return false;
    }

}
```

FIGURE 7-8

If you want to display traffic conditions on the map, use the `setTraffic()` method:

```
@Override
public void onCreate(Bundle savedInstanceState) {
    super.onCreate(savedInstanceState);
    setContentView(R.layout.activity_main);

    mapView = (MapView) findViewById(R.id.mapView);
    mapView.setBuiltInZoomControls(true);

    mapView.setSatellite(true);
    mapView.setTraffic(true);
}
```

Figure 7-9 shows the map displaying the current traffic conditions (you have to zoom in so that you can see the roads). The different colors (which you'll see on your phone, but not on the black and white figure, unfortunately) reflect the varying traffic conditions. In general, green equates to smooth traffic of about 50 miles per hour, yellow equates to moderate traffic of about 25–50 miles per hour, and red equates to slow traffic of about less than 25 miles per hour.

FIGURE 7-9

RECIPE 7.4 NAVIGATING THE MAP TO A PARTICULAR LOCATION

You want the Google Map to display a particular location.

Android Versions

    Level 1 and above

Permissions

    android.permission.INTERNET

Source Code to Download from Wrox.com

    Maps-Navigate.zip

Solution

One of the common uses of Google Maps is to display the current location of the user using the location information obtained through the `LocationManager` class.

To do so, you need to first obtain the controller for the `MapView`, and then use the `animateTo()` method to cause the map to display the particular location:

```
package net.learn2develop.maps;

import android.os.Bundle;

import com.google.android.maps.GeoPoint;
import com.google.android.maps.MapActivity;
import com.google.android.maps.MapController;
import com.google.android.maps.MapView;

public class MainActivity extends MapActivity {
    MapView mapView;
    MapController mc;

    @Override
    public void onCreate(Bundle savedInstanceState) {
        super.onCreate(savedInstanceState);
        setContentView(R.layout.activity_main);

        mapView = (MapView) findViewById(R.id.mapView);
        mapView.setBuiltInZoomControls(true);
```

```
        mc = mapView.getController();

        GeoPoint p = new GeoPoint(37423021,-122083739);

        mc.animateTo(p);
        mc.setZoom(13);
        mapView.invalidate();
    }

    @Override
    protected boolean isRouteDisplayed() {
        return false;
    }

}
```

Note that you need to call the `invalidate()` method to cause the map to redraw. Figure 7-10 shows the map displaying the specified location passed in through the `GeoPoint` object. Remember that the `GeoPoint`'s constructor takes the latitude and longitude in micro-degrees. Hence, remember to multiply the latitude and longitude by one million.

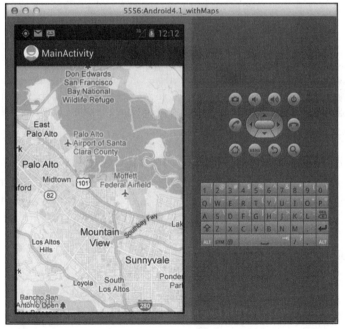

FIGURE 7-10

RECIPE 7.5 ADDING MARKERS TO THE MAP

Android Versions

Level 1 and above

Permissions

android.permission.INTERNET

android.permission.ACCESS_COARSE_LOCATION

android.permission.ACCESS_FINE_LOCATION

Source Code to Download from Wrox.com

Map-Overlays.zip

You want to add markers to the map indicating the current location, or locations of interest.

Solution

In the previous recipe, you learned how to make the Google Maps navigate to a particular location. Doing so pans the map, with the location you are navigating to be displayed at the center. A much more useful visual cue to the user would be a marker (commonly known as the *pushpin*) on the map so that the location is immediately clear to the user. The following sections show you the various ways to add this.

Solution Part 1: Displaying a Marker at the Current Location

One common request from developers is the capability to display the current location of the user without resorting to using the `LocationManager` class as described in Chapter 8, "Location-Based Services," Recipe 8.1.

To do so, you can use the `MyLocationOverlay` class. All you need is to do is create an instance of this class and then add it to the overlay lists of the `MapView`.

> **NOTE** *An overlay in `MapView` is a layer that can be added on top of the map. An overlay can contain bitmaps, drawings, etc.*

The following code snippet shows how to display the current location on the map using the `MyLocationOverlay` class:

```
package net.learn2develop.maps;

import android.os.Bundle;

import com.google.android.maps.MapActivity;
```

```
import com.google.android.maps.MapView;
import com.google.android.maps.MyLocationOverlay;

public class MainActivity extends MapActivity {
    MapView mapView;
    MapController mc;

    @Override
    public void onCreate(Bundle savedInstanceState) {
        super.onCreate(savedInstanceState);
        setContentView(R.layout.activity_main);

        mapView = (MapView) findViewById(R.id.mapView);
        mapView.setBuiltInZoomControls(true);

        mc = mapView.getController();

        //---get your current location and display a blue dot---
        MyLocationOverlay myLocationOverlay =
            new MyLocationOverlay(this, mapView);

        mapView.getOverlays().add(myLocationOverlay);
        myLocationOverlay.enableMyLocation();
    }

    @Override
    protected boolean isRouteDisplayed() {
        return false;
    }

}
```

As shown in Figure 7-11, the current location is represented on the map as a pulsating blue dot.

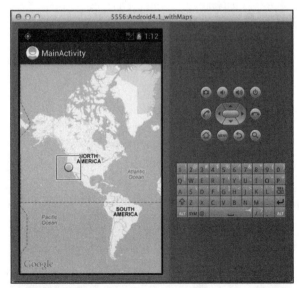

FIGURE 7-11

> **NOTE** *In order for the* `MyLocationOverlay` *class to locate your current location, you must add either the* `android.permission.ACCESS_COARSE_LOCATION` *or the* `android.permission.ACCESS_FINE_LOCATION` *permission.*

Solution Part 2: Displaying a Marker at Specific Locations

Besides displaying markers at the current location, you often want to display markers at specific locations (for instance, a particular destination). To do so, use the `ItemizedOverlay` class. The `ItemizedOverlay` class is an abstract class that consists of a list of `OverlayItem` (markers) objects. To use the `ItemizedOverlay` class, create a class that extends it, like this:

```
package net.learn2develop.maps;

import java.util.ArrayList;

import android.app.AlertDialog;
import android.content.Context;
import android.graphics.drawable.Drawable;

import com.google.android.maps.ItemizedOverlay;
import com.google.android.maps.OverlayItem;

public class MyItemizedOverlay extends ItemizedOverlay<OverlayItem> {
    //---array of OverlayItem objects---
    private ArrayList<OverlayItem> mOverlays = new ArrayList<OverlayItem>();
    Context mContext;

    public MyItemizedOverlay(Drawable defaultMarker) {
        super(boundCenterBottom(defaultMarker));
    }

    public MyItemizedOverlay(Drawable defaultMarker, Context context) {
        super(boundCenterBottom(defaultMarker));
        mContext = context;
    }

    //---add an OverlayItem object to the map---
    public void addOverlay(OverlayItem overlay) {
        mOverlays.add(overlay);
        //---call this to draw the OverLayItem objects---
        populate();
    }

    //---remove an OverlayItem object from the map---
    public void removeOverlay(OverlayItem overlay) {
        mOverlays.remove(overlay);
        //---call this to draw the OverLayItem objects---
        populate();
    }
```

```
//---called when populate() is called; returns each OverlayItem object
// in the array---
@Override
protected OverlayItem createItem(int i) {
    return mOverlays.get(i);
}

//---returns the number of OverlayItem objects---
@Override
public int size() {
    return mOverlays.size();
}

//---called when the user taps on the OverlayItem objects---
@Override
protected boolean onTap(int index) {
    OverlayItem item = mOverlays.get(index);
    AlertDialog.Builder dialog = new AlertDialog.Builder(mContext);
    dialog.setTitle(item.getTitle());
    dialog.setMessage(item.getSnippet());
    dialog.show();
    return true;
}
}
```

In the preceding code snippet, you implemented the abstract ItemizedOverlay class and overrode the following methods:

- ➤ The two constructors for the class
- ➤ The addOverlay() method, to allow an OverlayItem object to be added to the class
- ➤ The removeOverlay() method, to allow an OverlayItem object to be removed from the class
- ➤ The createItem() method, which returns each OverlayItem object contained in the class
- ➤ The size() method, which returns the total number of OverlayItem objects in the class
- ➤ The onTap() method, which displays an alert dialog whenever the user taps on an OverlayItem object

To use the MyItemizedOverlay class that you have just defined, create an instance of it and then add some OverlayItem objects to it. The constructor for the OverlayItem class takes a GeoPoint object indicating the location of the marker, as well as two strings indicating the title and description of the marker. Once the MyItemizedOverlay object is populated with OverlayItem objects, you can then add it to the overlay lists of the MapView. The following code snippet makes this clear:

```
package net.learn2develop.maps;

import java.util.List;

import android.graphics.drawable.Drawable;
import android.os.Bundle;
```

```
import com.google.android.maps.GeoPoint;
import com.google.android.maps.MapActivity;
import com.google.android.maps.MapController;
import com.google.android.maps.MapView;
import com.google.android.maps.MyLocationOverlay;
import com.google.android.maps.Overlay;
import com.google.android.maps.OverlayItem;

public class MainActivity extends MapActivity {
    MapView mapView;
    MapController mc;

    GeoPoint p1 = new GeoPoint(37423021,-122083739);
    GeoPoint p2 = new GeoPoint(37523021,-122183739);

    @Override
    public void onCreate(Bundle savedInstanceState) {
        super.onCreate(savedInstanceState);
        setContentView(R.layout.activity_main);

        mapView = (MapView) findViewById(R.id.mapView);
        mapView.setBuiltInZoomControls(true);

        mc = mapView.getController();

        //---get your current location and display a blue dot---
        MyLocationOverlay myLocationOverlay =
            new MyLocationOverlay(this, mapView);

        mapView.getOverlays().add(myLocationOverlay);
        myLocationOverlay.enableMyLocation();


        List<Overlay> listOfOverlays = mapView.getOverlays();
        Drawable drawable =
            this.getResources().getDrawable(R.drawable.ic_launcher);

        MyItemizedOverlay itemizedoverlay =
            new MyItemizedOverlay(drawable, this);
        OverlayItem overlayitem1 = new OverlayItem(
            p1, "Hello Google!", "I'm an Android!");

        //---add an overlayitem---
        itemizedoverlay.addOverlay(overlayitem1);

        OverlayItem overlayitem2= new OverlayItem(
            p2, "Hello Google!", "I'm swimming!");

        //---add an overlayitem---
        itemizedoverlay.addOverlay(overlayitem2);
```

```
        //---add the overlay---
        listOfOverlays.add(itemizedoverlay);

        mc.animateTo(p1);
        mc.setZoom(12);

    }

    @Override
    protected boolean isRouteDisplayed() {
        return false;
    }

}
```

Figure 7-12 shows the two markers added to the MapView.

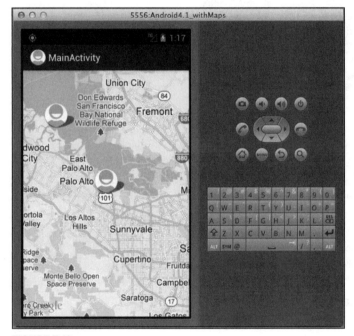

FIGURE 7-12

When you tap on a marker, the alert dialog will be displayed, showing the marker's title and description (see Figure 7-13).

FIGURE 7-13

To remove an `OverlayItem` object (such as when you no longer want to display a marker on the map) from the `MyItemizedOverlay` object, use the `removeOverlay()` method:

```
//---remove an overlayitem---
itemizedoverlay.removeOverlay(overlayitem1);
```

To remove the entire overlay from the map, use the `remove()` method of the `List` class:

```
//---remove an overlay---
listOfOverlays.remove(itemizedoverlay);
```

Solution Part 3: Drawing a Line Connecting Two Points

Often, you want to display two points on the map and then draw a line connecting them. This is useful when you have a series of points and you want to map out the path showing the series of locations that you have travelled.

To draw a line on the Google Maps, you use the `draw()` method inside an `Overlay` class. In the following code snippet, you implement the `draw()` method and then place the application icon on two locations on the map. You then set up a `Paint` object to draw a line connecting the two locations:

```
package net.learn2develop.maps;

import java.util.List;
```

```
import android.graphics.Bitmap;
import android.graphics.BitmapFactory;
import android.graphics.Canvas;
import android.graphics.Paint;
import android.graphics.Paint.Style;
import android.graphics.Point;
import android.os.Bundle;

import com.google.android.maps.GeoPoint;
import com.google.android.maps.MapActivity;
import com.google.android.maps.MapController;
import com.google.android.maps.MapView;
import com.google.android.maps.MyLocationOverlay;
import com.google.android.maps.Overlay;

public class MainActivity extends MapActivity {
    MapView mapView;
    MapController mc;

    GeoPoint p1 = new GeoPoint(37423021,-122083739);
    GeoPoint p2 = new GeoPoint(37523021,-122183739);

    private class MapOverlay extends com.google.android.maps.Overlay
    {

        @Override
        public boolean draw(Canvas canvas, MapView mapView,
        boolean shadow, long when)
        {
            super.draw(canvas, mapView, shadow);

            Bitmap bmp = BitmapFactory.decodeResource(
                    getResources(), R.drawable.ic_launcher);

            //---translate the GeoPoint to screen pixels---
            Point screenPts1 = new Point();
            mapView.getProjection().toPixels(p1, screenPts1);

            //---translate the GeoPoint to screen pixels---
            Point screenPts2 = new Point();
            mapView.getProjection().toPixels(p2, screenPts2);

            //---add the first marker---
            canvas.drawBitmap(bmp, screenPts1.x - bmp.getWidth()/2,
                                screenPts1.y - bmp.getHeight()/2, null);

            //---add the second marker---
            canvas.drawBitmap(bmp, screenPts2.x - bmp.getWidth()/2,
                                screenPts2.y - bmp.getHeight()/2, null);

            Paint paint = new Paint();
            paint.setStyle(Style.STROKE);
```

```
            paint.setColor(0xFF000000);
            paint.setAntiAlias(true);
            paint.setStrokeWidth(5);

            //---draws a line connecting the 2 points---
            canvas.drawLine(screenPts1.x, screenPts1.y,
                            screenPts2.x, screenPts2.y, paint);

            return true;
        }
    }

@Override
public void onCreate(Bundle savedInstanceState) {
    super.onCreate(savedInstanceState);
    setContentView(R.layout.activity_main);

    mapView = (MapView) findViewById(R.id.mapView);
    mapView.setBuiltInZoomControls(true);

    mc = mapView.getController();

    //---get your current location and display a blue dot---
    MyLocationOverlay myLocationOverlay =
        new MyLocationOverlay(this, mapView);

    mapView.getOverlays().add(myLocationOverlay);
    myLocationOverlay.enableMyLocation();

    /*
    //=============================
    List<Overlay> listOfOverlays = mapView.getOverlays();
    Drawable drawable =
        this.getResources().getDrawable(R.drawable.ic_launcher);

    MyItemizedOverlay itemizedoverlay =
        new MyItemizedOverlay(drawable, this);
    OverlayItem overlayitem1 = new OverlayItem(
        p1, "Hello Google!", "I'm an Android!");

    //---add an overlayitem---
    itemizedoverlay.addOverlay(overlayitem1);

    OverlayItem overlayitem2= new OverlayItem(
        p2, "Hello Google!", "I'm swimming!");

    //---add an overlayitem---
    itemizedoverlay.addOverlay(overlayitem2);

    //---add the overlay---
    listOfOverlays.add(itemizedoverlay);
```

```
        mc.animateTo(p1);
        mc.setZoom(12);
        */

        MapOverlay mapOverlay = new MapOverlay();
        List<Overlay> listOfOverlays = mapView.getOverlays();
        listOfOverlays.add(mapOverlay);

        mc.animateTo(p1);
        mc.setZoom(12);
    }

    @Override
    protected boolean isRouteDisplayed() {
        return false;
    }

}
```

The `toPixels()` method converts a `GeoPoint` object into screen coordinates so that you can draw the application icon on the map.

Figure 7-14 shows the black line connecting the two locations.

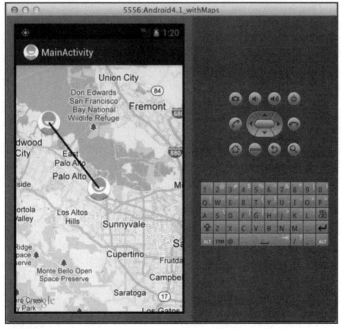

FIGURE 7-14

RECIPE 7.6 FINDING A USER-FRIENDLY ADDRESS USING REVERSE GEOCODING, AND VICE VERSA

Android Versions

Level 1 and above

Permissions

android.permission.INTERNET

android.permission.ACCESS_COARSE_LOCATION

android.permission.ACCESS_FINE_LOCATION

Source Code to Download from Wrox.com

Maps-Geocoding.zip

You want to determine the address of a location on the map simply by touching it. In addition, you want to be able to find the latitude and longitude of a given location.

Solution

While the users can pan the Google Maps to view the various locations graphically, it is useful to be able to touch the map and get the user-friendly address of the location being touched. To do so, you need to perform the following steps:

1. Get the latitude and longitude of the location being touched.

2. Perform a reverse geocoding operation to convert the latitude and longitude of a location into a user-friendly address.

The following sections show how to perform these operations using overlays in Google Maps.

Getting the Location That was Touched

To obtain the location that is being touched, you need to override the onTouchEvent() method within the Overlay class. This method is fired every time the user touches the map. This method has two parameters: MotionEvent and MapView. Using the MotionEvent parameter, you can determine whether the user has lifted his or her finger from the screen using the getAction() method.

In the following code snippet, you implement a class that extends the Overlay base class and then add an instance of it to the MapView object. When the user touches the screen and then lifts the finger, you display the latitude and longitude of the location touched:

```
package net.learn2develop.maps;

import java.util.List;
```

```java
import android.os.Bundle;
import android.view.MotionEvent;
import android.widget.Toast;

import com.google.android.maps.GeoPoint;
import com.google.android.maps.MapActivity;
import com.google.android.maps.MapController;
import com.google.android.maps.MapView;
import com.google.android.maps.Overlay;

public class MainActivity extends MapActivity {
    MapView mapView;
    MapController mc;

    private class MapOverlay extends Overlay
    {
        @Override
        public boolean onTouchEvent(MotionEvent event, MapView mapView)
        {
            //---when user lifts his finger---
            if (event.getAction() == 1) {
                GeoPoint p = mapView.getProjection().fromPixels(
                    (int) event.getX(),
                    (int) event.getY());
                    Toast.makeText(getBaseContext(),
                        "Location: "+
                        p.getLatitudeE6() / 1E6 + "," +
                        p.getLongitudeE6() /1E6 ,
                        Toast.LENGTH_SHORT).show();
            }
            return false;
        }
    }

    @Override
    public void onCreate(Bundle savedInstanceState) {
        super.onCreate(savedInstanceState);
        setContentView(R.layout.activity_main);

        mapView = (MapView) findViewById(R.id.mapView);
        mapView.setBuiltInZoomControls(true);

        mc = mapView.getController();

        MapOverlay mapOverlay = new MapOverlay();
        List<Overlay> listOfOverlays = mapView.getOverlays();
        listOfOverlays.add(mapOverlay);
    }

    @Override
    protected boolean isRouteDisplayed() {
        return false;
    }

}
```

The `getProjection()` method returns a projection for converting between screen-pixel coordinates and latitude/longitude coordinates. The `fromPixels()` method then converts the screen coordinates into a `GeoPoint` object.

Figure 7-15 shows the `Toast` class displaying the latitude and longitude of a location that was clicked on the Android emulator.

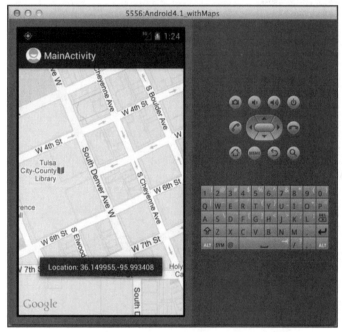

FIGURE 7-15

Reverse Geocoding

If you know the latitude and longitude of a location, you can find out its user-friendly address using a process known as *reverse geocoding*. Google Maps in Android supports this via the `Geocoder` class. The following code snippet shows how you can retrieve the address of a location just touched using the `getFromLocation()` method:

```
package net.learn2develop.maps;

import java.io.IOException;
import java.util.List;
import java.util.Locale;

import android.location.Address;
import android.location.Geocoder;
import android.os.AsyncTask;
import android.os.Bundle;
import android.view.MotionEvent;
import android.widget.Toast;
```

```
import com.google.android.maps.GeoPoint;
import com.google.android.maps.MapActivity;
import com.google.android.maps.MapController;
import com.google.android.maps.MapView;
import com.google.android.maps.Overlay;

public class MainActivity extends MapActivity {
    MapView mapView;
    MapController mc;

    /*
    private class MapOverlay extends Overlay
    {
        @Override
        public boolean onTouchEvent(MotionEvent event, MapView mapView)
        {
            //---when user lifts his finger---
            if (event.getAction() == 1) {
                GeoPoint p = mapView.getProjection().fromPixels(
                    (int) event.getX(),
                    (int) event.getY());
                    Toast.makeText(getBaseContext(),
                        "Location: "+
                        p.getLatitudeE6() / 1E6 + "," +
                        p.getLongitudeE6() /1E6 ,
                        Toast.LENGTH_SHORT).show();
            }
            return false;
        }
    }
    */

    private class MapOverlay extends Overlay
    {
        private class DoBackgroundTask extends AsyncTask
        <GeoPoint, Void, List<Address>> {

            protected List<Address> doInBackground(GeoPoint... locations) {
                Geocoder geoCoder = new Geocoder(
                        getBaseContext(), Locale.getDefault());
                try {
                    List<Address> addresses = geoCoder.getFromLocation(
                            locations[0].getLatitudeE6()  / 1E6,
                            locations[0].getLongitudeE6() / 1E6, 1);
                    return addresses;
                }
                catch (IOException e) {
                    e.printStackTrace();
                }
                return null;
            }

            protected void onPostExecute(List<Address> addresses) {
                String add = "";
                if (addresses.size() > 0)
```

```
                        {
                            for (int i=0;
                                     i<addresses.get(0).getMaxAddressLineIndex();
                                     i++)
                                add += addresses.get(0).getAddressLine(i) + "\n";
                        }
                        Toast.makeText(getBaseContext(), add,
                            Toast.LENGTH_SHORT).show();
                    }
                }


                @Override
                public boolean onTouchEvent(MotionEvent event, MapView mapView)
                {
                    //---when user lifts his finger---
                    if (event.getAction() == 1) {
                        GeoPoint p = mapView.getProjection().fromPixels(
                                (int) event.getX(),
                                (int) event.getY());
                        Toast.makeText(getBaseContext(),
                                "Location: "+
                                        p.getLatitudeE6() / 1E6 + "," +
                                        p.getLongitudeE6() /1E6 ,
                                        Toast.LENGTH_SHORT).show();

                        //---reverse geocoding---
                        new DoBackgroundTask().execute(p);
                        return true;
                    }
                    return false;
                }
            }

        @Override
        public void onCreate(Bundle savedInstanceState) {
            super.onCreate(savedInstanceState);
            setContentView(R.layout.activity_main);

            mapView = (MapView) findViewById(R.id.mapView);
            mapView.setBuiltInZoomControls(true);

            mc = mapView.getController();

            MapOverlay mapOverlay = new MapOverlay();
            List<Overlay> listOfOverlays = mapView.getOverlays();
            listOfOverlays.add(mapOverlay);
        }

        @Override
        protected boolean isRouteDisplayed() {
            return false;
        }


    }
```

Because the `getFromLocation()` method is a blocking call and may not return immediately, it is important to call it from a separate thread. In the preceding code snippet, you wrapped the call using an `AsyncTask` class. Figure 7-16 shows the reverse coding in action — it demonstrates the address of a location touched on the map.

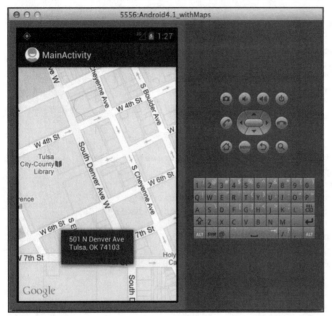

FIGURE 7-16

Geocoding

If you know the address of a location but want to know its latitude and longitude, you can do so via *geocoding*. You can use the `Geocoder` class for this purpose too. The following code shows how you can find the exact location of the Empire State Building by using the `getFromLocationName()` method:

```
@Override
public void onCreate(Bundle savedInstanceState) {
    super.onCreate(savedInstanceState);
    setContentView(R.layout.activity_main);

    mapView = (MapView) findViewById(R.id.mapView);
    mapView.setBuiltInZoomControls(true);

    mc = mapView.getController();

    MapOverlay mapOverlay = new MapOverlay();
    List<Overlay> listOfOverlays = mapView.getOverlays();
    listOfOverlays.add(mapOverlay);

    new DoBackgroundTask().execute("empire state building");
}
```

```
private class DoBackgroundTask extends AsyncTask
<String, Void, List<Address>> {
    protected List<Address> doInBackground(String... locationNames) {
        //---geo-coding---
        Geocoder geoCoder =
            new Geocoder(getBaseContext(), Locale.getDefault());
        try {
            //---maximum 5 results---
            List<Address> addresses = geoCoder.getFromLocationName(
                    locationNames[0], 5);
            return addresses;
        } catch (IOException e) {
            e.printStackTrace();
        }
        return null;
    }

    protected void onPostExecute(List<Address> addresses) {
        if (addresses.size() > 0) {
            GeoPoint p = new GeoPoint(
                    (int) (addresses.get(0).getLatitude() * 1E6),
                    (int) (addresses.get(0).getLongitude() * 1E6));
            mc.animateTo(p);
            mc.setZoom(20);
        }
    }
}
```

In the preceding code snippet, you took the first address returned by the getFromLocationName()
method and then displayed its location on the map (see Figure 7-17).

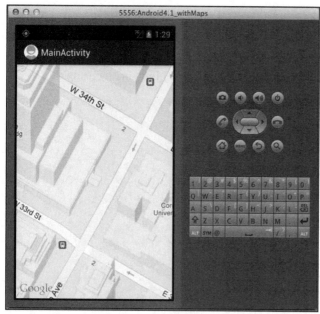

FIGURE 7-17

RECIPE 7.7 RESPONDING TO ZOOMING AND PANNING

Android Versions

Level 1 and above

Permissions

android.permission.INTERNET

Source Code to Download from Wrox.com

CustomMaps.zip

You want to create a listener that responds to the user's zooming and panning of the map.

Solution

The MapView provided by the Android SDK does not have APIs for you to monitor the zooming and panning of Google Maps. Sometimes it is useful for you to programmatically know the current location that the user is seeing on the map as well as the current zoom level that the map is displaying. You want to get all this information as the user is zooming and panning the map.

To do so, you need to create your custom MapView and implement a few additional methods. First, you need to create two Java class files under the current package name in your project (see Figure 7-18).

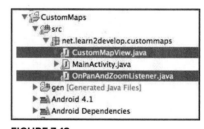

FIGURE 7-18

In the OnPanAndZoomListener.java file, create an interface that contains two method signatures:

```
package net.learn2develop.custommaps;

public interface OnPanAndZoomListener {

    //---called when the map is panned---
    public void onMapPan();

    //---called when the map is zoomed---
    public void onMapZoom();
}
```

In the CustomMapView.java file, create a class that extends the MapView class and implement the following methods:

```
package net.learn2develop.custommaps;

import android.content.Context;
import android.graphics.Canvas;
import android.util.AttributeSet;
```

```java
import android.view.MotionEvent;

import com.google.android.maps.GeoPoint;
import com.google.android.maps.MapView;

public class CustomMapView extends MapView {

    private int previousZoomLevel = -1;
    private GeoPoint previousMapCenter;
    private OnPanAndZoomListener panAndZoomListener;

    public CustomMapView(Context context, String apiKey) {
        super(context, apiKey);
    }

    public CustomMapView(Context context, AttributeSet attrs) {
        super(context, attrs);
    }

    public CustomMapView(Context context, AttributeSet attrs, int defStyle) {
        super(context, attrs, defStyle);
    }

    public void setOnPanAndZoomListener(OnPanAndZoomListener listener) {
        panAndZoomListener = listener;
    }

    @Override
    public boolean onTouchEvent(MotionEvent motionEvent) {

        if (motionEvent.getAction() == MotionEvent.ACTION_UP) {
            //---get the center of the map---
            GeoPoint currentMapCenter = this.getMapCenter();

            if (previousMapCenter == null ||
                (previousMapCenter.getLatitudeE6() !=
                    currentMapCenter.getLatitudeE6()) ||
                (previousMapCenter.getLongitudeE6() !=
                    currentMapCenter.getLongitudeE6()) ) {

                //---the user has panned the map---
                panAndZoomListener.onMapPan();
            }

            //---save the current map center for comparison later on---
            previousMapCenter = this.getMapCenter();
        }
        return super.onTouchEvent(motionEvent);
    }

    @Override
    protected void dispatchDraw(Canvas canvas) {
        super.dispatchDraw(canvas);

        if (getZoomLevel() != previousZoomLevel) {
            //---the user has zoomed the map---
```

```
                    panAndZoomListener.onMapZoom();

                    //---save the current zoom level for comparison later on---
            previousZoomLevel = getZoomLevel();
              }
          }
      }
```

The first three methods are the constructors for this custom `MapView` class. The `onTouch()` method is fired when the user taps (or clicks, for the emulator) on the map. Here, you compare the current location with the previously saved location. If there is a change, it means that the map has been panned, and hence you can call the `onMapPan()` method of the `OnPanAndZoomListener` object. The `dispatchDraw()` method is called whenever the map is about to be redrawn. Here, you compare the current zoom level with that of the previously recorded zoom level. If they are different, then the map is deemed to have changed the zoom level. Thus, you call the `onMapZoom()` method of the `OnPanAndZoomListener` object.

To use this custom `MapView`, simply use the `<net.learn2develop.CustomMaps.CustomMapView>` element in the `activity_main.xml` file:

```
<RelativeLayout xmlns:android="http://schemas.android.com/apk/res/android"
    xmlns:tools="http://schemas.android.com/tools"
    android:layout_width="match_parent"
    android:layout_height="match_parent" >

    <net.learn2develop.commmaps.CustomMapView
        android:id="@+id/mapView"
        android:layout_width="fill_parent"
        android:layout_height="fill_parent"
        android:apiKey="014sCTTyRmXQPd37eZiwVQHX9rQD08yVGM2iqTQ"
        android:clickable="true"
        android:state_enabled="true" />

</RelativeLayout>
```

The name of this element uses the following convention: `<package_name.class_name>`. Therefore, in this case the package name is `net.learn2develop.CustomMaps` and the class name of the custom `MapView` is `CustomMapView`, hence the element name is `<net.learn2develop.CustomMaps .CustomMapView>`.

In the activity, you need to create an instance of the `OnPanAndZoomListener` class and then override the two methods, `onMapZoom()` and `onMapPan()`. These two methods are called whenever the map is zoomed or panned, respectively:

```
package net.learn2develop.commmaps;

import android.os.Bundle;
import android.util.Log;

import com.google.android.maps.MapActivity;

public class MainActivity extends MapActivity  {
    CustomMapView mapView;

    @Override
```

```
public void onCreate(Bundle savedInstanceState) {
    super.onCreate(savedInstanceState);
    setContentView(R.layout.activity_main);

    OnPanAndZoomListener listener = new OnPanAndZoomListener() {
        @Override
        public void onMapZoom() {
            Log.d("CustomMaps","onMapZoom. Zoom level: " +
                    mapView.getZoomLevel());

        }
        @Override
        public void onMapPan() {
            Log.d("CustomMaps","onMapPan. Center: " +
                    mapView.getMapCenter().getLatitudeE6() / 1E6 + "," +
                    mapView.getMapCenter().getLongitudeE6() / 1E6);
        }
    };

    mapView = (CustomMapView) findViewById(R.id.mapView);
    mapView.setOnPanAndZoomListener(listener);
    mapView.setBuiltInZoomControls(true);
}

@Override
protected boolean isRouteDisplayed() {
    return false;
}

}
```

When you now run the application on the emulator, pan and/or zoom the map and you will be able to see the printout as shown in Figure 7-19 on the LogCat window in the DDMS perspective.

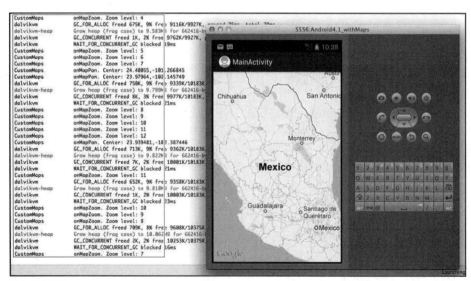

FIGURE 7-19

Location-Based Data Services

Nowadays, mobile devices are commonly equipped with GPS receivers. Because of the many satellites orbiting the earth, you can use a GPS receiver to find your location easily. However, GPS requires a clear sky to work and hence does not always work indoors or where satellites can't penetrate (such as a tunnel through a mountain).

Another effective way to locate your position is through *cell tower triangulation*. When a mobile phone is switched on, it is constantly in contact with base stations surrounding it. By knowing the identity of cell towers, it is possible to translate this information into a physical location through the use of various databases containing the cell towers' identities and their exact geographical locations. The advantage of cell tower triangulation is that it works indoors, without the need to obtain information from satellites. However, it is not as precise as GPS because its accuracy depends on overlapping signal coverage, which varies quite a bit. Cell tower triangulation works best in densely populated areas where the cell towers are closely located.

A third method of locating your position is to rely on Wi-Fi triangulation. Rather than connect to cell towers, the device connects to a Wi-Fi network and checks the service provider against databases to determine the location serviced by the provider. Of the three methods described here, Wi-Fi triangulation is the least accurate.

On the Android platform, the SDK provides the `LocationManager` class to help your device determine the user's physical location. The recipes in this chapter describe the various ways to get your location data, and how you can capture locations into a database.

RECIPE 8.1 OBTAINING GEOGRAPHICAL LOCATION USING GPS, WI-FI, OR CELLULAR NETWORKS

> **Android Versions**
> Level 1 and above
>
> **Permissions**
> android.permission.ACCESS_FINE_LOCATION
> android.permission.ACCESS_COARSE_LOCATION
>
> **Source Code to Download from Wrox.com**
> LBSGPS.zip
> LBSNetwork.zip

Your application needs to obtain the geographical location of the user using GPS, Wi-Fi, or cellular network triangulations.

Solution

To obtain the user's geographical location, you need to make use of the LocationManager class together with the LocationListener interface:

```
package net.learn2develop.lbsgps;

import android.app.Activity;
import android.location.LocationListener;
import android.location.LocationManager;
import android.os.Bundle;

public class MainActivity extends Activity {
    LocationManager lm;
    LocationListener locationListener;

    @Override
    public void onCreate(Bundle savedInstanceState) {
        super.onCreate(savedInstanceState);
        setContentView(R.layout.activity_main);
    }

}
```

To listen for changes in location, you need to create a class that implements the `LocationListener` interface:

```
package net.learn2develop.lbsgps;

import android.app.Activity;
import android.location.Location;
import android.location.LocationListener;
import android.location.LocationManager;
import android.os.Bundle;
import android.widget.Toast;

public class MainActivity extends Activity {
    LocationManager lm;
    LocationListener locationListener;

    private class MyLocationListener implements LocationListener
    {
        @Override
        public void onLocationChanged(Location loc) {
            if (loc != null) {
                Toast.makeText(getBaseContext(),
                        "Location changed : Lat: " + loc.getLatitude() +
                        " Lng: " + loc.getLongitude(),
                        Toast.LENGTH_SHORT).show();
            }
        }

        @Override
        public void onProviderDisabled(String provider) {
            Toast.makeText(getBaseContext(),
                    "Provider: " + provider + " disabled",
                    Toast.LENGTH_SHORT).show();
        }

        @Override
        public void onProviderEnabled(String provider) {
            Toast.makeText(getBaseContext(),
                    "Provider: " + provider + " enabled",
                    Toast.LENGTH_SHORT).show();
        }

        @Override
        public void onStatusChanged(String provider, int status,
                Bundle extras) {
            String statusString = "";
            switch (status) {
                case android.location.LocationProvider.AVAILABLE:
                    statusString = "available";
                case android.location.LocationProvider.OUT_OF_SERVICE:
                    statusString = "out of service";
                case
                    android.location.LocationProvider.TEMPORARILY_UNAVAILABLE:
                    statusString = "temporarily unavailable";
            }
```

```
            Toast.makeText(getBaseContext(),
                    provider + " " + statusString,
                    Toast.LENGTH_SHORT).show();
        }
    }

    @Override
    public void onCreate(Bundle savedInstanceState) {
        super.onCreate(savedInstanceState);
        setContentView(R.layout.activity_main);
    }

}
```

Within the `LocationListener` interface, you need to override four methods:

➤ `onLocationChanged()` — Called when the location has changed

➤ `onProviderDisabled()` — Called when the user has disabled the location provider

➤ `onProviderEnabled()` — Called when the user has enabled the location provider

➤ `onStatusChanged()` — Called when the location provider's status has changed

In the preceding implementation, you simply use the `Toast` class to display the information, such as the location and the status of the provider.

When the location has changed, the `onLocationChanged()` method's argument will contain the location information. From this argument, you can obtain the location's latitude and longitude, among other useful information such as accuracy, altitude, speed, and so on.

To instantiate the `LocationManager` class, use the `getSystemService()` method, followed by creating an instance of the `MyLocationListener` class that you just implemented:

```
import android.content.Context;
...

    @Override
    public void onCreate(Bundle savedInstanceState) {
        super.onCreate(savedInstanceState);
        setContentView(R.layout.activity_main);

        //---use the LocationManager class to obtain locations data---
        lm = (LocationManager)
                getSystemService(Context.LOCATION_SERVICE);
        locationListener = new MyLocationListener();
    }
```

To subscribe to location updates provided by the `MyLocationListener` class, call the `requestLocationUpdates()` method of the `LocationManager` object and pass it four arguments:

```
    @Override
    public void onResume() {
        super.onResume();
```

```
        //---request for location updates using GPS---
        lm.requestLocationUpdates(
                LocationManager.GPS_PROVIDER,
                0,
                0,
                locationListener);
    }
```

The four arguments are as follows:

➤ `provider` — The name of the provider with which you register. In this case, use the GPS_
   PROVIDER constant ("gps") if you are using GPS to obtain your geographical location data,
   or use NETWORK_PROVIDER ("network") if you are using Wi-Fi and cellular triangulations:

```
        //---request for location updates using WiFi and Cellular
        // triangulations---
        lm.requestLocationUpdates(
                LocationManager.NETWORK_PROVIDER,
                0,
                0,
                locationListener);
```

➤ `minTime` — The minimum time interval for notifications, in milliseconds. 0 indicates that you
   want to be continually informed of location changes.

➤ `minDistance` — The minimum distance interval for notifications, in meters. 0 indicates that
   you want to be continually informed of location changes.

➤ `listener` — An object whose onLocationChanged() method will be called for each location
   update.

> **NOTE** *Which provider should you use? If you are indoors, you should use the*
> NETWORK_PROVIDER, *as it does not require line of sight to the sky (as is needed*
> *by GPS). However, using the* NETWORK_PROVIDER *requires you to have Internet*
> *access (either 3G or Wi-Fi) because the provider needs to contact external servers*
> *in order to triangulate your position. If you want higher precision, you should use*
> *the* GPS_PROVIDER.

Because listening for location changes is a costly affair (in terms of battery consumption), you
should remove the updates whenever you are done with the location tracking. You can do so via
the removeUpdates() method of the LocationManager object:

```
        @Override
        public void onDestroy() {
            super.onDestroy();

            //---remove the location listener---
            lm.removeUpdates(locationListener);
        }
```

When using the `GPS_PROVIDER`, you need to add the `android.permission.ACCESS_FINE_LOCATION` permission in your `AndroidManifest.xml` file. If you are using the `NETWORK_PROVIDER`, you need to add the `android.permission.ACCESS_COARSE_LOCATION` permission.

> **NOTE** *The* `NETWORK_PROVIDER` *will not work on the Android emulator. If your code uses it and you test the application on the emulator, it will result in an illegal argument exception. You need to test the code on a real device.*

RECIPE 8.2 CHOOSING THE BEST LOCATION PROVIDER TO USE

Android Versions

   Level 1 and above

Permissions

   android.permission.ACCESS_FINE_LOCATION

   android.permission.ACCESS_COARSE_LOCATION

Source Code to Download from Wrox.com

   LocationProviders.zip

You want to be able to choose the best provider possible to help you determine your location.

Solution

In the previous recipe, you saw how to use the `GPS_PROVIDER` and the `NETWORK_PROVIDER` to obtain your current location information using the various techniques (GPS, Wi-Fi, or cellular triangulation). However, sometimes you might want to let the OS determine which provider is best depending on your specific requirements. In this case, you can use the `getBestProvider()` method of the `LocationManager` class to help the application decide based on the specified criteria.

First, create an object of type `LocationManager`:

```
package net.learn2develop.locationproviders;

import android.app.Activity;
import android.location.LocationManager;
import android.os.Bundle;

public class MainActivity extends Activity {
    LocationManager lm;
```

```
    @Override
    public void onCreate(Bundle savedInstanceState) {
        super.onCreate(savedInstanceState);
        setContentView(R.layout.activity_main);
    }

}
```

Instantiate the `LocationManager` class by calling the `getSystemService()` method:

```
    /** Called when the activity is first created. */
    @Override
    public void onCreate(Bundle savedInstanceState) {
        super.onCreate(savedInstanceState);
        setContentView(R.layout.main);

        lm = (LocationManager) getSystemService(LOCATION_SERVICE);
    }
```

To get a list of location providers, use the `getAllProviders()` method of the `LocationManager` class, which returns a list of location providers:

```
package net.learn2develop.locationproviders;

import java.util.List;

import android.app.Activity;
import android.location.LocationManager;
import android.os.Bundle;
import android.util.Log;

public class MainActivity extends Activity {
    LocationManager lm;

    @Override
    public void onCreate(Bundle savedInstanceState) {
        super.onCreate(savedInstanceState);
        setContentView(R.layout.activity_main);

        lm = (LocationManager) getSystemService(LOCATION_SERVICE);

        //---print out all the location providers---
        List<String> locationProviders = lm.getAllProviders();
        for (String provider : locationProviders) {
            Log.d("LocationProviders", provider);
        }
    }

}
```

To specify the set of criteria to determine the best location provider, create an instance of the `Criteria` class and set its various methods as follows:

```
package net.learn2develop.locationproviders;

import java.util.List;
```

```
import android.app.Activity;
import android.location.Criteria;
import android.location.LocationManager;
import android.os.Bundle;
import android.util.Log;

public class MainActivity extends Activity {
    LocationManager lm;

    @Override
    public void onCreate(Bundle savedInstanceState) {
        super.onCreate(savedInstanceState);
        setContentView(R.layout.activity_main);

        lm = (LocationManager) getSystemService(LOCATION_SERVICE);

        //---print out all the location providers---
        List<String> locationProviders = lm.getAllProviders();
        for (String provider : locationProviders) {
            Log.d("LocationProviders", provider);
        }

        //---set the criteria for best location provider---
        Criteria c = new Criteria();
        c.setAccuracy(Criteria.ACCURACY_FINE);
        //---OR---
        //c.setAccuracy(Criteria.ACCURACY_COARSE);
        c.setAltitudeRequired(false);
        c.setBearingRequired(false);
        c.setCostAllowed(true);
        c.setPowerRequirement(Criteria.POWER_HIGH);
    }

}
```

To get the best location provider available on the device based on the list of criteria, call the
`getBestProvider()` method:

```
    @Override
    public void onCreate(Bundle savedInstanceState) {
        super.onCreate(savedInstanceState);
        setContentView(R.layout.activity_main);

        lm = (LocationManager) getSystemService(LOCATION_SERVICE);

        //---print out all the location providers---
        List<String> locationProviders = lm.getAllProviders();
        for (String provider : locationProviders) {
            Log.d("LocationProviders", provider);
        }

        //---set the criteria for best location provider---
        Criteria c = new Criteria();
        c.setAccuracy(Criteria.ACCURACY_FINE);
```

```
//---OR---
//c.setAccuracy(Criteria.ACCURACY_COARSE);
c.setAltitudeRequired(false);
c.setBearingRequired(false);
c.setCostAllowed(true);
c.setPowerRequirement(Criteria.POWER_HIGH);

//---get the best location provider---
String bestProvider = lm.getBestProvider(c, true);
Log.d("LocationProviders", "Best provider is " + bestProvider);
}
```

If you want to quickly get the last known location without requesting an update using the `LocationManager` object, call the `getLastKnownLocation()` method and pass it the name of the location provider (either "gps", or "network"). If a location is available, it will be returned as a `Location` object:

```
import android.location.Location;
...

@Override
public void onCreate(Bundle savedInstanceState) {
    super.onCreate(savedInstanceState);
    setContentView(R.layout.activity_main);

    lm = (LocationManager) getSystemService(LOCATION_SERVICE);

    //---print out all the location providers---
    List<String> locationProviders = lm.getAllProviders();
    for (String provider : locationProviders) {
        Log.d("LocationProviders", provider);
    }

    //---set the criteria for best location provider---
    Criteria c = new Criteria();
    c.setAccuracy(Criteria.ACCURACY_FINE);
    //---OR---
    //c.setAccuracy(Criteria.ACCURACY_COARSE);
    c.setAltitudeRequired(false);
    c.setBearingRequired(false);
    c.setCostAllowed(true);
    c.setPowerRequirement(Criteria.POWER_HIGH);

    //---get the best location provider---
    String bestProvider = lm.getBestProvider(c, true);
    Log.d("LocationProviders", "Best provider is " + bestProvider);

    //---get the last known location---
    Location location = lm.getLastKnownLocation(bestProvider);
    if (location!=null) Log.d("LocationProviders", location.toString());
}
```

RECIPE 8.3 MONITORING A LOCATION

Android Versions

Level 1 and above

Permissions

android.permission.ACCESS_FINE_LOCATION

Source Code to Download from Wrox.com

MonitorLocation.zip

Your application wants to monitor a particular location, and when the device is near that location you want to perform some actions. This is very useful if you are writing an application that reminds you when you are near places of interest, for example.

Solution

One very cool feature of the `LocationManager` class is its ability to monitor a specific location. This is achieved using the `addProximityAlert()` method.

The following code snippet shows how to monitor a particular location so that if the user is within a five-meter radius of that location, your application will fire a `PendingIntent` object to launch the web browser:

```
package net.learn2develop.monitorlocation;

import android.app.Activity;
import android.app.PendingIntent;
import android.content.Context;
import android.content.Intent;
import android.location.LocationManager;
import android.net.Uri;
import android.os.Bundle;

public class MainActivity extends Activity {
    LocationManager lm;
    PendingIntent pendingIntent;

    @Override
    public void onCreate(Bundle savedInstanceState) {
        super.onCreate(savedInstanceState);
        setContentView(R.layout.activity_main);

        //---use the LocationManager class to obtain locations data---
        lm = (LocationManager)
            getSystemService(Context.LOCATION_SERVICE);
```

```
    }

    @Override
    public void onResume() {
        super.onResume();

        //---PendingIntent to launch activity if the user is within
        // some locations---
        pendingIntent = PendingIntent.getActivity(
            this, 0, new
            Intent(android.content.Intent.ACTION_VIEW,
              Uri.parse("http://www.amazon.com")), 0);

        lm.addProximityAlert(37.422006, -122.084095, 5, -1, pendingIntent);
    }

    @Override
    public void onDestroy() {
        super.onDestroy();

        lm.removeProximityAlert(pendingIntent);
    }

}
```

The `addProximityAlert()` method takes five arguments: latitude, longitude, radius (in meters), expiration (time for the proximity alert to be valid, after which it will be deleted; -1 for no expiration), and the `PendingIntent` object.

> **NOTE** *If the Android device's screen goes to sleep, the proximity is also checked once every four minutes in order to preserve the battery life of the device.*

RECIPE 8.4 USING A BROADCASTRECEIVER TO OBTAIN LOCATIONS

Android Versions

Level 3 and above

Permissions

android.permission.ACCESS_FINE_LOCATION

Source Code to Download from Wrox.com

LBSReceiver.zip

Rather than use the `LocationListener` class to obtain location data, you can instead use a `PendingIntent` object together with a `BroadcastReceiver` class. Using this approach, you can continue to listen for location data even if your application is closed by the user.

Solution

In the first recipe in this chapter ("Obtaining Geographical Location Using GPS, Wi-Fi, or Cellular Networks"), you learned how to obtain your geographical location using an instance of the `LocationListener` class. The `LocationListener` class is useful if you are monitoring the location from within an activity. However, if the activity is destroyed, the `LocationListener` object would also be destroyed, and you would no longer be able to track your location. An alternative for getting your location is to create a `BroadcastReceiver` class together with a `PendingIntent` object. To see how it works, create a class in your package and name it `MyLocationReceiver.java`. Code it as follows:

```java
package net.learn2develop.lbsreceiver;

import android.content.BroadcastReceiver;
import android.content.Context;
import android.content.Intent;
import android.location.Location;
import android.location.LocationManager;
import android.widget.Toast;

public class MyLocationReceiver extends BroadcastReceiver {
    @Override
    public void onReceive(Context context, Intent intent) {
        String locationKey = LocationManager.KEY_LOCATION_CHANGED;
        String providerEnabledKey = LocationManager.KEY_PROVIDER_ENABLED;
        if (intent.hasExtra(providerEnabledKey)) {
            if (!intent.getBooleanExtra(providerEnabledKey, true)) {
                Toast.makeText(context,
                        "Provider disabled",
                        Toast.LENGTH_SHORT).show();
            } else {
                Toast.makeText(context,
                        "Provider enabled",
                        Toast.LENGTH_SHORT).show();
            }
        }

        if (intent.hasExtra(locationKey)) {
            Location loc = (Location)intent.getExtras().get(locationKey);
            Toast.makeText(context,
                    "Location changed : Lat: " + loc.getLatitude() +
                    " Lng: " + loc.getLongitude(),
                    Toast.LENGTH_SHORT).show();
        }
    }
}
```

When the `BroadcastReceiver` class's `onReceive()` method is fired due to a change in location, its `Intent` argument contains location information. This information can be identified using the keys `LocationManager.KEY_LOCATION_CHANGED` and `LocationManager.KEY_PROVIDER_ENABLED`, which indicate the location information and whether the location provider is enabled, respectively.

To obtain location data using the `BroadcastReceiver` class that you just created, add the following code to your activity:

```
package net.learn2develop.lbsreceiver;

import android.app.Activity;
import android.app.PendingIntent;
import android.content.Context;
import android.content.Intent;
import android.location.LocationManager;
import android.os.Bundle;

public class MainActivity extends Activity {
    LocationManager lm;
    PendingIntent pendingIntent;

    @Override
    public void onCreate(Bundle savedInstanceState) {
        super.onCreate(savedInstanceState);
        setContentView(R.layout.activity_main);

        //---use the LocationManager class to obtain locations data---
        lm = (LocationManager)
                getSystemService(Context.LOCATION_SERVICE);
        Intent i = new Intent(this, MyLocationReceiver.class);
        pendingIntent = PendingIntent.getBroadcast(
                this, 0, i, PendingIntent.FLAG_UPDATE_CURRENT);

        //---request for location updates using GPS---
        lm.requestLocationUpdates(
                LocationManager.GPS_PROVIDER,
                60000,
                100,
                pendingIntent);
    }

}
```

Like Recipe 8.1, you use the `requestLocationUpdates()` method of the `LocationManager` object to request location updates. However, unlike that recipe, you now pass in a `PendingIntent` object instead of a `LocationListener` object. When there is a change in location, you fire the `onReceive()` method of the `BroadcastReceiver`.

Finally, remember to add the `<receiver>` element to the `AndroidManifest.xml` file:

```xml
<manifest xmlns:android="http://schemas.android.com/apk/res/android"
    package="net.learn2develop.lbsreceiver"
    android:versionCode="1"
    android:versionName="1.0" >

    <uses-sdk
        android:minSdkVersion="8"
        android:targetSdkVersion="15" />

    <uses-permission android:name="android.permission.ACCESS_FINE_LOCATION"/>

    <application
        android:icon="@drawable/ic_launcher"
        android:label="@string/app_name"
        android:theme="@style/AppTheme" >
        <activity
            android:name=".MainActivity"
            android:label="@string/title_activity_main" >
            <intent-filter>
                <action android:name="android.intent.action.MAIN" />

                <category android:name="android.intent.category.LAUNCHER" />
            </intent-filter>
        </activity>

        <receiver android:name=".MyLocationReceiver"/>

    </application>

</manifest>
```

With this, your application will continually receive location updates, even if the activity is killed.

> **NOTE** *Note that to preserve battery, I set the location update intervals to be 60,000 milliseconds and 100 meters. That is, you won't receive another location update until at least one minute after you have received your last update or you have moved at least 100 meters from your last location. Hence, if you are testing this application on the emulator, be sure to take note of this, and change the latitude and longitude in the DDMS in between updates.*

Keep a reference to the `PendingIntent` object so that when you are done with the location tracking, you can remove the location updates using it:

```java
lm.removeUpdates(pendingIntent);
```

RECIPE 8.5 LOCATION DATA LOGGING

Android Versions

Level 3 and above

Permissions

android.permission.ACCESS_FINE_LOCATION

Source Code to Download from Wrox.com

LBSReceiver-DataLogging.zip

You want to log the location data to a database so that the locations can be retrieved later for other purposes, such as plotting a track on Google Maps.

Solution

In the previous recipe, you saw how to track your location using a PendingIntent object and a BroadcastReceiver object. A good use of these is to perform location data logging. For example, you might want to save all the location data to a database so that the locations can be retrieved later.

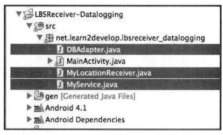

For this recipe, add three Java class files to the project as shown in Figure 8.1.

FIGURE 8-1

The DBAdapter.java file is the helper class for saving your location data to a SQLite database. Populate it with the following code:

```
package net.learn2develop.lbsreceiver_datalogging;

import java.text.SimpleDateFormat;
import java.util.Calendar;

import android.content.ContentValues;
import android.content.Context;
import android.database.Cursor;
import android.database.SQLException;
import android.database.sqlite.SQLiteDatabase;
import android.database.sqlite.SQLiteOpenHelper;

public class DBAdapter {
    static final String KEY_DATE = "date";
    static final String KEY_LAT = "lat";
    static final String KEY_LNG = "lng";
    static final String TAG = "DBAdapter";

    static final String DATABASE_NAME = "MyDB";
```

```
static final String DATABASE_TABLE = "Locations";
static final int DATABASE_VERSION = 1;

final Context context;

DatabaseHelper DBHelper;
SQLiteDatabase db;
Calendar currentDate;
SimpleDateFormat formatter;

public DBAdapter(Context ctx)
{
    this.context = ctx;
    DBHelper = new DatabaseHelper(context);
    currentDate = Calendar.getInstance();
    formatter = new SimpleDateFormat("yyyy/MMM/dd HH:mm:ss");
}

private static class DatabaseHelper extends SQLiteOpenHelper
{
    DatabaseHelper(Context context)
    {
        super(context, DATABASE_NAME, null, DATABASE_VERSION);
    }

    @Override
    public void onCreate(SQLiteDatabase db) { }

    @Override
    public void onUpgrade(SQLiteDatabase db, int oldVersion,
    int newVersion) { }
}

//---opens the database---
public DBAdapter open() throws SQLException
{
    db = DBHelper.getWritableDatabase();
    return this;
}

//---closes the database---
public void close()
{
    DBHelper.close();
}

//---insert a location into the database---
public long insertLocation(String lat, String lng)
{
    ContentValues initialValues = new ContentValues();
    initialValues.put(KEY_DATE, formatter.format(currentDate.getTime()));
    initialValues.put(KEY_LAT, lat);
    initialValues.put(KEY_LNG, lng);
    return db.insert(DATABASE_TABLE, null, initialValues);
}
```

```
        //---retrieves all the locations---
        public Cursor getAllLocations()
        {
            return db.query(DATABASE_TABLE, new String[] {
                KEY_DATE, KEY_LAT, KEY_LNG},
                null, null, null, null, null);
        }
    }
```

For this recipe, you need to create a new SQLite database named `mydb` containing a table named `Locations`, with the following fields:

➤ date — text

➤ lat — text

➤ lng — text

> **NOTE** *You can easily create a SQLite database using the SQLite Database Browser, which can be downloaded from* `http://sourceforge.net/projects/sqlitebrowser.`

Drag and drop the database onto the `assets` folder of your project (see Figure 8-2).

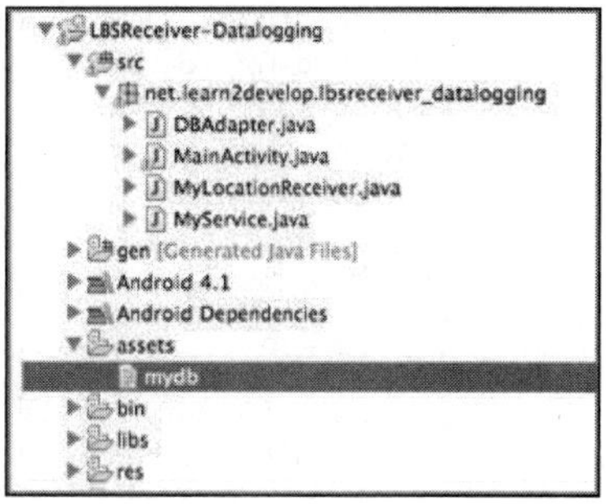

You also need a `BroadcastReceiver` class in your package. For this recipe, the `BroadcastReceiver` class is named `MyLocationReceiver.java`. This class receives the location information and saves the information to the database. Populate it with the following code:

FIGURE 8-2

```
package net.learn2develop.lbsreceiver_datalogging;

import android.content.BroadcastReceiver;
import android.content.Context;
import android.content.Intent;
import android.location.Location;
import android.location.LocationManager;
import android.widget.Toast;

public class MyLocationReceiver extends BroadcastReceiver {
    @Override
    public void onReceive(Context context, Intent intent) {
        String locationKey = LocationManager.KEY_LOCATION_CHANGED;
        String providerEnabledKey = LocationManager.KEY_PROVIDER_ENABLED;

        if (intent.hasExtra(providerEnabledKey)) {
            if (!intent.getBooleanExtra(providerEnabledKey, true)) {
                Toast.makeText(context,
                        "Provider disabled",
                        Toast.LENGTH_SHORT).show();
            } else {
                Toast.makeText(context,
```

```
                                "Provider enabled",
                                Toast.LENGTH_SHORT).show();
                    }
            }

            if (intent.hasExtra(locationKey)) {
                Location loc = (Location)intent.getExtras().get(locationKey);
                Toast.makeText(context,
                        "Location changed : Lat: " + loc.getLatitude() +
                        " Lng: " + loc.getLongitude(),
                        Toast.LENGTH_SHORT).show();

                DBAdapter db = new DBAdapter(context);
                db.open();
                db.insertLocation(String.valueOf(loc.getLatitude()),
                                String.valueOf(loc.getLongitude()));
                db.close();
            }
        }
    }
```

You also need a `Service` to run in the background so that it can listen for changes in location. This file is named `MyService.java`. Populate it with the following code:

```
package net.learn2develop.lbsreceiver_datalogging;

import android.app.PendingIntent;
import android.app.Service;
import android.content.Context;
import android.content.Intent;
import android.location.LocationManager;
import android.os.IBinder;
import android.widget.Toast;

public class MyService extends Service {
    LocationManager lm;
    PendingIntent pendingIntent;

    @Override
    public IBinder onBind(Intent arg0) {
        return null;
    }

    @Override
    public int onStartCommand(Intent intent, int flags, int startId) {
        Toast.makeText(this, "Service Started", Toast.LENGTH_LONG).show();

        //---use the LocationManager class to obtain locations data---
        lm = (LocationManager)
                getSystemService(Context.LOCATION_SERVICE);
        Intent i = new Intent(this, MyLocationReceiver.class);
        pendingIntent = PendingIntent.getBroadcast(
                this, 0, i, PendingIntent.FLAG_UPDATE_CURRENT);
```

```
        //---request for location updates using GPS---
        lm.requestLocationUpdates(
                LocationManager.GPS_PROVIDER,
                60000,
                100,
                pendingIntent);

        return START_STICKY;
    }

    @Override
    public void onDestroy() {
        //---remove the pending intent---
        lm.removeUpdates(pendingIntent);

        super.onDestroy();
        Toast.makeText(this, "Service Destroyed", Toast.LENGTH_LONG).show();
    }
}
```

In the main activity, add the following code in bold:

```
package net.learn2develop.lbsreceiver_datalogging;

import java.io.File;
import java.io.FileNotFoundException;
import java.io.FileOutputStream;
import java.io.IOException;
import java.io.InputStream;
import java.io.OutputStream;

import android.app.Activity;
import android.content.Intent;
import android.os.Bundle;
import android.view.View;

public class MainActivity extends Activity {

    public void CopyDB(InputStream inputStream,
            OutputStream outputStream) throws IOException {
        //---copy 1K bytes at a time---
        byte[] buffer = new byte[1024];
        int length;
        while ((length = inputStream.read(buffer)) > 0) {
            outputStream.write(buffer, 0, length);
        }
        inputStream.close();
        outputStream.close();
    }

    @Override
    public void onCreate(Bundle savedInstanceState) {
        super.onCreate(savedInstanceState);
        setContentView(R.layout.activity_main);
```

```
        String destDir = "/data/data/" + getPackageName() +
                "/databases/";
        String destPath = destDir + "MyDB";
        File f = new File(destPath);
        if (!f.exists()) {
            //---make sure directory exists---
            File directory = new File(destDir);
            directory.mkdirs();
            //---copy the db from the assets folder into
            // the databases folder---
            try {
                CopyDB(getBaseContext().getAssets().open("mydb"),
                        new FileOutputStream(destPath));
            } catch (FileNotFoundException e) {
                e.printStackTrace();
            } catch (IOException e) {
                e.printStackTrace();
            }
        }
    }

    public void onStart(View view) {
        startService(new Intent(getBaseContext(), MyService.class));
    }

    public void onStop(View view) {
        stopService(new Intent(getBaseContext(), MyService.class));
    }

}
```

When the activity is created, the preceding code copies the SQLite database from the `assets` folder and pastes it into the `data` folder of the application on the device. To start and stop the service, add the following statements to the `activity_main.xml` file:

```xml
<LinearLayout xmlns:android="http://schemas.android.com/apk/res/android"
    android:layout_width="fill_parent"
    android:layout_height="fill_parent"
    android:orientation="vertical" >

    <Button
        android:id="@+id/button1"
        android:layout_width="match_parent"
        android:layout_height="wrap_content"
        android:text="Start"
        android:onClick="onStart" />

    <Button
        android:id="@+id/button2"
        android:layout_width="match_parent"
        android:layout_height="wrap_content"
        android:text="Stop"
        android:onClick="onStop" />

</LinearLayout>
```

Finally, remember to add the `<receiver>` and `<service>` elements to the `AndroidManifest.xml` file, plus the permission:

```xml
<manifest xmlns:android="http://schemas.android.com/apk/res/android"
    package="net.learn2develop.lbsreceiver_datalogging"
    android:versionCode="1"
    android:versionName="1.0" >

    <uses-sdk
        android:minSdkVersion="8"
        android:targetSdkVersion="15" />

    <uses-permission android:name="android.permission.ACCESS_FINE_LOCATION"/>

    <application
        android:icon="@drawable/ic_launcher"
        android:label="@string/app_name"
        android:theme="@style/AppTheme" >
        <activity
            android:name=".MainActivity"
            android:label="@string/title_activity_main" >
            <intent-filter>
                <action android:name="android.intent.action.MAIN" />

                <category android:name="android.intent.category.LAUNCHER" />
            </intent-filter>
        </activity>

        <receiver android:name=".MyLocationReceiver"/>
        <service android:name=".MyService" />

    </application>

</manifest>
```

That's it! Click the Start button and the application will start logging the location data.

> **NOTE** *See Chapter 9 for information about how to examine the database stored on the emulator.*

Accessing the Hardware

In this chapter, you explore the different ways to access the hardware features of your Android device. You will learn how to use the built-in camera to take pictures, how to activate the flashlight, how to detect the various hardware features on your device, and how to determine whether the GPS or location service is enabled on the Android device.

RECIPE 9.1 CAPTURING PICTURES WITH THE CAMERA

Android Versions

Level 1 and above

Permissions

CAMERA

Source Code to Download from Wrox.com

Camera.zip

Most Android phones nowadays include built-in cameras — one at the front and one at the back. This recipe shows you how to programmatically invoke the camera to take a picture and then save the picture to external storage.

Solution

First, add a Button in your application UI, such as `activity_main.xml`:

```xml
<?xml version="1.0" encoding="utf-8"?>
<LinearLayout xmlns:android="http://schemas.android.com/apk/res/android"
    android:layout_width="fill_parent"
```

```
        android:layout_height="fill_parent"
        android:orientation="vertical" >

    <Button
        android:layout_width="match_parent"
        android:layout_height="wrap_content"
        android:onClick="btnTakePhoto"
        android:text="Take Photo" />

</LinearLayout>
```

In the activity, code the following lines in bold:

```
package net.learn2develop.camera;

import java.io.File;

import android.app.Activity;
import android.content.Intent;
import android.net.Uri;
import android.os.Bundle;
import android.os.Environment;
import android.provider.MediaStore;
import android.view.Menu;
import android.view.View;
import android.widget.Toast;

public class MainActivity extends Activity {
    static int TAKE_PICTURE = 1;
    Uri outputFileUri;

    @Override
    public void onCreate(Bundle savedInstanceState) {
        super.onCreate(savedInstanceState);
        setContentView(R.layout.activity_main);
    }

    @Override
    public boolean onCreateOptionsMenu(Menu menu) {
        getMenuInflater().inflate(R.menu.activity_main, menu);
        return true;
    }

    public void btnTakePhoto(View view) {
        Intent intent = new Intent(MediaStore.ACTION_IMAGE_CAPTURE);
        File file = new File(Environment.getExternalStorageDirectory(),
            "MyPhoto.jpg");
        outputFileUri = Uri.fromFile(file);
        intent.putExtra(MediaStore.EXTRA_OUTPUT, outputFileUri);
        startActivityForResult(intent, TAKE_PICTURE);
    }
```

```
        @Override
        protected void onActivityResult(int requestCode, int resultCode,
        Intent data)
        {
            if (requestCode == TAKE_PICTURE && resultCode==RESULT_OK){
                Toast.makeText(this, outputFileUri.toString(),
                    Toast.LENGTH_LONG).show();
    }
        }


    }
```

Essentially, you are using an `Intent` object to invoke the camera, using the `MediaStore.ACTION_IMAGE_CAPTURE` action. At the same time, you are telling the camera that you want to save the captured picture to external storage and name the saved picture `MyPhoto.jpg`. Finally, you call the `startActivityForResult()` method to fire the `Intent` object. This ensures that once the picture has been saved, its path will be displayed using the `Toast` class. This is done through the `onActivityResult()` callback function.

To ensure that your application can only be installed on devices with a camera, you need to add the `<uses-feature>` element to your `AndroidManifest.xml` file:

```
<manifest xmlns:android="http://schemas.android.com/apk/res/android"
    package="net.learn2develop.camera"
    android:versionCode="1"
    android:versionName="1.0" >

    <uses-sdk
        android:minSdkVersion="8"
        android:targetSdkVersion="15" />

    <uses-feature android:name="android.hardware.camera" />

    <application
        android:icon="@drawable/ic_launcher"
        android:label="@string/app_name"
        android:theme="@style/AppTheme" >
        <activity
            android:name=".MainActivity"
            android:label="@string/title_activity_main" >
            <intent-filter>
                <action android:name="android.intent.action.MAIN" />

                <category android:name="android.intent.category.LAUNCHER" />
            </intent-filter>
        </activity>
    </application>

</manifest>
```

Figure 9-1 shows the `Toast` class displaying the location of the image saved on external storage.

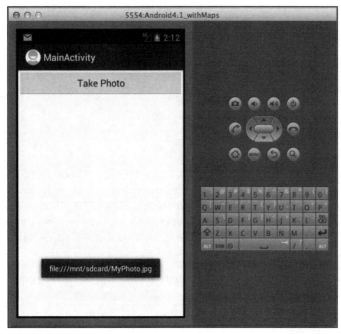

FIGURE 9-1

> **NOTE** *Specifying the* `<uses-feature>` *element in your* `AndroidManifest.xml`
> *file ensures that your application can only be installed on a device with a built-in
> camera.*

RECIPE 9.2 DETECTING THE PRESENCE OF HARDWARE FEATURES

Android Versions

Level 1 and above (unless otherwise indicated in code)

Permissions

None

Source Code to Download from Wrox.com

DetectHardwareFeatures.zip

One great advantage of the Android platform is the wide variety of devices from which users can select. However, with choice comes fragmentation — devices in all shapes and sizes, each supporting different sets of features. This fragmentation problem causes a lot of headaches for developers, who have to ensure that their application runs on the widest range of devices available. This recipe demonstrates how to determine whether a particular hardware feature is supported on the device.

Solution

Several methods enable you to detect hardware features on your devices:

➤   `getResources()` — This method returns an instance of the `Resources` class for your package. Using this instance, you can use the `getConfiguration()` method to get the current configuration for your package. This technique enables you to find information such as whether a hardware keyboard is attached to your device, whether the device supports landscape orientation, and so on.

➤   `ViewConfiguration.get()` — This method returns a `ViewConfiguration` object that enables you to check whether a device has a hardware MENU key, and other information such as the scrollbar size, the time needed for a long press gesture, and more.

➤   `getPackageManager()` — This method returns a `PackageManager` object that enables you to check for certain hardware features using the `hasSystemFeature()` method, such as the presence of a front camera, GPS, various sensors, and more.

The following code snippet enables you to check for the presence of the following:

➤   GPS

➤   Front camera

➤   Near Field Communication (NFC)

➤   Hardware MENU button

➤   Hardware keyboard

```
import android.annotation.SuppressLint;
import android.content.pm.PackageManager;
import android.content.res.Configuration;
import android.view.ViewConfiguration;

    private boolean IsKeyboardPresent() {
        return getResources().getConfiguration().keyboard !=
        Configuration.KEYBOARD_NOKEYS;
    }

    //---requires level 14---
    @SuppressLint("NewApi")
    private boolean IsHardwareMenuButtonPresent() {
        return ViewConfiguration.get(this).hasPermanentMenuKey();
    }

    private boolean IsNFCPresent() {
        return getPackageManager().hasSystemFeature(PackageManager.FEATURE_NFC);
```

```
    }

    private boolean IsFrontCameraPresent() {
        return getPackageManager().hasSystemFeature(
            PackageManager.FEATURE_CAMERA_FRONT);
    }

    private boolean IsGPSPresent() {
        return getPackageManager().hasSystemFeature(
            PackageManager.FEATURE_LOCATION_GPS);
    }
```

RECIPE 9.3 CHECKING NETWORK STATE

Android Versions

Level 1 and above

Permissions

ACCESS_NETWORK_STATE

CHANGE_WIFI_STATE

Source Code to Download from Wrox.com

CheckNetworkState.zip

If you are writing a network application, it is important that you check whether the device is currently connected to a network, such as a Wi-Fi network, or the data network (3G or 4G). This recipe shows how to do this using the ConnectivityManager class.

Solution

To check for network connectivity, use the ConnectivityManager class. In the following code snippet, you first obtain an instance of the ConnectivityManager class and then use the getNetworkInfo() method to get information about the Wi-Fi (ConnectivityManager.TYPE_WIFI) and data network (ConnectivityManager.TYPE_MOBILE). The getNetworkInfo() method returns an instance of the NetworkInfo class. Using this instance, you can determine whether a network type is connected or not:

```
package com.example.checknetworkstate;

import android.app.Activity;
import android.content.Context;
```

```java
import android.net.ConnectivityManager;
import android.net.NetworkInfo;
import android.net.wifi.WifiManager;
import android.os.Bundle;
import android.view.Menu;
import android.widget.Toast;

public class MainActivity extends Activity {
    ConnectivityManager connectivity;
    NetworkInfo wifiNetworkInfo, mobileNetworkInfo;

    @Override
    public void onCreate(Bundle savedInstanceState) {
        super.onCreate(savedInstanceState);
        setContentView(R.layout.activity_main);

        connectivity = (ConnectivityManager)
            getSystemService(Context.CONNECTIVITY_SERVICE);

        wifiNetworkInfo =
                connectivity.getNetworkInfo(
                        ConnectivityManager.TYPE_WIFI);
        mobileNetworkInfo =
                connectivity.getNetworkInfo(
                        ConnectivityManager.TYPE_MOBILE);
        if (wifiNetworkInfo.isConnected())
            Toast.makeText(this, "WiFi is connected", Toast.LENGTH_LONG).show();
        else
            Toast.makeText(this, "WiFi not connected", Toast.LENGTH_LONG).show();
        if (mobileNetworkInfo.isConnected())
            Toast.makeText(this, "3G/4G is connected", Toast.LENGTH_LONG).show();
        else
            Toast.makeText(this, "3G/4G not connected", Toast.LENGTH_LONG).show();
    }
```

To access the network state on your device, you need to add the permission for ACCESS_NETWORK_ STATE in the AndroidManifest.xml file:

```xml
<uses-permission android:name="android.permission.ACCESS_NETWORK_STATE"/>
```

In the event that Wi-Fi is not enabled, you can programmatically turn it on using the WifiManager class:

```java
WifiManager wifiManager = (WifiManager)
    getSystemService(Context.WIFI_SERVICE);
wifiManager.setWifiEnabled(true);
```

If you use the WiFiManager class to enable the Wi-Fi, you need to add the CHANGE_WIFI_STATE permission:

```xml
<uses-permission android:name="android.permission.CHANGE_WIFI_STATE"/>
```

RECIPE 9.4 TURNING GPS ON/OFF

Android Versions

Level 1 and above

Permissions

ACCESS_FINE_LOCATION

ACCESS_COARSE_LOCATION

Source Code to Download from Wrox.com

ToggleGPS.zip

If you have a location-based service (LBS) application that relies on the Global Positioning System (GPS) or network triangulation, you need to ensure that the relevant settings in the Location Services page in the Settings application are enabled. This recipe demonstrates how to detect whether the relevant settings are turned on; and if not, how to direct the page to the user to enable the settings.

Solution

To determine if location services are enabled on the device, you first obtain an instance of the `LocationManager` class. Using this instance, you can then check whether the GPS or network provider is enabled by using the `isProviderEnabled()` method, as demonstrated in the following code snippet:

```
package net.learn2develop.togglegps;

import android.app.Activity;
import android.content.Context;
import android.content.Intent;
import android.location.LocationManager;
import android.os.Bundle;
import android.view.Menu;

public class MainActivity extends Activity {

    @Override
    public void onCreate(Bundle savedInstanceState) {
        super.onCreate(savedInstanceState);
        setContentView(R.layout.activity_main);

        LocationManager lm = (LocationManager)
            getSystemService(Context.LOCATION_SERVICE);

        //---check if GPS_PROVIDER is enabled---
        boolean gpsStatus = lm.isProviderEnabled(LocationManager.GPS_PROVIDER);
```

```
//---check if NETWORK_PROVIDER is enabled---
boolean networkStatus = lm.isProviderEnabled(
    LocationManager.NETWORK_PROVIDER);

if (!gpsStatus || !networkStatus) {
    //---display the "Location services" settings page---
    Intent in = new
        Intent(
    android.provider.Settings.ACTION_LOCATION_SOURCE_SETTINGS);
    startActivity(in);
}
}
```

If a particular setting is not enabled, you use an Intent object to direct the user to the Settings page (see Figure 9-2).

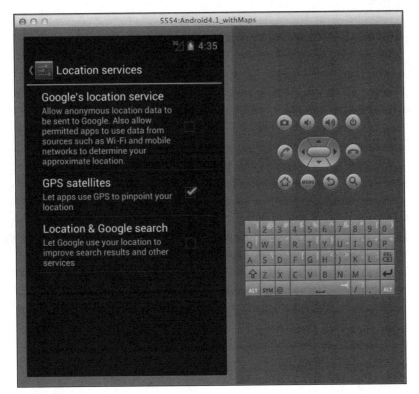

FIGURE 9-2

You also need to ensure that you add the relevant permission in your AndroidManifest.xml file:

```
<uses-permission android:name="android.permission.ACCESS_FINE_LOCATION"/>

<uses-permission android:name="android.permission.ACCESS_COARSE_LOCATION"/>
```

Note that you are not allowed to programmatically turn on the GPS or network provider, like this:

```
//---the following statement will crash---
//---having WRITE_SECURE_SETTINGS permission will not help---
Settings.Secure.putString(getContentResolver(),
    Settings.Secure.LOCATION_PROVIDERS_ALLOWED, "network,gps");
```

RECIPE 9.5 CAPTURING HARDWARE BUTTONS PROGRAMMATICALLY

Android Versions

Level 1 and above

Permissions

None

Source Code to Download from Wrox.com

CaptureHardwareButtons.zip

In addition to the standard hardware buttons such as Home, MENU, Back, and Search, some Android devices have built-in keyboards and a directional pad. This recipe shows you how to programmatically capture the pressing of these buttons so that your application can override their built-in functions. For example, the default behavior of the Back button on an Android device will remove the current active activity and display the previous activity. You may want to override this behavior by capturing the Back button so that the application can perform something else (such as confirming with the user if he really wants to quit the current activity) when the Back button is pressed.

Solution

To capture the various hardware buttons on your Android device, you need to implement the onKeyDown() method in your activity, as shown in the following example:

```java
package com.example.capturehardwarebuttons;

import android.app.Activity;
import android.os.Bundle;
import android.view.KeyEvent;
import android.view.Menu;
import android.widget.Toast;

public class MainActivity extends Activity {

    @Override
```

```
public void onCreate(Bundle savedInstanceState) {
    super.onCreate(savedInstanceState);
    setContentView(R.layout.activity_main);
}

@Override
public boolean onCreateOptionsMenu(Menu menu) {
    getMenuInflater().inflate(R.menu.activity_main, menu);
    return true;
}

public boolean onKeyDown(int keyCode, KeyEvent event) {
    switch (keyCode) {
    case KeyEvent.KEYCODE_DPAD_CENTER:
        Toast.makeText(this, "The Center key was pressed",
                Toast.LENGTH_SHORT).show();
        return true;

    case KeyEvent.KEYCODE_DPAD_RIGHT:
        Toast.makeText(this, "The Right key was pressed",
                Toast.LENGTH_SHORT).show();
        return true;

    case KeyEvent.KEYCODE_DPAD_LEFT:
        Toast.makeText(this, "The Left key was pressed", Toast.LENGTH_SHORT)
                .show();
        return true;

    case KeyEvent.KEYCODE_BACK:
        Toast.makeText(this, "The Back key was pressed", Toast.LENGTH_SHORT)
                .show();

        //---this event has been handled---
        return true;
    }

    //---this event has not been handled---
    return false;
}

}
```

In the preceding code snippet, you identify the various buttons using the `keyCode` argument of the `OnKeyDown()` method. Here, you specifically trap the various buttons on the directional page (center, right, and left) as well as the Back button.

> **NOTE** *Most modern Android devices do not have the directional keypad, which was popularized by device makers such as Samsung and HTC. Figure 9-3 shows the directional pad of the Samsung Galaxy I7500.*

FIGURE 9-3

Figure 9-4 shows the `Toast` class displaying which button was pressed when you click the directional pad on the emulator.

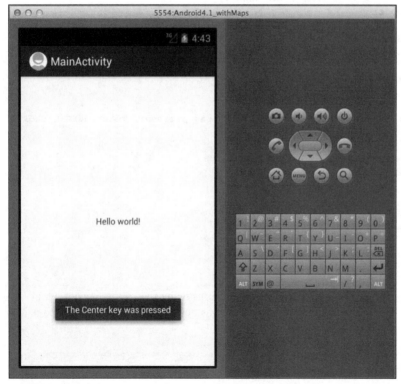

FIGURE 9-4

Note that the preceding example disables the Back key, so you will not be able to dismiss the activity anymore. To dismiss the activity, you have two options. If you want to move the entire task to the background, use the `moveTaskToBack()` method, like this:

```
case KeyEvent.KEYCODE_BACK:
    Toast.makeText(this, "The Back key was pressed",
        Toast.LENGTH_SHORT).show();

    //---move the entire task to the background---
    moveTaskToBack(true);

    //---this event has been handled---
    return true;
}
```

This moves the activity to the background but does not destroy it. If you do want the activity to be destroyed when the user presses the Back button, use the `finish()` method:

```
case KeyEvent.KEYCODE_BACK:
    Toast.makeText(this, "The Back key was pressed",
        Toast.LENGTH_SHORT).show();

    //---destroy the current activity---
    finish();

    //---this event has been handled---
    return true;
}
```

RECIPE 9.6 SWITCHING ON THE FLASHLIGHT

Android Versions

Level 1 and above

Permissions

CAMERA

FLASHLIGHT

Source Code to Download from Wrox.com

Flashlight.zip

Along with the built-in cameras that most Android devices offer, a flashlight is usually included next to the camera on the back of the device. This recipe shows you how to activate the flashlight of your camera.

Solution

To activate the flashlight on your Android device, you first need to declare two permissions:

```
<uses-permission android:name="android.permission.CAMERA" />

<uses-permission android:name="android.permission.FLASHLIGHT"/>
```

You also need to have a `SurfaceView` in your UI to display the preview of images taken with the camera:

```
<LinearLayout xmlns:android="http://schemas.android.com/apk/res/android"
    android:layout_width="fill_parent"
    android:layout_height="fill_parent"
    android:orientation="vertical" >

    <Button
        android:id="@+id/button1"
        android:layout_width="match_parent"
        android:layout_height="wrap_content"
        android:text="Turn On Flash"
        android:onClick="TurnOn"/>

    <Button
        android:id="@+id/button2"
        android:layout_width="match_parent"
        android:layout_height="wrap_content"
        android:text="Turn Off Flash"
        android:onClick="TurnOff"/>

    <SurfaceView
        android:id="@+id/surface1"
        android:layout_width="match_parent"
        android:layout_height="200dp"/>

</LinearLayout>
```

The `SurfaceView` view provides a dedicated drawing surface to display the images captured by your camera.

In your activity, you also need to implement the `SurfaceHolder.Callback` interface and the various methods declared in this interface:

```
package net.learn2develop.flashlight;

import java.io.IOException;

import android.app.Activity;
import android.content.pm.PackageManager;
import android.hardware.Camera;
import android.hardware.Camera.Parameters;
import android.os.Bundle;
import android.util.Log;
import android.view.Menu;
```

```
import android.view.SurfaceHolder;
import android.view.SurfaceView;
import android.view.View;

public class MainActivity extends Activity implements SurfaceHolder.Callback {

    SurfaceView surfaceView;
    SurfaceHolder surfaceHolder;
    Camera camera;

    @Override
    public void onCreate(Bundle savedInstanceState) {
        super.onCreate(savedInstanceState);
        setContentView(R.layout.activity_main);

        surfaceView = (SurfaceView) this.findViewById(R.id.surface1);
        surfaceHolder = surfaceView.getHolder();
        surfaceHolder.addCallback(this);
    }

    @Override
    public boolean onCreateOptionsMenu(Menu menu) {
        getMenuInflater().inflate(R.menu.activity_main, menu);
        return true;
    }

    public void surfaceChanged(SurfaceHolder arg0, int arg1, int arg2, int arg3) {
    }

    public void surfaceCreated(SurfaceHolder arg0) {
    }

    public void surfaceDestroyed(SurfaceHolder arg0) {
    }

    @Override
    public void onResume() {
        super.onResume();
        try {
            camera = Camera.open();
        } catch (Exception e) {
            //---exception handling here---
            Log.d("Flashlight", e.toString());
        }
    }

    @Override
    public void onPause() {
        super.onPause();
        TurnOff(null);
        camera.release();
    }

    public void TurnOn(View view) {
        if (FlashAvailable() && camera != null) {
            Parameters p = camera.getParameters();
```

```
            //---works with Android 2.x as well---
            p.setFlashMode(Parameters.FLASH_MODE_TORCH);
            camera.setParameters(p);
            camera.startPreview();
            try {
                camera.setPreviewDisplay(surfaceHolder);
            } catch (IOException e) {
                e.printStackTrace();
            }
        }
    }

    public void TurnOff(View view) {
        if (FlashAvailable() && camera != null) {
            Parameters p = camera.getParameters();
            p.setFlashMode(Parameters.FLASH_MODE_OFF);
            camera.setParameters(p);
            camera.stopPreview();
        }
    }

    private Boolean FlashAvailable() {
        return getPackageManager().hasSystemFeature(
            PackageManager.FEATURE_CAMERA_FLASH);
    }

}
```

In the `onCreate()` method, you basically get a reference to the `SurfaceView` and its holder (display surface) and then add a callback interface to this holder:

```
surfaceView = (SurfaceView) this.findViewById(R.id.surface1);
surfaceHolder = surfaceView.getHolder();
surfaceHolder.addCallback(this);
```

Before you activate the flash, you need to check its availability:

```
private Boolean FlashAvailable() {
    return getPackageManager().hasSystemFeature(
        PackageManager.FEATURE_CAMERA_FLASH);
}
```

To create a `Camera` object, call the `open()` method of the `Camera` class:

```
camera = Camera.open();
```

To turn on the camera and the flash, obtain an instance of the `Parameters` class, which enables you to set the various parameters of the camera. To turn on the flash, use the `setFlashMode()` method together with the `FLASH_MODE_TORCH` constant. Finally, the `startPreview()` method starts the camera together with the flash:

```
if (FlashAvailable() && camera != null) {
    Parameters p = camera.getParameters();
    //---works with Android 2.x as well---
    p.setFlashMode(Parameters.FLASH_MODE_TORCH);
    camera.setParameters(p);
```

```
        camera.startPreview();
        try {
            camera.setPreviewDisplay(surfaceHolder);
        } catch (IOException e) {
            e.printStackTrace();
        }
    }
```

To turn off the flash, simply use the FLASH_MODE_OFF constant:

```
if (FlashAvailable() && camera != null) {
    Parameters p = camera.getParameters();
    p.setFlashMode(Parameters.FLASH_MODE_OFF);
    camera.setParameters(p);
    camera.stopPreview();
}
```

Figure 9-5 shows that when the flash is enabled, the SurfaceView view displays images captured by the camera.

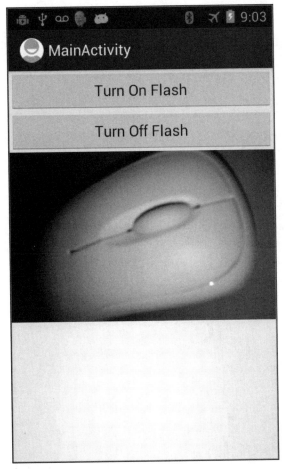

FIGURE 9-5

> **NOTE** *You need to ensure that the* SurfaceView *has at least 1 pixel for the width as well as the height. Otherwise, the flashlight will not work.*

If you want to turn on the flashlight without showing the preview of the camera, you can hide the SurfaceView behind some other views. The following code snippet shows the SurfaceView hidden behind an ImageView using the FrameLayout:

```xml
<LinearLayout xmlns:android="http://schemas.android.com/apk/res/android"
    android:layout_width="fill_parent"
    android:layout_height="fill_parent"
    android:orientation="vertical" >

    <Button
        android:id="@+id/button1"
        android:layout_width="match_parent"
        android:layout_height="wrap_content"
        android:onClick="TurnOn"
        android:text="Turn On Flash" />

    <Button
        android:id="@+id/button2"
        android:layout_width="match_parent"
        android:layout_height="wrap_content"
        android:onClick="TurnOff"
        android:text="Turn Off Flash" />

    <FrameLayout
        android:id="@+id/mainlayout"
        android:layout_width="fill_parent"
        android:layout_height="fill_parent"
        android:orientation="vertical" >

        <SurfaceView
            android:id="@+id/surface1"
            android:layout_width="200dp"
            android:layout_height="200dp" />

        <ImageView
            android:layout_width="200dp"
            android:layout_height="200dp"
            android:src="@drawable/android" />
    </FrameLayout>

</LinearLayout>
```

Figure 9-6 shows the SurfaceView hidden by the ImageView.

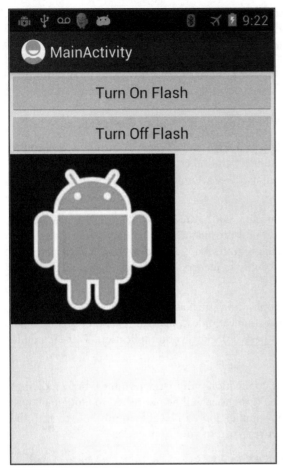

FIGURE 9-6

RECIPE 9.7 CAPTURING BARCODES

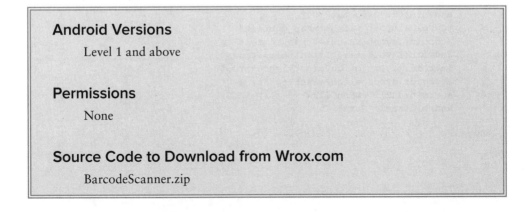

Android Versions

Level 1 and above

Permissions

None

Source Code to Download from Wrox.com

BarcodeScanner.zip

Because most currently sold Android devices include a built-in camera, it would be nice to get the most out of it. For example, you can put it to good use by enabling it to scan barcodes. This recipe describes how to enable your Android application to scan the different types of barcodes available on the market today.

Solution

There are a number of ways to make use of your built-in camera as a barcode scanner:

➤ Write your own image processing routine to interpret the image captured by the camera. This approach is not for the faint of heart and takes considerable effort to achieve. Moreover, you are reinventing the wheel, as there are many libraries available on the market that do exactly that.

➤ Make use of third-party libraries that you can incorporate into your application. ZXing is one such library. ZXing is an open-source, multi-format 1D/2D barcode image processing library implemented in Java. This approach requires knowing how to use a library in your project, but it provides the maximum flexibility to incorporate barcode scanning capability into your project.

➤ Use an `Intent` object to call a barcode application (such as ZXing's Barcode Scanner) installed on the Android device so that the application can perform the barcode scanning. Once the barcode is scanned, the result is passed back to your application. This method is the easiest.

This recipe demonstrates the third method. Your application will first determine whether ZXing's Barcode Scanner is installed on the device. If it isn't, the user will be redirected to Google Play to download the app. Once the app is installed, your application will be able to invoke it to scan the barcodes. Once a barcode is scanned, the result is returned to your application.

First, add a button to the UI of your application, such as the `activity_main.xml` file:

```
<RelativeLayout xmlns:android="http://schemas.android.com/apk/res/android"
    xmlns:tools="http://schemas.android.com/tools"
    android:layout_width="match_parent"
    android:layout_height="match_parent" >

    <Button
        android:id="@+id/button1"
        android:layout_width="wrap_content"
        android:layout_height="wrap_content"
        android:layout_alignParentLeft="true"
        android:layout_alignParentRight="true"
        android:layout_alignParentTop="true"
        android:onClick="onClick"
        android:text="Scan" />

</RelativeLayout>
```

To use ZXing's Barcode Scanner, you need to add two Java class files to your project (see Figure 9-7).

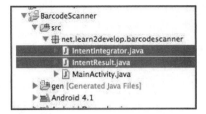

The `IntentIntegrator` class contains code that checks whether the Android device has the ZXing Barcode Scanner installed. If it does not have the application, it redirects the user to Google Play to download it.

FIGURE 9-7

> **NOTE** *The source of the* `IntentIntegrator` *class is* `http://code.google.com/p/zxing/source/browse/trunk/android-integration/src/com/google/zxing/integration/android/IntentIntegrator.java`.

Populate the `IntentIntegrator.java` file with the content found from the `http://code.google.com/p/zxing/source/browse/trunk/android-integration/src/com/google/zxing/integration/android/IntentIntegrator.java`.

The `IntentResult` class is for encapsulating the result of the scan obtained by the ZXing Barcode Scanner.

> **NOTE** *The source for the* `IntentResult` *class is* `http://code.google.com/p/zxing/source/browse/trunk/android-integration/src/com/google/zxing/integration/android/IntentResult.java?r=1273`.

Populate the `IntentResult.java` file from the content found on this URL: `http://code.google.com/p/zxing/source/browse/trunk/android-integration/src/com/google/zxing/integration/android/IntentResult.java?r=1273`.

Finally, add the following statements in bold to the `MainActivity.java` file:

```
package net.learn2develop.barcodescanner;

import android.app.Activity;
import android.content.Intent;
import android.os.Bundle;
import android.view.Menu;
import android.view.View;
import android.widget.Toast;

public class MainActivity extends Activity {

    @Override
    public void onCreate(Bundle savedInstanceState) {
        super.onCreate(savedInstanceState);
        setContentView(R.layout.activity_main);
    }
```

```
@Override
public boolean onCreateOptionsMenu(Menu menu) {
    getMenuInflater().inflate(R.menu.activity_main, menu);
    return true;
}

public void onClick(View v) {
    IntentIntegrator integrator = new IntentIntegrator(this);
    integrator.initiateScan();
}

public void onActivityResult(int requestCode, int resultCode,
Intent intent)
{
    IntentResult scanResult = IntentIntegrator.parseActivityResult(
            requestCode, resultCode, intent);
    if (scanResult != null) {
        //---handle scan result---
        Toast.makeText(this, scanResult.getContents(),
            Toast.LENGTH_LONG).show();
    }
}
}
```

To start scanning, you call the `initiateScan()` method from the `IntentIntegrator` class. When the barcode is obtained, you can get it from the `IntentResult` object, which is obtained from the `parseActivityResult()` method of the `IntentIntegrator` class.

When you run the application (by tapping the Scan button) on a device that does not have the ZXing Barcode Scanner installed, it will prompt you to install it (see Figure 9-8).

You will be redirected to Google Play (see Figure 9-9) to download and install it.

After the ZXing Barcode Scanner is installed, return to the application and tap the Scan button again. This time it will activate the camera to scan for barcodes (see Figure 9-10). Once a barcode is scanned, your application displays the barcode in a `Toast` class.

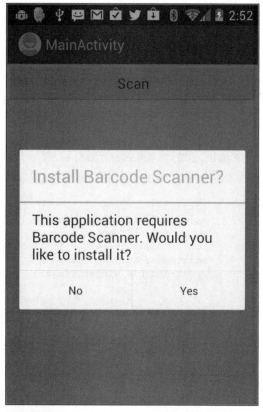

FIGURE 9-8

FIGURE 9-9

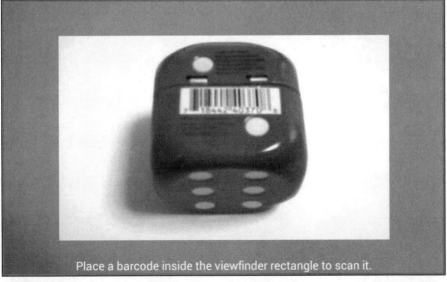

Place a barcode inside the viewfinder rectangle to scan it.

FIGURE 9-10

10

Persisting Data

In this chapter, you will learn how to persist data in your Android applications. Persisting data is an important topic in application development, as users expect to reuse the data some time at a later stage. For Android, there are primarily three basic ways of persisting data:

➤ A lightweight mechanism known as *shared preferences* to save small chunks of data

➤ Traditional filesystems

➤ A relational database management system through the support of SQLite databases

The recipes discussed in this chapter enable your Android applications to persist data to permanent storage.

RECIPE 10.1 SAVING AND LOADING USER PREFERENCES

Android versions

Level 1 and above

Permissions

None

Source code to download from Wrox.com

Preferences.zip

Android provides the SharedPreferences object to help you save simple application data. Using the SharedPreferences object, you can save the data you want through the use of key/value pairs — specify a key for the data you want to save, and then both it and its value will be saved automatically to an XML file. This feature is known as *shared preferences* in Android.

Solution

To use the SharedPreferences object, create a variable of type SharedPreferences:

```
package net.learn2develop.preferences;

import android.app.Activity;
import android.content.SharedPreferences;
import android.os.Bundle;

public class MainActivity extends Activity {
    SharedPreferences prefs;
    String prefName = "MyPref";

    @Override
    public void onCreate(Bundle savedInstanceState) {
        super.onCreate(savedInstanceState);
        setContentView(R.layout.activity_main);
    }

}
```

In the preceding code snippet, you also created a string variable to store the name of the preference file that will be created later by the SharedPreferences object.

Before using the SharedPreferences object, use the getSharedPreferences() method to obtain an instance of the SharedPreferences object, passing it the name of the preference file, as well as the operating mode (MODE_PRIVATE is the default):

```
    @Override
    public void onCreate(Bundle savedInstanceState) {
        super.onCreate(savedInstanceState);
        setContentView(R.layout.activity_main);

        //---get the SharedPreferences object---
        prefs = getSharedPreferences(prefName, MODE_PRIVATE);
    }
```

To save some values into the SharedPreferences object, you need to create an instance of the SharedPreferences.Editor class so that the values can be added in batches:

```
        //---get the SharedPreferences object---
        prefs = getSharedPreferences(prefName, MODE_PRIVATE);

        SharedPreferences.Editor editor = prefs.edit();
```

You can now add key/value pairs to the `Editor` object using its various methods (which one you use depends on the type of data you are saving):

```
SharedPreferences.Editor editor = prefs.edit();

//---save some values using the SharedPreferences object---
editor.putFloat("temperature", 85);
editor.putBoolean("authenticated", true);
editor.putString("username", "Wei-Meng Lee");
```

Finally, you use the `commit()` method to commit your changes back to the `SharedPreferences` object so that the values can be saved to persistent storage:

```
//---save some values using the SharedPreferences object---
editor.putFloat("temperature", 85);
editor.putBoolean("authenticated", true);
editor.putString("username", "Wei-Meng Lee");

//---saves the values---
editor.commit();
```

Retrieving data from the `SharedPreferences` object is similar — you obtain an instance of the `SharedPreferences` object and then use the various methods (depending on the type of data you are retrieving) to get the values based on the keys:

```
public void readPrefValues() {
    prefs = getSharedPreferences(prefName, MODE_PRIVATE);
    float temperature = prefs.getFloat("temperature", 50);
    boolean authenticated = prefs.getBoolean("authenticated", false);
    String username = prefs.getString("username", "");
}

@Override
public void onCreate(Bundle savedInstanceState) {
    super.onCreate(savedInstanceState);
    setContentView(R.layout.activity_main);

    //---get the SharedPreferences object---
    prefs = getSharedPreferences(prefName, MODE_PRIVATE);

    SharedPreferences.Editor editor = prefs.edit();

    //---save some values using the SharedPreferences object---
    editor.putFloat("temperature", 85);
    editor.putBoolean("authenticated", true);
    editor.putString("username", "Wei-Meng Lee");

    //---saves the values---
    editor.commit();

    readPrefValues();
}
```

Note that each method allows you to specify a default value in the event that the key you are retrieving cannot be found.

The key/value pairs saved by the `SharedPreferences` object will be saved in the `/data/data/<package_name>/shared_prefs` folder and named `MyPref.xml` (see Figure 10-1).

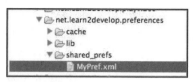

FIGURE 10-1

RECIPE 10.2 CREATING A PREFERENCE SCREEN

Android versions

Level 1 and above

Permissions

None

Source code to download from Wrox.com

PreferenceScreens.zip

The previous recipe shows how to use the `SharedPreferences` object to store key/value pairs programmatically from within your Android application. If you want to let the users edit the values of these data directly, you can use a *preference activity*.

Solution

Instead of programmatically creating the key/value pairs to store in the `SharedPreferences` object, you can define the various keys in an XML file. To do so, create a new `xml` folder under the `res` folder in your project. Within this folder, create an XML file and name it something meaningful, such as `myapppreferences.xml`. Populate the `myapppreferences.xml` file as follows:

```
<PreferenceScreen xmlns:android="http://schemas.android.com/apk/res/android" >
    <PreferenceCategory android:title="Category 1" >
        <CheckBoxPreference
            android:defaultValue="false"
            android:key="checkboxPref"
            android:summary="True or False"
            android:title="Checkbox" />
    </PreferenceCategory>

    <PreferenceCategory android:title="Category 2" >
        <EditTextPreference
            android:defaultValue="[Enter a string here]"
            android:key="editTextPref"
```

```
            android:summary="Enter a string"
            android:title="Edit Text" />

        <RingtonePreference
            android:key="ringtonePref"
            android:summary="Select a ringtone"
            android:title="Ringtones" />

        <PreferenceScreen
            android:key="secondPrefScreenPref"
            android:summary="Click here to go to the second Preference Screen"
            android:title="Second Preference Screen" >
            <EditTextPreference
                android:key="secondEditTextPref"
                android:summary="Enter a string"
                android:title="Edit Text (second Screen)" />
        </PreferenceScreen>
    </PreferenceCategory>
</PreferenceScreen>
```

In the package of your project, add a new Java class file and name it `AppPreferenceActivity.java`. Populate it as follows:

```
package net.learn2develop.preferencescreens;

import android.os.Bundle;
import android.preference.PreferenceActivity;

public class AppPreferenceActivity extends PreferenceActivity {
    @Override
    public void onCreate(Bundle savedInstanceState) {
        super.onCreate(savedInstanceState);

        //---load the preferences from an XML file---
        addPreferencesFromResource(R.xml.myapppreferences);
    }
}
```

Observe that the `AppPreferenceActivity` class extends the `PreferenceActivity` base class. When it is created, it uses the `addPreferencesFromResource()` method to load the preference keys from the `myapppreferences.xml` file.

To make the `AppPreferenceActivity` class callable, you need to declare it in the `AndroidManifest.xml` file:

```
<manifest xmlns:android="http://schemas.android.com/apk/res/android"
    package="net.learn2develop.preferencescreens"
    android:versionCode="1"
    android:versionName="1.0" >

    <uses-sdk
        android:minSdkVersion="8"
        android:targetSdkVersion="15" />
```

```xml
<application
    android:icon="@drawable/ic_launcher"
    android:label="@string/app_name"
    android:theme="@style/AppTheme" >
    <activity
        android:name=".MainActivity"
        android:label="@string/title_activity_main" >
        <intent-filter>
            <action android:name="android.intent.action.MAIN" />

            <category android:name="android.intent.category.LAUNCHER" />
        </intent-filter>
    </activity>

    <activity android:name=".AppPreferenceActivity"
            android:label="@string/app_name">
        <intent-filter>
            <action
                android:name="net.learn2develop.AppPreferenceActivity" />
            <category android:name="android.intent.category.DEFAULT" />
        </intent-filter>
    </activity>

</application>

</manifest>
```

To display the `AppPreferenceActivity` class, you use an `Intent` object, like this:

```java
package net.learn2develop.preferencescreens;

import android.app.Activity;
import android.content.Intent;
import android.os.Bundle;

public class MainActivity extends Activity {

    @Override
    public void onCreate(Bundle savedInstanceState) {
        super.onCreate(savedInstanceState);
        setContentView(R.layout.activity_main);

        Intent i = new Intent("net.learn2develop.AppPreferenceActivity");
        startActivity(i);
    }

}
```

When the `AppPreferenceActivity` class is displayed, it will look like Figure 10-2.

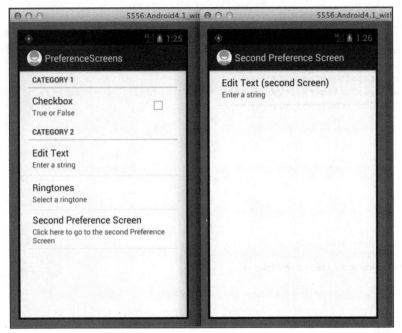

FIGURE 10-2

The key/value pairs are saved in the /data/ data/<package_name>/shared_prefs folder and named <package_name>_preferences.xml (see Figure 10-3).

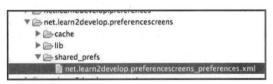

FIGURE 10-3

To programmatically retrieve the saved key/value pairs in the preferences file, you can use the get-SharedPreferences() method as shown in the previous recipe:

```
package net.learn2develop.preferencescreens;

import android.app.Activity;
import android.content.SharedPreferences;
import android.os.Bundle;
import android.widget.Toast;

public class MainActivity extends Activity {

    @Override
    public void onCreate(Bundle savedInstanceState) {
        super.onCreate(savedInstanceState);
        setContentView(R.layout.activity_main);

        /*
        Intent i = new Intent("net.learn2develop.AppPreferenceActivity");
        startActivity(i);
        */
```

```
        SharedPreferences appPrefs = getSharedPreferences(
            "net.learn2develop.PreferenceScreens_preferences",
            MODE_PRIVATE);

        Toast.makeText(getBaseContext(),
            appPrefs.getString("editTextPref", ""),
            Toast.LENGTH_LONG).show();
    }

}
```

If you want to change the default name of the preferences file, you can use the `PreferenceManager` class and then use the `setSharedPreferencesName()` method to set the name you want:

```
package net.learn2develop.preferencescreens;

import android.os.Bundle;
import android.preference.PreferenceActivity;
import android.preference.PreferenceManager;

public class AppPreferenceActivity extends PreferenceActivity {
    @Override
    public void onCreate(Bundle savedInstanceState) {
        super.onCreate(savedInstanceState);

        PreferenceManager prefMgr = getPreferenceManager();
        prefMgr.setSharedPreferencesName("appPreferences");

        //---load the preferences from an XML file---
        addPreferencesFromResource(R.xml.myapppreferences);
    }
}
```

The preceding code snippet sets the preferences file as `appPreferences.xml`. You can verify this by looking at the `shared_prefs` folder again. This time, the `appPreferences.xml` file is created.

To programmatically retrieve the newly named preferences file, make sure you change the name passed to the `getSharedPreferences()` method accordingly:

```
    @Override
    public void onCreate(Bundle savedInstanceState) {
        super.onCreate(savedInstanceState);
        setContentView(R.layout.activity_main);

        /*
        Intent i = new Intent("net.learn2develop.AppPreferenceActivity");
        startActivity(i);
        */

        /*
        SharedPreferences appPrefs = getSharedPreferences(
            "net.learn2develop.PreferenceScreens_preferences",
            MODE_PRIVATE);
        */
```

```
SharedPreferences appPrefs =
        getSharedPreferences("appPreferences", MODE_PRIVATE);

Toast.makeText(getBaseContext(),
    appPrefs.getString("editTextPref", ""),
    Toast.LENGTH_LONG).show();
}
```

RECIPE 10.3 SAVING FILES TO THE DATA DIRECTORY

Android versions

Level 1 and above

Permissions

None

Source code to download from Wrox.com

Files.zip

If the data you want to preserve cannot be best represented as key/value pairs, then you might want to use the primitive method of saving it directly to the filesystem as files. This option is useful for saving long strings of text, or binary data.

Solution

To create a file for saving, you can use the openFileOutput() method, specifying the filename and the mode in which you want the file to be opened. This method will then return a FileOutputStream object:

```
package net.learn2develop.files;

import java.io.FileOutputStream;
import java.io.IOException;

import android.app.Activity;
import android.os.Bundle;

public class MainActivity extends Activity {

    @Override
    public void onCreate(Bundle savedInstanceState) {
        super.onCreate(savedInstanceState);
        setContentView(R.layout.activity_main);
```

```
            //---writing to files---
            try {
                FileOutputStream fOut =
                    openFileOutput("textfile.txt", MODE_PRIVATE);
            } catch (IOException ioe) {
                ioe.printStackTrace();
            }
        }


    }
```

For writing bytes to a file, use the `OutputStreamWriter` class and use its `write()` method to write a string to the file. To save the changes to the file, use its `close()` method:

```
package net.learn2develop.files;

import java.io.FileOutputStream;
import java.io.IOException;
import java.io.OutputStreamWriter;

import android.app.Activity;
import android.os.Bundle;
import android.widget.Toast;

public class MainActivity extends Activity {

    @Override
    public void onCreate(Bundle savedInstanceState) {
        super.onCreate(savedInstanceState);
        setContentView(R.layout.activity_main);

        //---writing to files---
        try {
            FileOutputStream fOut =
                openFileOutput("textfile.txt", MODE_PRIVATE);

            OutputStreamWriter osw = new OutputStreamWriter(fOut);

            //---write the string to the file---
            osw.write("The quick brown fox jumps over the lazy dog");
            osw.close();

            //---display file saved message---
            Toast.makeText(getBaseContext(), "File saved successfully!",
                    Toast.LENGTH_SHORT).show();
        } catch (IOException ioe) {
            ioe.printStackTrace();
        }
    }


}
```

When the file is created, it will be saved in the `/data/data/`
`<package_name>/files` folder (see Figure 10-4).

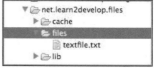

FIGURE 10-4

> **NOTE** *Files that are stored in the* `files` *folder are persistent. They remain there until you explicitly delete them.*

Likewise, you use the `openFileInput()` method to open a file for reading. It returns a `FileInputStream` object, which you can pass to an `InputStreamReader` object for reading:

```java
package net.learn2develop.files;

import java.io.FileInputStream;
import java.io.FileOutputStream;
import java.io.IOException;
import java.io.InputStreamReader;
import java.io.OutputStreamWriter;

import android.app.Activity;
import android.os.Bundle;
import android.widget.Toast;

public class MainActivity extends Activity {

    @Override
    public void onCreate(Bundle savedInstanceState) {
        super.onCreate(savedInstanceState);
        setContentView(R.layout.activity_main);

        //---writing to files---
        try {
            FileOutputStream fOut =
                openFileOutput("textfile.txt", MODE_PRIVATE);

            OutputStreamWriter osw = new OutputStreamWriter(fOut);

            //---write the string to the file---
            osw.write("The quick brown fox jumps over the lazy dog");
            osw.close();

            //---display file saved message---
            Toast.makeText(getBaseContext(), "File saved successfully!",
                    Toast.LENGTH_SHORT).show();
        } catch (IOException ioe) {
            ioe.printStackTrace();
        }

        //---reading from files---
        try
        {
            FileInputStream fIn =
                openFileInput("textfile.txt");
            InputStreamReader isr = new
                InputStreamReader(fIn);
        }
```

```
                    catch (IOException ioe) {
                        ioe.printStackTrace();
                    }
                }

            }
```

Because you do not know how many characters need to be read from the file, you use the `read()` method from the `InputStreamReader` object to read in the characters in blocks of 100 bytes (you can change this to a value reasonable to you). The `read()` method returns the number of characters read, and reading continues until there are no more unread characters (it returns -1 when the end of the file is reached):

> **NOTE** *In this example, you read from the file in blocks of 100 bytes. But what about increasing the block size to 1000 bytes, or decreasing it to 50 bytes? You definitely can do that, but the size of the block is largely determined by the size of your files. If you usually have large files, then it makes more sense to have a large block size as more bytes can be read per iteration of the loop. On the other hand, large block size also takes up more memory since at any point in time you have to reserve memory for the buffer. In general, block sizes of up to 8K are reasonable.*

```
package net.learn2develop.files;

import java.io.FileInputStream;
import java.io.FileOutputStream;
import java.io.IOException;
import java.io.InputStreamReader;
import java.io.OutputStreamWriter;

import android.app.Activity;
import android.os.Bundle;
import android.widget.Toast;

public class MainActivity extends Activity {
    static final int READ_BLOCK_SIZE = 100;
    @Override
    public void onCreate(Bundle savedInstanceState) {
        super.onCreate(savedInstanceState);
        setContentView(R.layout.activity_main);

        //---writing to files---
        try {
            FileOutputStream fOut =
                openFileOutput("textfile.txt", MODE_PRIVATE);

            OutputStreamWriter osw = new OutputStreamWriter(fOut);
```

```
        //---write the string to the file---
        osw.write("The quick brown fox jumps over the lazy dog");
        osw.close();

        //---display file saved message---
        Toast.makeText(getBaseContext(), "File saved successfully!",
                Toast.LENGTH_SHORT).show();
    } catch (IOException ioe) {
        ioe.printStackTrace();
    }

    //---reading from files---
    try
    {
        FileInputStream fIn =
            openFileInput("textfile.txt");
        InputStreamReader isr = new
            InputStreamReader(fIn);

        char[] inputBuffer = new char[READ_BLOCK_SIZE];
        String s = "";
        int charRead;
        while ((charRead = isr.read(inputBuffer))>0)
        {
            //---convert the chars to a String---
            String readString =
                String.copyValueOf(inputBuffer, 0,
                charRead);
            s += readString;

            inputBuffer = new char[READ_BLOCK_SIZE];
        }
        isr.close();

        Toast.makeText(getBaseContext(),
            "File loaded successfully! " + s,
            Toast.LENGTH_SHORT).show();
    }
    catch (IOException ioe) {
        ioe.printStackTrace();
    }
}

}
```

> **NOTE** *The entire* /data/data/<package_name> *folder will be deleted when the user uninstalls the application.*

RECIPE 10.4 SAVING FILES TO THE CACHE DIRECTORY

Android versions

Level 1 and above

Permissions

None

Source code to download from Wrox.com

Cache.zip

Files stored in the `files` folder are persistent; they will always be there until you explicitly delete them. Sometimes, however, you may not want this to happen because you only need to save the files temporarily and do not need them again later. For this purpose, you should save the files into the `cache` folder.

> **NOTE** *Files stored in the cache folder are not persistent and will be removed by the OS when it is low on internal storage. However, it is always a good practice to clean up the folder yourself and restrict your application to using no more than 1MB.*

Solution

To save files to the cache directory, use the `getCacheDir()` method to return the absolute path to the application-specific cache directory on the filesystem. You can then use the `File` class to create a full path for the file that you want to store in the cache folder.

The following code snippet shows how to save a file into the cache folder and then read back its content:

```java
package net.learn2develop.cache;

import java.io.File;
import java.io.FileInputStream;
import java.io.FileOutputStream;
import java.io.IOException;
import java.io.InputStreamReader;
import java.io.OutputStreamWriter;

import android.app.Activity;
import android.os.Bundle;
import android.widget.Toast;
```

```java
public class MainActivity extends Activity {
    static final int READ_BLOCK_SIZE = 100;
    @Override
    public void onCreate(Bundle savedInstanceState) {
        super.onCreate(savedInstanceState);
        setContentView(R.layout.activity_main);

        //---Saving to the file in the Cache folder---
        try
        {
            //---get the Cache directory---
            File cacheDir = getCacheDir();
            File file = new File(cacheDir.getAbsolutePath(), "textfile.txt");

            FileOutputStream fOut = new
                FileOutputStream(file);

            OutputStreamWriter osw = new
                OutputStreamWriter(fOut);

            //---write the string to the file---
            osw.write("The quick brown fox jumps over the lazy dog");
            osw.flush();
            osw.close();

            //---display file saved message---
            Toast.makeText(getBaseContext(),
                "File saved successfully!",
                Toast.LENGTH_SHORT).show();
        }
        catch (IOException ioe)
        {
            ioe.printStackTrace();
        }

        //---Reading from the file in the Cache folder---
        try
        {
            //---get the Cache directory---
            File cacheDir = getCacheDir();
            File file = new File(cacheDir, "textfile.txt");
            FileInputStream fIn = new FileInputStream(file);

            InputStreamReader isr = new
                InputStreamReader(fIn);

            char[] inputBuffer = new char[READ_BLOCK_SIZE];
            String s = "";
            int charRead;
            while ((charRead = isr.read(inputBuffer))>0)
            {
                //---convert the chars to a String---
                String readString =
                    String.copyValueOf(inputBuffer, 0,
```

```
            charRead);
        s += readString;

    inputBuffer = new char[READ_BLOCK_SIZE];
    }
                isr.close();

    Toast.makeText(getBaseContext(),
        "File loaded successfully! " + s,
        Toast.LENGTH_SHORT).show();
    }
    catch (IOException ioe) {
        ioe.printStackTrace();
    }
}

}
```

When the preceding code snippet is run, the `textfile.txt` file will be created in the `/data/data/<package_name>/cache` folder (see Figure 10-5).

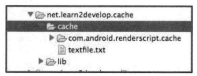

FIGURE 10-5

> **NOTE** *The entire* `/data/data/<package_name>` *folder will be deleted when the user uninstalls the application.*

RECIPE 10.5 SAVING FILES TO EXTERNAL STORAGE

Android versions

Level 1 and above

Permissions

android.permission.WRITE_EXTERNAL_STORAGE

Source code to download from Wrox.com

ExternalStorage.zip

The previous recipes show you how to save data to the application's filesystem on the device. In some cases, you might want to save the files to the device's external storage, such as the SD card.

> **NOTE** *In the context of Android, external storage does not necessarily mean physically external storage such as the SD card. It may also refer to storage on the device that is separate from the protected internal storage. External storage can be mounted by a user as a filesystem, and it may not always be accessible when it is mounted or removed.*

Solution

Before you write or read files from the external storage, it is always important to check whether it is available and writeable. The following method checks that:

```
package net.learn2develop.externalstorage;

import android.app.Activity;
import android.os.Bundle;
import android.os.Environment;

public class MainActivity extends Activity {

    @Override
    public void onCreate(Bundle savedInstanceState) {
        super.onCreate(savedInstanceState);
        setContentView(R.layout.activity_main);
    }

    public boolean IsExternalStorageAvailableAndWriteable() {
        boolean externalStorageAvailable = false;
        boolean externalStorageWriteable = false;
        String state = Environment.getExternalStorageState();

        if (Environment.MEDIA_MOUNTED.equals(state)) {
            //---you can read and write the media---
            externalStorageAvailable = externalStorageWriteable = true;
        } else if (Environment.MEDIA_MOUNTED_READ_ONLY.equals(state)) {
            //---you can only read the media---
            externalStorageAvailable = true;
            externalStorageWriteable = false;
        } else {
            //---you cannot read nor write the media---
            externalStorageAvailable = externalStorageWriteable = false;
        }
        return externalStorageAvailable && externalStorageWriteable;
    }

}
```

To save a file to the application's specific folder on the external storage, use the `getExternalFilesDir()` method (available only for API level 8 and above), passing it a type argument. If the type is `null`, then it returns the absolute path to the application's directory on the external filesystem:

```
package net.learn2develop.externalstorage;

import java.io.File;
import java.io.FileOutputStream;
import java.io.IOException;
import java.io.OutputStreamWriter;

import android.app.Activity;
import android.os.Bundle;
import android.os.Environment;
import android.widget.Toast;

public class MainActivity extends Activity {

    @Override
    public void onCreate(Bundle savedInstanceState) {
        super.onCreate(savedInstanceState);
        setContentView(R.layout.activity_main);

        //---writing to files---
        try
        {
            if (IsExternalStorageAvailableAndWriteable()) {
                //---external Storage---
                File extStorage =
                        getExternalFilesDir(null);
                File file = new File(extStorage, "textfile.txt");

                FileOutputStream fOut = new
                        FileOutputStream(file);

                OutputStreamWriter osw = new
                        OutputStreamWriter(fOut);

                //---write the string to the file---
                osw.write("The quick brown fox jumps over the lazy dog");
                osw.flush();
                osw.close();

                //---display file saved message---
                Toast.makeText(getBaseContext(),
                        "File saved successfully!",
                        Toast.LENGTH_SHORT).show();
            }
        }
        catch (IOException ioe)
        {
            ioe.printStackTrace();
        }
    }
```

```
    public boolean IsExternalStorageAvailableAndWriteable() {
        ...
    }

}
```

The preceding code snippets create the `textfile.txt` file in the `/mnt/sdcard/Android/data/<package_name>/files` folder.

> **NOTE** *The entire* `/mnt/sdcard/Android/data/<package_name>` *folder will be deleted when the user uninstalls the application.*

The following code snippet reads the same file from external storage:

```
package net.learn2develop.externalstorage;

import java.io.File;
import java.io.FileInputStream;
import java.io.FileOutputStream;
import java.io.IOException;
import java.io.InputStreamReader;
import java.io.OutputStreamWriter;

import android.app.Activity;
import android.os.Bundle;
import android.os.Environment;
import android.widget.Toast;

public class MainActivity extends Activity {
    static final int READ_BLOCK_SIZE = 100;

    @Override
    public void onCreate(Bundle savedInstanceState) {
        super.onCreate(savedInstanceState);
        setContentView(R.layout.activity_main);

        //---writing to files---
        try
        {
            if (IsExternalStorageAvailableAndWriteable()) {
                ...
            }
        }
        catch (IOException ioe)
        {
            ioe.printStackTrace();
        }

        //---reading from files---
        try
        {
```

```
            if (IsExternalStorageAvailableAndWriteable()) {
                //---External Storage---
                File extStorage =
                        getExternalFilesDir(null);
                File file = new File(extStorage, "textfile.txt");

                FileInputStream fIn = new FileInputStream(file);

                InputStreamReader isr = new
                        InputStreamReader(fIn);

                char[] inputBuffer = new char[READ_BLOCK_SIZE];
                String s = "";
                int charRead;
                while ((charRead = isr.read(inputBuffer))>0)
                {
                    //---convert the chars to a String---
                    String readString =
                            String.copyValueOf(inputBuffer, 0,
                                    charRead);
                    s += readString;

                    inputBuffer = new char[READ_BLOCK_SIZE];
                }
                isr.close();
                Toast.makeText(getBaseContext(),
                        "File loaded successfully! " + s,
                        Toast.LENGTH_SHORT).show();
            }
        }
        catch (IOException ioe) {
            ioe.printStackTrace();
        }
    }

    public boolean IsExternalStorageAvailableAndWriteable() {
        ...
    }

}
```

If you want to save your file in special directories that can be automatically discovered by the system, you can pass in a string constant to the getExternalFilesDir() method (available only for API level 8 and above), like this:

```
File extStorage =
        getExternalFilesDir(Environment.DIRECTORY_PICTURES);
```

The preceding code saves the file inside the /mnt/sdcard/Android/data/<package_name>/Pictures folder.

If you want to save to one of the public directories on the external storage, use the `getExternalStoragePublicDirectory()` method (available only for API level 8 and above):

```
File extStorage =
        Environment.getExternalStoragePublicDirectory(
        Environment.DIRECTORY_PICTURES);
```

The preceding code stores the file inside the `/mnt/sdcard/Pictures` folder. When you save the file to one of the public directories, the file remains there even if the user uninstalls your application.

If you want to save the file to the external storage's root folder, you can use the `getExternalStorageDirectory()` method (API level 1 and above):

```
File extStorage =
        Environment.getExternalStorageDirectory();
File directory = new File
        (extStorage.getAbsolutePath() + "/MyFiles");
directory.mkdirs();
File file = new File(directory, "textfile.txt");
```

The preceding code stores the file into the `/mnt/sdcard/MyFiles` folder.

Finally, note that to save a file to external storage, you need to add the `WRITE_EXTERNAL_STORAGE` permission to the `AndroidManifest.xml` file:

```
<uses-permission
    android:name="android.permission.WRITE_EXTERNAL_STORAGE" />
```

RECIPE 10.6 ATTACHING FILES TO YOUR PROJECT

Android versions

Level 1 and above

Permissions

None

Source code to download from Wrox.com

FileAttachment.zip

Besides creating files during runtime, it is also very common for developers to attach documents to a project during design time so that they are available during runtime. For example, you might want to attach HTML files to your project so that you can load them onto a `WebView` view later.

Solution

To attach a file to your project, create a `raw` folder under the `res` folder (see Figure 10-6). Add a file to it and name it, say, `textfile.txt`. Populate it with the string shown in the figure.

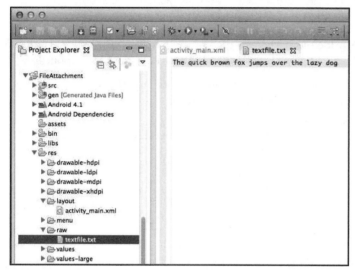

FIGURE 10-6

To read from the text file, use the `InputStream` class and refer to the file stored in the `raw` folder using the `get.Resources().openRawResource()` method:

```
package net.learn2develop.fileattachment;

import java.io.BufferedReader;
import java.io.IOException;
import java.io.InputStream;
import java.io.InputStreamReader;

import android.app.Activity;
import android.os.Bundle;
import android.widget.Toast;

public class MainActivity extends Activity {

    @Override
    public void onCreate(Bundle savedInstanceState) {
        super.onCreate(savedInstanceState);
        setContentView(R.layout.activity_main);

        InputStream is =
                this.getResources().openRawResource(R.raw.textfile);
        BufferedReader br =
```

```
            new BufferedReader(new InputStreamReader(is));
        String str = null;
        try {
            while ((str = br.readLine()) != null) {
                Toast.makeText(getBaseContext(), str,
                        Toast.LENGTH_SHORT).show();
            }
            is.close();
            br.close();
        } catch (IOException e) {
            e.printStackTrace();
        }
    }
}
```

RECIPE 10.7 CREATING AND USING SQLITE DATABASES PROGRAMMATICALLY

Android versions

Level 1 and above

Permissions

None

Source code to download from Wrox.com

Databases.zip

So far, all the recipes you have seen in this chapter are useful for saving simple sets of data. To save relational data, using a database is much more efficient. For example, to store the results of all the students in a school, it is much more efficient to use a database to represent them because you can use database querying to retrieve the results of specific students. Moreover, using databases enables you to enforce data integrity by specifying the relationships between different sets of data.

Android uses the SQLite database system. The database that you create for an application is only accessible to itself; other applications will not be able to access it.

In this recipe, you will learn how to programmatically create a SQLite database in your Android application. For Android, the SQLite database that you create programmatically in an application is always stored in the /data/data/<package_name>/databases folder.

Solution

A good practice for dealing with databases is to create a helper class to encapsulate all the complexities of accessing the data so that it is transparent to the calling code. Hence, for this recipe, you will create a helper class called DBAdapter (named DBAdapter.java) that creates, opens, closes, and uses a SQLite database.

In this example, you are going to create a database named MyDB containing one table named contacts. This table will have three columns: _id, name, and email (see Figure 10-7).

_id	name	email

FIGURE 10-7

The content of the DBAdapter class looks like this:

```
package net.learn2develop.databases;

import android.content.ContentValues;
import android.content.Context;
import android.database.Cursor;
import android.database.SQLException;
import android.database.sqlite.SQLiteDatabase;
import android.database.sqlite.SQLiteOpenHelper;
import android.util.Log;

public class DBAdapter {
    static final String KEY_ROWID = "_id";
    static final String KEY_NAME = "name";
    static final String KEY_EMAIL = "email";
    static final String TAG = "DBAdapter";

    static final String DATABASE_NAME = "MyDB";
    static final String DATABASE_TABLE = "contacts";
    static final int DATABASE_VERSION = 1;

    static final String DATABASE_CREATE =
        "create table contacts (_id integer primary key autoincrement, "
        + "name text not null, email text not null);";

    final Context context;

    DatabaseHelper DBHelper;
    SQLiteDatabase db;

    public DBAdapter(Context ctx)
    {
        this.context = ctx;
        DBHelper = new DatabaseHelper(context);
    }
```

```java
private static class DatabaseHelper extends SQLiteOpenHelper
{
    DatabaseHelper(Context context)
    {
        super(context, DATABASE_NAME, null, DATABASE_VERSION);
    }

    @Override
    public void onCreate(SQLiteDatabase db)
    {
        try {
            db.execSQL(DATABASE_CREATE);
        } catch (SQLException e) {
            e.printStackTrace();
        }
    }

    @Override
    public void onUpgrade(SQLiteDatabase db, int oldVersion, int newVersion)
    {
        Log.w(TAG, "Upgrading database from version " + oldVersion + " to "
                + newVersion + ", which will destroy all old data");
        db.execSQL("DROP TABLE IF EXISTS contacts");
        onCreate(db);
    }
}

//---opens the database---
public DBAdapter open() throws SQLException
{
    db = DBHelper.getWritableDatabase();
    return this;
}

//---closes the database---
public void close()
{
    DBHelper.close();
}

//---insert a contact into the database---
public long insertContact(String name, String email)
{
    ContentValues initialValues = new ContentValues();
    initialValues.put(KEY_NAME, name);
    initialValues.put(KEY_EMAIL, email);
    return db.insert(DATABASE_TABLE, null, initialValues);
}

//---deletes a particular contact---
public boolean deleteContact(long rowId)
{
    return db.delete(DATABASE_TABLE, KEY_ROWID + "=" + rowId, null) > 0;
}
```

```
        //---retrieves all the contacts---
        public Cursor getAllContacts()
        {
            return db.query(DATABASE_TABLE, new String[] {KEY_ROWID, KEY_NAME,
                    KEY_EMAIL}, null, null, null, null, null);
        }

        //---retrieves a particular contact---
        public Cursor getContact(long rowId) throws SQLException
        {
            Cursor mCursor =
                    db.query(true, DATABASE_TABLE, new String[] {KEY_ROWID,
                    KEY_NAME, KEY_EMAIL}, KEY_ROWID + "=" + rowId, null,
                    null, null, null, null);
            if (mCursor != null) {
                mCursor.moveToFirst();
            }
            return mCursor;
        }

        //---updates a contact---
        public boolean updateContact(long rowId, String name, String email)
        {
            ContentValues args = new ContentValues();
            args.put(KEY_NAME, name);
            args.put(KEY_EMAIL, email);
            return db.update(
                DATABASE_TABLE, args, KEY_ROWID + "=" + rowId, null) > 0;
        }
    }
```

In this class, you did the following:

➤ You first defined several constants to contain the various fields for the table that you are going to create in your database.

➤ You declared the DATABASE_CREATE constant to contain the SQL statement for creating the contacts table within the MyDB database.

➤ Within the DBAdapter class, you also added a private class that extends the SQLiteOpenHelper class, which is a helper class in Android for database creation and version management. In particular, you override the onCreate() and onUpgrade() methods.

> ➤ The onCreate() method creates a new database if the required database is not present.

> ➤ The onUpgrade() method is called when the database needs to be upgraded. This is achieved by checking the value defined in the DATABASE_VERSION constant. For this implementation of the onUpgrade() method, you simply drop the table and create it again.

You then define the various methods for opening and closing the database, as well as the methods for adding/editing/deleting rows in the table.

> **NOTE** *Android uses the* Cursor *class as a return value for queries. Think of the* Cursor *as a pointer to the result set from a database query. Using* Cursor *enables Android to more efficiently manage rows and columns as needed.*

➤ You use a ContentValues object to store key/value pairs. Its put() method enables you to insert keys with values of different data types.

To create a database in your application using the DBAdapter class, you create an instance of the DBAdapter class:

```
public DBAdapter(Context ctx)
{
    this.context = ctx;
    DBHelper = new DatabaseHelper(context);
}
```

The constructor of the DBAdapter class will then create an instance of the DatabaseHelper class to create a new database:

```
DatabaseHelper(Context context)
{
    super(context, DATABASE_NAME, null, DATABASE_VERSION);
}
```

To use the DBAdapter class that you have just defined, use the following methods (AddContact(), GetContacts(), GetContact(), UpdateContact(), DeleteContact(), and DisplayContact()):

```
package net.learn2develop.databases;

import android.app.Activity;
import android.database.Cursor;
import android.os.Bundle;
import android.widget.Toast;

public class MainActivity extends Activity {
    DBAdapter db;

    @Override
    public void onCreate(Bundle savedInstanceState) {
        super.onCreate(savedInstanceState);
        setContentView(R.layout.activity_main);

        db = new DBAdapter(this);

        AddContact();
        GetContacts();
        GetContact();
        UpdateContact();
        DeleteContact();
    }
```

```java
public void AddContact() {
    //---add a contact---
    db.open();
    if (db.insertContact(
        "Wei-Meng Lee", "weimenglee@learn2develop.net") >= 0){
        Toast.makeText(this, "Add successful.", Toast.LENGTH_LONG).show();
    }

    if (db.insertContact("Mary Jackson", "mary@jackson.com") >= 0) {
        Toast.makeText(this, "Add successful.", Toast.LENGTH_LONG).show();
    }
    db.close();
}

public void GetContacts() {
    //--get all contacts---
    db.open();
    Cursor c = db.getAllContacts();
    if (c.moveToFirst())
    {
        do {
            DisplayContact(c);
        } while (c.moveToNext());
    }
    db.close();
}

public void GetContact() {
    //---get a contact---
    db.open();
    Cursor c = db.getContact(2);
    if (c.moveToFirst())
        DisplayContact(c);
    else
        Toast.makeText(this, "No contact found", Toast.LENGTH_LONG).show();
    db.close();
}

public void UpdateContact() {
    //---update a contact---
    db.open();
    if (db.updateContact(1, "Wei-Meng Lee", "weimenglee@gmail.com"))
        Toast.makeText(this, "Update successful.", Toast.LENGTH_LONG).show();
    else
        Toast.makeText(this, "Update failed.", Toast.LENGTH_LONG).show();
    db.close();
}

public void DeleteContact() {
    db.open();
    if (db.deleteContact(1))
        Toast.makeText(this, "Delete successful.", Toast.LENGTH_LONG).show();
```

```
        else
            Toast.makeText(this, "Delete failed.", Toast.LENGTH_LONG).show();
        db.close();
    }

    public void DisplayContact(Cursor c)
    {
        Toast.makeText(this,
                "id: " + c.getString(0) + "\n" +
                    "Name: " + c.getString(1) + "\n" +
                    "Email:  " + c.getString(2),
                    Toast.LENGTH_LONG).show();
    }

}
```

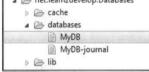

When the database is created, you can find it in the /data/data/
<package_name>/databases folder (see Figure 10-8).

FIGURE 10-8

RECIPE 10.8 PRE-CREATING THE SQLITE DATABASES

Android versions

Level 1 and above

Permissions

None

Source code to download from Wrox.com

Precreated.zip

In real-life applications, sometimes it would be more efficient to pre-create the database at design time rather than run time. To pre-create a SQLite database, many free tools are available on the Internet. One such tool is the SQLite Database Browser, which is available free for different platforms (see http://sourceforge.net/projects/sqlitebrowser/).

Solution

The first thing to do once you have installed the SQLite Database Browser it to create a database using it. Figure 10-9 shows that I have created a contacts table with the fields indicated.

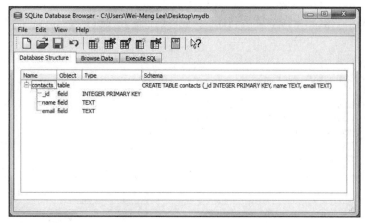

FIGURE 10-9

Populating the table with rows is straightforward. Figure 10-10 shows how you can fill the table with data using the Browse Data tab.

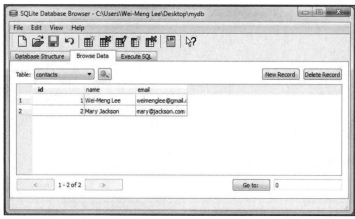

FIGURE 10-10

Once the database is created, drag and drop it into the `assets` folder of your project (see Figure 10-11).

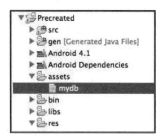

FIGURE 10-11

Next, you define the `CopyDB()` method to copy the database file from one location to another:

```
package net.learn2develop.precreated;

import java.io.IOException;
import java.io.InputStream;
import java.io.OutputStream;

import android.app.Activity;
import android.os.Bundle;

public class MainActivity extends Activity {

    @Override
    public void onCreate(Bundle savedInstanceState) {
        super.onCreate(savedInstanceState);
        setContentView(R.layout.activity_main);
    }

    public void CopyDB(InputStream inputStream, OutputStream outputStream)
    throws IOException {
        //---copy 1K bytes at a time---
        byte[] buffer = new byte[1024];
        int length;
        while ((length = inputStream.read(buffer)) > 0) {
            outputStream.write(buffer, 0, length);
        }
        inputStream.close();
        outputStream.close();
    }

}
```

Note that in this case you use the `InputStream` object to read from the source file, and then write it to the destination file using the `OutputStream` object.

When the activity is created, you copy the database file located in the `assets` folder into the `/data/data/net.learn2develop.Databases/databases/` folder on the Android device:

```
package net.learn2develop.precreated;

import java.io.File;
import java.io.FileNotFoundException;
import java.io.FileOutputStream;
import java.io.IOException;
import java.io.InputStream;
import java.io.OutputStream;

import android.app.Activity;
import android.os.Bundle;

public class MainActivity extends Activity {
    DBAdapter db;
```

```
@Override
public void onCreate(Bundle savedInstanceState) {
    super.onCreate(savedInstanceState);
    setContentView(R.layout.activity_main);

    String destDir = "/data/data/" + getPackageName() +
        "/databases/";
    String destPath = destDir + "MyDB";
    File f = new File(destPath);
    if (!f.exists()) {
        //---make sure directory exists---
        File directory = new File(destDir);
        directory.mkdirs();
        //---copy the db from the assets folder into
        // the databases folder---
        try {
                CopyDB(getBaseContext().getAssets().open("mydb"),
                        new FileOutputStream(destPath));
            } catch (FileNotFoundException e) {
                e.printStackTrace();
            } catch (IOException e) {
                e.printStackTrace();
            }
    }

    db = new DBAdapter(this);
}

public void CopyDB(InputStream inputStream, OutputStream outputStream)
throws IOException {
    ...
}
}
```

> **WARNING** *You copy the database file only if it does not exist in the destination folder. If you don't perform this check, every time the activity is created you will overwrite the database file with the one in the* assets *folder. This may not be desirable, as your application may make changes to the database file during run time, and this will wipe out all the changes you have made so far.*

To ensure that the database is correctly copied, check the /data/data/<package_name>/databases folder to verify that it contains a database file named MyDB.

You can now use the database as is described in Recipe 10.7.

11

Deploying Your
Android Applications

This chapter demonstrates the various methods available to deploy your Android application. While there are a number of different ways to sell your applications through vendor-supported portals, such as Google Play, Amazon.com's Appstore, and so on, this chapter focuses on:

➤ Localization issues

➤ Freely distributing your applications to users, including via email, the web, and an SD card

➤ Setting an installation location

RECIPE 11.1 LOCALIZING YOUR APPLICATION

Android Versions

Level 1 and above

Permissions

None

Source Code to Download from Wrox.com

Localization.zip

Most applications today are developed for the world market — it is likely that your application will be used by people residing in countries other than your own. As such, it is important that you make provisions to ensure that your app is easily localizable to other languages. This recipe shows how to localize the UI of your application to display the language with which the user is familiar.

Solution

The first rule of localizing your Android application is to ensure that all the string literals used in the UI of the application are stored in the `strings.xml` file located in the `res/values` folder of your project. For example, consider the following `activity_main.xml` file:

```
<RelativeLayout xmlns:android="http://schemas.android.com/apk/res/android"
    xmlns:tools="http://schemas.android.com/tools"
    android:layout_width="match_parent"
    android:layout_height="match_parent" >

    <TextView
        android:layout_width="wrap_content"
        android:layout_height="wrap_content"
        android:layout_centerHorizontal="true"
        android:layout_centerVertical="true"
        android:padding="@dimen/padding_medium"
        android:text="@string/quotation"
        tools:context=".MainActivity" />

</RelativeLayout>
```

In the preceding example, the string displayed by the `TextView` is stored as a key named `quotation` in the `strings.xml` file (located in the `res/values` folder), like this:

```
<resources>

    <string name="app_name">Localization</string>
    <string name="hello_world">Hello world!</string>
    <string name="menu_settings">Settings</string>
    <string name="title_activity_main">MainActivity</string>
    <string name="quotation">One small step for a man, a giant leap
    for mankind</string>

</resources>
```

When the Android system loads your application, it will look for the `res/values` folder to find the key named `quotation`. Figure 11-1 shows the UI displayed when the application is loaded.

To localize your application to display other languages, make a copy of the `values` folder under the `res` folder and name it using the following format:

```
values-<LanguageCode>-r<CountryCode>
```

FIGURE 11-1

For example, if you want to support the French language in Canada, create the `values-fr-rCA` folder under the `res` folder, as shown in Figure 11-2. Similarly, to support the Chinese language in China, you would create the folder `values-zh-rCN`.

Translate the strings (consider hiring a professional translator for this) into the language to which you are localizing. The following `strings.xml` file shows the string represented by the `quotation` key translated into French:

FIGURE 11-2

```
<resources>

    <string name="app_name">Localization</string>
    <string name="hello_world">Hello world!</string>
    <string name="menu_settings">Settings</string>
    <string name="title_activity_main">MainActivity</string>
    <string name="quotation">Un petit pas pour un homme, un bond de
    géant pour l\'humanité</string>

</resources>
```

That's all you need to do. When the application is compiled, the language displayed will vary according to the language settings chosen by the user.

To change the language settings on your Android device, go to the Settings application and select Language & input (see Figure 11-3) and then Language (see Figure 11-4).

FIGURE 11-3

FIGURE 11-4

Select the language you want to display. Figure 11-5 shows the French language in Canada selected.

FIGURE 11-5

When the application is reloaded, it will now display the UI in French (see Figure 11-6).

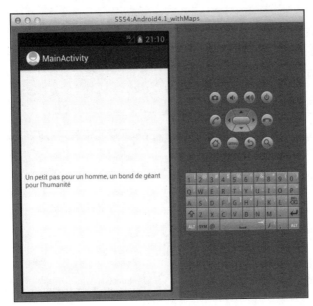

FIGURE 11-6

To target all French-speaking users without regard to the country, you can instead name the folder `values-fr`. In this case, as long as the user selects the French language, the UI of your application will always display French regardless of the country selected. How does your application determine which `strings.xml` file to use? It goes from the most specific to the most generic. For example, suppose your project has the following folders:

➤   `res/values-fr-rCA`

➤   `res/values-fr`

➤   `res/values`

The preceding folders are listed from the most specific to the most generic. If the user's device has the French (Canada) language selected, Android will first check whether the `strings.xml` file is in the `res/values-fr-rCA` folder. If so, it will get the strings from the `strings.xml` file. If not, it will next look in the `res/values-fr` folder, followed by the `res/values` folder. If the user chose the French language in France, then it will load the `strings.xml` file from the `res/values-fr` folder.

RECIPE 11.2   EXPORTING YOUR APPLICATION AS AN APK FILE

Android Versions

Level 1 and above

Permissions

None

Source Code to Download from Wrox.com

MyApp.zip

When your application is completed and tested, and therefore ready to hit the market, you need to package it as an APK (Android Package) file. This recipe shows how you can do that in Eclipse.

Solution

To export your application as an APK file, first ensure that the application compiles successfully. Then, right-click on the project name in Eclipse and select Export... (see Figure 11-7).

In the Export dialog, expand the Android item and select Export Android Application (see Figure 11-8). Click Next.

FIGURE 11-7

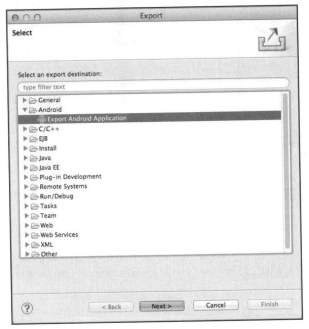

FIGURE 11-8

You are asked to select a project to export. Because you have already selected the project to export, the project name is filled in for you automatically (see Figure 11-9). Click Next.

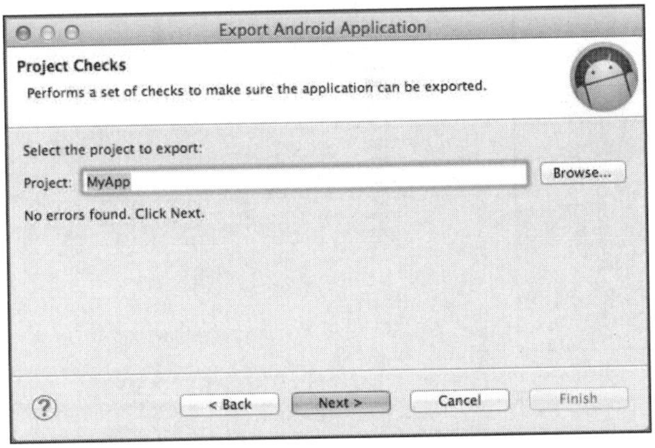

FIGURE 11-9

You are now asked for a keystore (certificate) to code-sign the application. You can either use an existing keystore or create a new one. If you do not already have your own self-generated keystore, you can create a new one here. Enter a location to save the new keystore and supply a password to protect it (see Figure 11-10). Click Next.

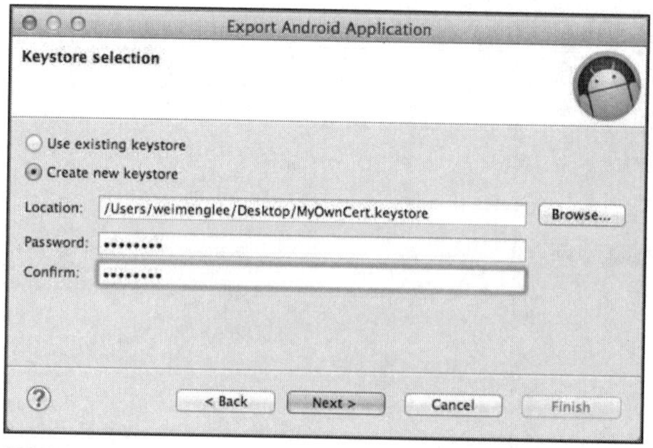

FIGURE 11-10

Next, enter the information shown in Figure 11-11. In particular, all Android applications must be signed with a keystore that is valid until at least 22 October 2033. Hence, enter a validity period that satisfies this requirement. Click Next.

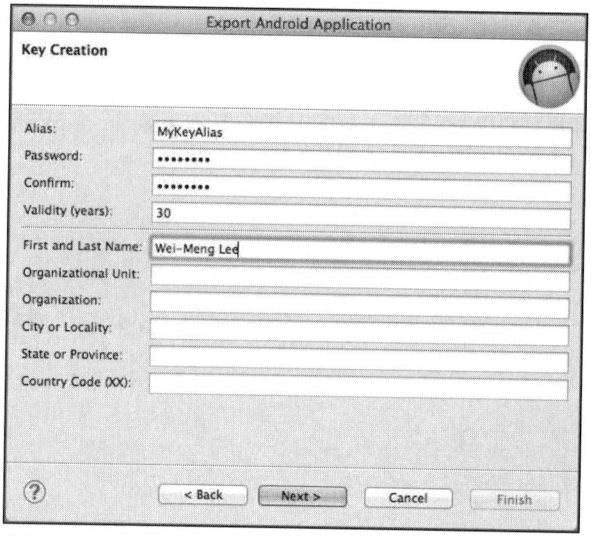

FIGURE 11-11

Specify the location to store your APK file (see Figure 11-12) and then click Finish. Once this is done, your APK will be available in the folder that you have specified.

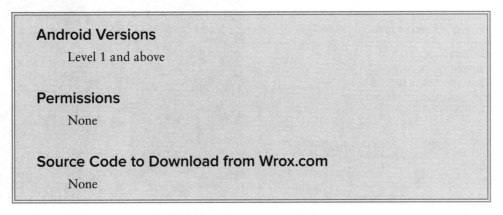

FIGURE 11-12

The next couple of recipes show how you can deploy this APK to your users.

RECIPE 11.3 DEPLOYING YOUR APP THROUGH E-MAIL

Android Versions

Level 1 and above

Permissions

None

Source Code to Download from Wrox.com

None

Once the APK file for your application is generated, you can deliver it to your users so that they can install it onto their Android devices. This recipe demonstrates how to do that by sending it to users through e-mail.

Solution

The easiest way to deploy your application to users is to send them your APK file. Once they receive it, they can install your application directly from their mail application. Figure 11-13 shows the APK file sent as an e-mail attachment. Tapping on the INSTALL button will directly install the application.

As shown in Figure 11-14, the user is prompted for the necessary permission required by the application. In this case, no permission is required by the application.

FIGURE 11-13

FIGURE 11-14

NOTE *Not all mail applications will display the INSTALL button. For example, when the e-mail containing the APK attachment is received in the Mail application on the Android emulator, the INFO button is displayed instead of the INSTALL button (see Figure 11-15). In this case, installation through e-mail may not be available.*

FIGURE 11-15

RECIPE 11.4 DEPLOYING YOUR APP THROUGH THE WEB

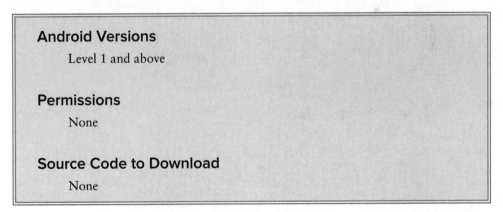

Android Versions

Level 1 and above

Permissions

None

Source Code to Download

None

Another easy way to deploy your application is through a web server. You can use the web server to host your APK file, and give the URL to users. This recipe shows you how.

Solution

If you have your own web server, you can use it to host the APK file and then share the URL with your users, who can use the built-in browser on their device to browse to the URL and download the APK file directly onto their device.

> **NOTE** *On some web servers, you may need to configure the MIME type for the APK file so that it can be served correctly. The MIME type for the APK file is* `application/vnd.android.package-archive`.

Once the APK file is downloaded, users will be able to see that from the notification window (see Figure 11-16).

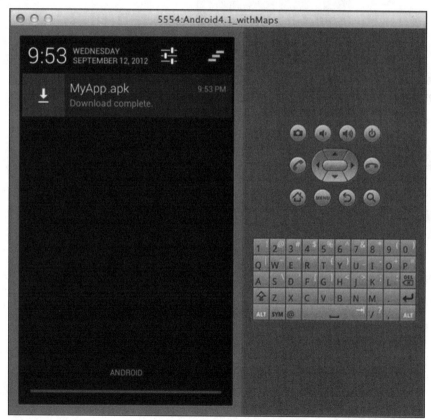

FIGURE 11-16

Tapping on the notification will prompt the user to install the application.

> **NOTE** *You can deploy your APK file very easily if you have Dropbox (`http://www.dropbox.com`). Simply copy the APK file into the `Public` folder of your `Dropbox` folder and you will be able to get the public URL of the APK file and share it with your users.*
>
> *The typical path of a Dropbox `Public` folder is `https://dl.dropbox.com/u/<user_account>/MyApp.apk`.*
>
> *Using this method, there is no need to configure your own web server. Of course, the downside to this approach is that your APK file is publicly available to anyone, anywhere.*

RECIPE 11.5   DEPLOYING YOUR APP THROUGH AN SD CARD

Android Versions

   Level 1 and above

Permissions

   None

Source Code to Download from Wrox.com

   None

Besides sending the APK file to users through the web or e-mail, you can also pass it physically through an external storage medium, such as an SD card. This recipe shows you how.

Solution

To deploy your app through an SD card, simply copy your APK file to the SD card and then pass it to your users. On the Android device, users need to use a third-party file manager, such as the Astro File Manager, to view the content of the SD card. Figure 11-17 shows the Astro File Manager displaying the content of the SD card.

FIGURE 11-17

To install the app, simply tap on it. The dialog shown in Figure 11-18 will appear.

FIGURE 11-19

FIGURE 11-18

From here, the user can directly install the app or select Open App Manager to examine the content of the app before installing (see Figure 11-19).

RECIPE 11.6 SPECIFYING THE APPLICATION INSTALLATION LOCATION

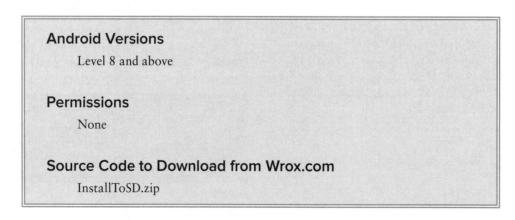

Android Versions

Level 8 and above

Permissions

None

Source Code to Download from Wrox.com

InstallToSD.zip

Beginning with Android level 8, you can now install your application on external storage media (such as the SD card). This recipe shows how you can support this feature in your Android app.

Solution

To support the feature of installing your application on the external storage of your user's device, you need to use the `android:installLocation` attribute in the `AndroidManifest.xml` file, like this:

```xml
<?xml version="1.0" encoding="utf-8"?>
<manifest xmlns:android="http://schemas.android.com/apk/res/android"
    package="net.learn2develop.InstallToSD"
    android:versionCode="1"
    android:versionName="1.0"
    android:installLocation="preferExternal" >
<!-- the values for installLocation can be
     "auto", "preferExternal", or "internalOnly" -->

<uses-sdk android:minSdkVersion="15" />

<application
    android:icon="@drawable/ic_launcher"
    android:label="@string/app_name" >
    <activity
        android:name=".InstallToSDActivity"
        android:label="@string/app_name" >
        <intent-filter>
            <action android:name="android.intent.action.MAIN" />

            <category android:name="android.intent.category.LAUNCHER" />
        </intent-filter>
    </activity>
</application>

</manifest>
```

If you do not specify the `android:installLocation` attribute, the application will be installed in the internal memory of the device and cannot be moved to the external memory. The default value of the `android:installLocation` attribute is `internalOnly`.

If you specify `auto`, the system will determine the best way to install the application based on several factors.

If you specify `preferExternal`, the system will try to install on external storage if it is adequate. If not, it will install onto internal memory.

As shown in Figure 11-20, when an app is installed to external storage, its App info page will display a "Move to phone" button that enables the user to move the application to internal storage.

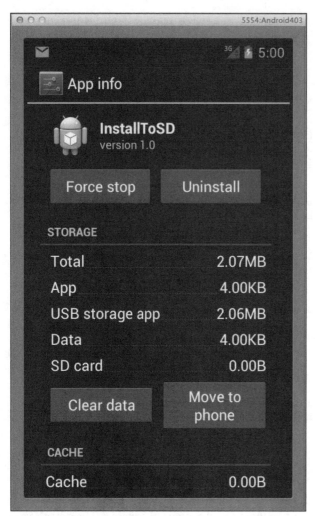

FIGURE 11-20

INDEX

Q

R

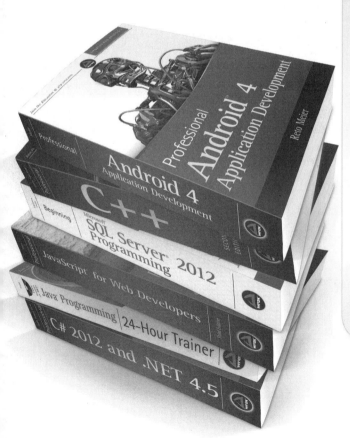